Johannes Suitner
Imagineering Cultural Vienna

Urban Studies

Johannes Suitner (Dipl.-Ing. Dr.) is PostDoc researcher at Vienna University of Technology, where he is doing research on planning cultures, urban imaginaries, culture-led urban transformation, urban politics, and metropolitan development.

Johannes Suitner
Imagineering Cultural Vienna
On the Semiotic Regulation of Vienna's
Culture-led Urban Transformation

[transcript]

Printed with the support of:

ÖFG // ÖSTERREICHISCHE
FORSCHUNGSGEMEINSCHAFT

Bibliographic information published by the Deutsche Nationalbibliothek
The Deutsche Nationalbibliothek lists this publication in the Deutsche Nationalbibliografie; detailed bibliographic data are available in the Internet at http://dnb.d-nb.de

© 2015 transcript Verlag, Bielefeld

All rights reserved. No part of this book may be reprinted or reproduced or utilized in any form or by any electronic, mechanical, or other means, now known or hereafter invented, including photocopying and recording, or in any information storage or retrieval system, without permission in writing from the publisher.

Cover layout: Kordula Röckenhaus, Bielefeld
Cover illustration: Johannes Suitner, Wien, 2012.
Printed in Germany
Print-ISBN 978-3-8376-2978-1
PDF-ISBN 978-3-8394-2978-5

Contents

Cultural Imagineering. A first encounter | 7
Planning with culture between materiality and meaning | 9
Research approach | 27

Contextualizing urban development. Cities between materiality and meaning. | 39
A spatial turn: The city as discursive process? | 40
The multi-scalar city: Between local and global | 42
Urban economies in transition: From production to consumption | 48
Pluralization, fragmentation, and an urban revival in a postmodern age | 51

The contested politics of planning. Ideology and power, accumulation and representation | 57
The changed face of the state: New coalitions, new development goals | 58
New modes of planning: Constructing identity and difference | 63
The political in planning: Contests over accumulation and representation | 69

Linking culture, city, and planning. Entering a cultural era in urban development | 77
An agent of change: The salient narratives of culturalization for capitalization | 83
Culture for representation: Between hegemony and cultural pluralism | 90

Theorizing Cultural Imagineering. Conceptualizing the discursive regulation of culture-led place transformation | 95

Empirical research design. De- and reconstructing Cultural Imagineering in practice | 103
Material context: Vienna's development trajectory | 104
The construction of cultural imaginaries: Critical Discourse Analysis | 105
Triangulation and hidden information: Narrative interviews | 109
Confronting discourse with material practice | 110

Contextualizing "Cultural Vienna". Retracing the cultural development trajectory | 113
Morphology, urban structures and spatial development | 113

Vienna's socio-economic development path | 117
Urban politics and the culture of planning | 119
The institutional setting | 123
The strategic layer: Vienna's politics of planning | 127
Strategically approaching culture: Vienna between hub and heritage | 133

Karlsplatz: A cultural economy for global tourism | 145
Development background | 145
The discursive construction of Karlsplatz | 149
Materializations of the cultural imaginary | 156
Transformation as hegemonic material practice? | 160

Seestadt Aspern: Cultural symbolism for entrepreneurial urbanism | 163
Development background | 163
The discursive construction of Seestadt Aspern | 168
Materializations of the cultural imaginary | 180
Transformation as hegemonic material practice? | 184

Brunnenviertel: Capitalizing on cultural diversity | 187
Development background | 187
The discursive construction of Brunnenviertel | 191
Materializations of the cultural imaginary | 200
Transformation as hegemonic material practice? | 204

Cultural Vienna revisited. Rationales, imaginaries, and hegemonic practice | 207
Uncerlying rationales of planning the city with culture | 207
Culture-led hegemonic economic and ideological projects | 216

Towards a culturized planning practice. Conclusions on Cultural Imagineering | 225
The Cultural Imagineering of Vienna | 225
Planning for cultural development: Towards a culturized planning practice in Vienna | 230

List of Figures & Tables | 239

Bibliography | 241

Cultural Imagineering
A first encounter

In a globalizing world, often equated with increasing sameness, cities and their places can still be characterized by unique qualities (Kelly, 1999; Marcuse & van Kempen, 2000). If we see their pictures and hear their stories, we can still distinguish Paris from Rome, or New York from Chicago. Asking for the reasons to that, the answer often is "culture". Today we are aware that culture is deeply linked with space. Even more, in the past decades planning research and practice have come to find that it is culture, which signifies places. Thus it has become a regular practice in recent planning to actively employ culture for highlighting the qualities of place (Mumford, 1970; Miles, 2007; Springer, 2007; Benneworth & Hospers, 2009). Herewith, culture has attained a pivotal position as a tool in governing urban development.

But the practice of culture-led place transformation is today stuck in a tension between two conflictive goals that build upon dichotomous interpretations of culture and cultural identities. On the one hand, powerful actors of the city increasingly utilize the forming forces of culture to promote individual economic and ideological projects in urban development (Zukin, 1989, 1995, 1996, 1998; Harvey, 1990; Jameson, 1998; Young, 2008). In this regard, they turn to approved cultural strategies that build upon dominant historic narratives and narrow interpretations of a culture that speaks a global language, while the "*plural pasts*" (Ashworth et al., 2007) and diverse identities of a local population are largely neglected (Kearns & Philo, 1993; Gupta & Ferguson, 1997a, 1997b; Porter, 2008; Turnbridge, 2008). On the other hand, the increasing cultural diversity of globalizing cities is actively fostered as a driver of development. It is an indispensable precondition to successfully cope with recent urban change, as the underlying interpretation of culture as diverse identities, lifestyles, and practices is considered a resource of democratizing urban development (Jacobs & Fincher, 1998; Moulaert et al., 2004; Puype, 2004; Bauman, 2011). Thus, the tension inherent in cultural planning today is that between an instrumental view of culture, and preparing the ground for cultural diversity to unfold; between planning *with* culture for individual and elite interests, or planning *for* cultural development, a democratic city, and pluralized hegemony[1] (Mouffe, 2007).

I make this tension the point of departure of this research. Yet, numerous well-formulated critical accounts of the utilizations of cultural specificity for capitalist and undemocratic planning projects already exist (cf. Zukin, 1989, 1995, 1996, 1998; Harvey, 1990; Scott, 1997; Jameson, 1998 to name but a few). Hence, *Cultural Imagineering* explicitly embeds the clinch between planning with culture and planning for cultural development in a differentiated conceptualization of urban space as consisting of materiality and meaning (Cresswell, 2004). Herewith it accentuates the so far under-investigated influence of discursive constructs of individual cultural visions on the outcomes of material place transformation. It builds upon the notion that urban discourses are more than just the sphere where the marketable recreations of urban cultural environments are created. Instead, they are increasingly understood as *the* tool for constructing powerful visions of an urban future (Healey et al., 1999; Torfing, 1999; Hajer & Wagenaar, 2003; Smith, 2005). Acknowledging the deep links between practice and discourse, between materiality and meaning in urban space and its development, *Cultural Imagineering* assumes that actors intervening in discourse have the ability to influence material planning outcomes by constructing reductionist cultural visions of urban development – so-called *"cultural imaginaries"* (Taylor, 2004; Jessop, 2004, 2008). The depiction of such imaginaries and their conflation with the analysis of transformed material practice allows for answering a central question in the framework of current cultural planning practice: *Which and whose cultural visions succeed to influence place transformation, and who benefits from the so-created material cultural places?* This book contributes to the wide array of Cultural Political Economy research by theorizing the influence of cultural imaginaries on place transformation and empirically investigating Vienna as a case study of *Cultural Imagineering*.

---

1 The term hegemony refers to "[...] moral and intellectual leadership which treats the aspirations and views of subaltern people as an active element within the political and cultural programme of the hegemonizing bloc." (Jones, 2006: 55)

PLANNING WITH CULTURE BETWEEN MATERIALITY AND MEANING

> "When it comes to art and culture, Vienna is not only a big city, but a world city."
> MICHAEL HÄUPL, MAYOR OF VIENNA[2]

Cities are fascinating. As David Harvey outlines, they are somehow capable of accommodating the most diverse, maybe even opposing forces, *"[...] not necessarily so as to harmonize them, but to channel them into so many possibilities of both creative and destructive social transformation."* (Harvey, 1985: 222) Reasonably, cities must then be understood as processes of constant change, undergoing boom, bust and revival (Hall, 1998). It is here that urban politics attempts to find ways of stabilizing periods of success, accelerating uplift and averting crisis. And while ever-deepening insight into the versatile capabilities of urbanity sustains the success story of urbanization per se (Jacobs, 1969; Mumford, 1970; Harvey, 1985, 1997), an evolving cognizance of the city's multi-layered character and increasing diversity also makes it an ever more complex subject of active transformation in material terms. And here, Cultural Imagineering comes into play.

Contemporary cities are fuzzy concepts of loose ties, blurry scales, societal diversity and cultural difference. One could say that they have become *"an inordinately complex world"* (Jessop, 2008: 239). The transformation and utilization of urban space in favor of individual interests thus demands new instruments that are able of reducing urban complexity to support the accomplishment of these development visions. It demands an imaginary – a discursive construct of a *"[...] common understanding that makes possible common practices and a widely shared sense of legitimacy"* (Taylor, 2004: 330). The imaginary is a political tool; a constructed, objectified common interest; a simplified narrative of a symbolic urban vision that "keeps things going" in an urban world that would otherwise be too complex to handle (Jessop, 2004, 2008; Jessop & Oosterlynck, 2008).

For cities that are increasingly judged by such narratives, symbols and place-specific meaning (Kearns & Philo, 1993; Ward, 1998; Madanipour, 1999, 2003; Evans, 2001, 2003, 2006), the discursive layer thus needs to be understood as being more than an emotional representation of material urban environments. It serves as an objectified interpretation of what an urban future *should* look like

---

2   Cf. SPÖ Wien, 2012.

(Taylor, 2004). The discursive layer has become the contested arena where the construction of visions and stories of future urban development are fought out (Eade & Mele, 2002). The so-created imaginaries become the political legitimation and regulative framework of an urban future, thereby also shaping the materializations in urban space (Jessop, 2004, 2008).

The planning-political mechanisms mediating between contesting expectations towards urban development are thus more than ever signified by communication, negotiation, and mediatization as the means to re-shaping such imaginaries (Healey, 1992, 1997; Healey et al., 1999; Helbrecht, 1993, 1994; Häußermann et al., 2008; Lundby, 2009). Consequently, the politics of planning, where opposing visions and values of urban development collide to form political antagonisms, and where power is obtained and exercised, condense in discourse (Torfing, 1999; Lees, 2004; Jacobs, 2006). Here, objectified knowledge is constructed, and the symbols of place are shaped to form an urban imaginary that decisively influences urban politics and planning practice (Davoudi & Strange, 2009; Keller, 2011).

Adopting the notion of a spatial turn, this book builds upon the duality of materiality and meaning and the notion of space as constituted by both material processes and discourse (Cresswell, 2004; Döring & Thielmann, 2008; Soja, 2008; Davoudi & Strange, 2009). The initial quote is a telling example in this regard. It originates from one of Vienna's most influential political figures of the past two decades, the city's mayor, Michael Häupl. I consider it expressive for two reasons. First, it reveals how powerful actors actively engage in urban development discourses by constructing a picture of political confidence, local power and scale in order to show "the right way" for the future of a city. Second, it also shows the pivotal position culture reached in urban development politics and recent planning, obviously being a decisive factor of a city's position in a world economy. It hints at the wide-ranging turn to culture in planning and its increasing recognition as a representation instrument of both the powerful and marginalized people of a city (Berndt & Pütz, 2007; Young, 2008; Eckardt & Nyström, 2009). At the same time it leaves no doubt about culture's fundamental role as economic resource utilized in postmodern, entrepreneurial politics of capital accumulation in a global capitalist economy (Zukin, 1995, 1996, 1998; Hall & Hubbard, 1996; Scott, 1997, 2000; du Gay & Pryke, 2002; Harvey, 2002).

The influential character of culture in recent planning forms the second pillar to the concept of Cultural Imagineering. The wide-ranging cultural turn emphasizes the deep links between cultural specificity and space to form distinct locations of cultural uniqueness (Zukin, 1989, 1995, 1996, 1998; Jameson, 1998; Springer, 2007; Young, 2008). Furthermore, culture is increasingly employed in planning to bridge the gap between identity and difference in cities consisting of many instead of one culture (Fohrbeck & Wiesand, 1989; Gupta & Ferguson, 1997a, 1997b; Madanipour, 2003; Bauman, 2011). As an elastic concept, it can be the constructed common interest to create acceptance in planning (Bassett et al., 2005) – either for the prospect of surplus value (Harvey, 2002; Lagendijk, 2004), or as symbolic expressions representing identities, value sets and political power (Kearns, 1993; Hall, 1997; Schulz, 2006; De Frantz, 2011; Grubbauer, 2011a, 2011b). In cities struggling with multiple crises, culture thus seems to having become the one answer to a number of questions on an urban revival (Göschel & Kirchberg, 1998; Evans, 2001; Garcia, 2004; Miles, 2007; Benneworth & Hospers, 2009). Hence, it comes as no surprise that material planning and the imaginaries influencing it are often based on conceptualizations of culture.

Although the term itself obviously implies numerous interpretations, in this work I refer to culture as an agent of change (Zukin, 1995). Herewith I point to its recent employment in economic and political strategies, i.e. its targeted utilization by actors of the city as a tool to secure, accelerate or stabilize desired urban transformations. In this regard cultural expression doesn't even have to be the central planning goal, but often only serves as the medium through which change is legitimized, hence serving as an instrument for gaining or maintaining power and safeguarding economic profits. These utilizations are based on both the material cultural substance of place and the discursively formed imaginary, which attempts to employ a certain cultural vision for the benefit of individual interests in a city's material transformation. The present book concentrates on the formation of such cultural imaginaries by reconstructing the discursive formation of planning decisions in culture-led urban development. It identifies urban discourses as important processes of meaning-making in the production of space (Cresswell, 2004; Schmid, 2008) and influencing factors of planning and political decisions concerning urban development. By unhiding the prevailing arguments and underlying rationales that influence culture-led urban development, it reveals the dominant value constructs and actors affecting a city's cultural development. Thereby it sketches a picture of who has power in planning and power over space (Flyvbjerg, 2002, 2003, 2004) when it comes to employing culture as a resource of urban development.

To put this approach into practice, this piece of work builds upon a political-economic understanding of processes of urban transformation and urban planning. It considers urban development as a highly contested process of developing and utilizing urban space for capitalist and political principles of accumulation and representation (Harvey, 1985, 1989, 1990; Jessop, 1997, 2004, 2008;

Madanipour, 1999, 2003; Brenner, 2000; Jones, 2006; Bieling, 2006a; Stäheli, 2006). It refers to planning as processes embedded in urban politics (Häußermann et al., 2008), where imaginaries are constructed and translated into material realities.

At the same time, it dissociates itself from a radical constructivist perspective that considers discourse as the only source of power and determinant of materiality (cf. for instance Berger & Luckmann, 1980). Instead it stresses the notion of materiality and meaning as equally important influencing factors and determinants of space. So while its primary aim is to empirically detect influences of powerful discursive constructions on material planning outcomes, it still acknowledges the influence of materiality, i.e. history, path-dependency[3], institutions and practices, as a determinant of certain discourse formations (Jessop, 2004, 2008; Jessop & Oosterlynck, 2008). Hence, embedding discourse in the material practice of urban development is important for at least two reasons: first, it is a necessary precondition for understanding locally specific development paths and discursive strategies, and second, it constitutes the central assessment criterion for critically reviewing the actual influence of discursive cultural constructs on material planning outcomes.

Imagineering and the case of ALCOA

By speaking of *Imagineering*, I deploy a term that was first uttered in an advertisement from the Aluminum Company of America, ALCOA, in Time Magazine in 1942 (Time, 1942). ALCOA created the word *Imagineering* to describe its effort of producing a versatile, easily applicable product for almost all purposes. The advertisement states: *"Imagineering is letting your imagination soar, and then engineering it down to earth."* (Time, 1942: 56) Transferring this definition to the making of contemporary cities, it highlights the conception of the urban as a material *and* discursive site of society (Helbrecht, 2001). It stresses that under conditions of wide-ranging mediatization (Lundby, 2009) and an increasing emphasis on communicative politics (Healey, 1992, 1997; Helbrecht, 1993, 1994; Schneider, 1997), "letting your imagination soar" allows for the cognitive con-

---

3 Path-dependency describes "[...] how existing institutions and structures, internal and external to the places under consideration, condition the latter's trajectories." (Martinelli & Novy, 2013: 296) Contrastingly, path-shaping refers to active interventions in these institutions and structures to form specific futures, while path-breaking indicates the opposing process of overcoming development dependencies and hegemonic formations (ibid.).

struction of an urban future, which might become so powerful as to be "engineered down to earth". In urban development, Imagineering thus stands for the discursive construction of an imaginary, i.e. a simplistic logic of planning, which might be powerful enough to influence the development paths of a city. In its out-and-out manifestation it leads to hegemony (Bieling, 2006a; Jones, 2006) – the implementation of discursively objectified planning rationales by subordinates, without them challenging these rationales or related objectives and structures.

In urban development, such imaginaries have been influencing planning practice since long. In European cities, for instance, the unquestioned distinction between public and private has long been a determinant of these cities' spatial organization, legal regulations, and development visions. Current planning practice would be unimaginable without taking into account property ownership, which is due to a powerful social imaginary that conceptualized public and private as two oppositional, incompatible conditions (Taylor, 2004). Consequently, we all take public spaces, private properties and the related restrictions or permissions of their use for granted in our perception of today's cities.

Fig. 1: ALCOA's Imagineering: imaginary, materialization, hegemony

Source: ALCOA Inc., 2002: adapted presentation

Ironically, ALCOA did not just invent the term Imagineering for marketing reasons. The case of ALCOA is itself a great metaphor of how Imagineering successfully established hegemony in terms of economic production and consumption. The permeation of global markets and our everyday lives with their product, aluminum, speaks for itself. Although products made of aluminum hadn't been a success story since the very beginning, ALCOA persistently engaged in promoting what they do (Smith, 1988). While during Second World War the ability of producing almost any military equipment from a cheap, light-weight and versatile material made ALCOA a prospering company, its definitive triumph came afterwards (ALCOA Inc., 2002). Under a post-war economic regime of industrial production and mass consumption, and boosted further by the vast American political and economic power (Hall, 1998), the company further pushed its agenda, constructing a picture of a world unimaginable without aluminum (Smith, 1988).

In fact, this picture greatly influences our everyday lives still today. The company's effort of *"covering the world in aluminum"* (ibid.: 308) is the reason why today we eat and drink literally everything from a can. Only naturally, anything from juice and coffee to fruits and vegetables is packed in aluminum – worldwide. What this impressively demonstrates, is how ALCOA has successfully conducted Imagineering. They have constructed an imaginary – a simplistic idea of a mode of production and consumption as a solution to a simplistic problem – and embedded it in public discourse via advertising. The imaginary legitimizes a certain form of production, frames consumer behavior and thereby stabilizes an economic model that has become hegemonic, as it permeates a global economy of production and consumption without question (cf. Fig. 1).

Apparently, the case of ALCOA holds a striking analogy to the process of Cultural Imagineering in the politics of planning. Here the cultural imaginary is the discursively constructed abstraction of the complex and overlapping matters of culture, city, and planning and their interaction to "get things going" in urban development. It delineates a simplistic, objectified planning reality that builds the legitimizing argument for the materialization of certain values and visions in urban space. As a perpetual discourse, it can even reach unquestioned ideological supremacy and become a hegemonic rationale of how modes of cultural production and consumption, the creation of wealth upon a certain form of culture, and urban culture-led development should function (Bieling, 2006a; Jones, 2006). As Evans (2001: 1) aptly puts it, *"How and why culture is planned is a reflection of the place of the arts and culture in society."* And this place in society is of course influenced by the imaginaries that inform material practice.

The concept of imaginary

As a great variety of research has shown, discourses need to be understood as frameworks of urban social and political life (Salet & Faludi, 2000; Martin et al., 2003; McCann, 2003; Hajer & Versteeg, 2005; Jessop & Oosterlynck, 2008; Lundby, 2009; Schipper, 2012). Hence, they are important factors in the politics of planning. Discourses can be interpreted as public negotiations about what is possible in the development of the city, and what is not. It might seem in the first place as if this conceptualization of planning as a discursive process builds upon a communicative rationale (Healey, 1992; Schneider, 1997), putting the notion of an open debate about urban futures into practice by realizing broad discussions. Yet, discourses are permeated by unequally distributed power and constant fights for pushing through individual ideologies, opinions, and planning visions. It is obvious nowadays that the most diverse actors engage heavily in these processes of discursive meaning-making (Helbrecht, 1993; Zukin, 1998; Scott, 2001; Miles & Paddison, 2005). Thus, the fact that actors might use discourses strategically in the politics of planning must be a focal point of analysis (Hajer & Versteeg, 2005) – particularly in the highly contested approaches to culture-led development (Kearns & Philo, 1993, Zukin, 1995, 1998, Evans, 2003).

As processes of meaning-making, discourses have the ability to frame active urban development (Eade & Mele, 2002; McCann, 2003, 2004). For the case of Cultural Imagineering this implies that the actually overlapping and multiply interacting entities of culture, city, and planning are being reduced to a simplistic ideal of interaction, which I refer to as a *cultural imaginary*. Herewith I build upon the conception of "imaginary" as developed in recent accounts of Cultural Political Economy (henceforth CPE) (Jessop, 2004, 2008, 2013; Jessop & Sum, 2006; Jessop & Oosterlynck, 2008). The origin of the concept lies in different fields from psychoanalysis to anthropology and political philosophy, all putting a different emphasis on its actual meaning (Strauss, 2006). Referring to Lacan, an imaginary obscures the real (ibid.), while for Castoriadis it is *"a society's unifying core conception"* (ibid.: 324). Yet, I take philosopher Charles Taylor's definition of modern social imaginaries as my point of departure. In this sense, it is both a cultural and ideological model of how things go and how they *should* go, serving as a legitimation of certain actions:

"I speak of imaginary because I'm talking about the way ordinary people 'imagine' their social surroundings [...]. [T]he social imaginary is that common understanding that makes possible common practices and a widely shared sense of legitimacy." (Taylor, 2004: 106)

Yet, for employing the concept in processes of culture-led urban development, I move from Taylor's definition to Jessop's recently developed interpretation of the imaginary as a discursive construct established by a governing coalition to *legitimize and stabilize* certain economic regimes (Jessop, 2004, 2008, 2013). Taylor analyzes the imaginary at a structural level in order to explain how unquestioned beliefs or ideas of a society come into being in the long term (Taylor, 2004). CPE, on the other hand, interprets the imaginary in its instrumental form, i.e. as a discursive tool to actively establish a reductionist view of complex relations for individual interests. Jessop explains the phenomenon of imaginary by pointing at the economy as a field of political intervention. As this field is far too complex to be fully grasped by the diverse actors involved, it needs a simplified, abstracted vision in the form of an economic imaginary.

"The totality of economic activities is so unstructured and complex that it cannot be an object of calculation, management, governance, or guidance. Instead such practices are always oriented to subsets of economic relations (economic systems or subsystems) that have been discursively and, perhaps organizationally and institutionally, fixed as objects of intervention. This involves 'economic imaginaries' that rely on semiosis to constitute these subsets." (Jessop, 2004: 5)

While imaginaries conceptualized that way might end up in determinant beliefs as well in the long run, it is the declared goal of this research to analyze only those discursive constructs that aim at regulating single projects in planning. Such imaginaries form a framework of legitimacy. They construct an abstraction and simplification of complex fields, relations, activities or systems (e.g. the contextual culture of a city) for that complex thing to become operable in a multi-scalar and multi-sectoral governing coalition (Jessop, 2004). Thus, an imaginary can be considered as the selective projection of complex processes in discourse (Jessop & Oosterlynck, 2008). It can inform and shape economic strategies on all organizational and territorial scales, it can inform and shape state projects and hegemonic visions, integrating private, institutional, and wider public narratives about past experiences, present difficulties, and future prospects (Albrechts, 2004; Jessop, 2004). As Jessop (2004, 2008) deduces so plausibly for economic imaginaries, the multifaceted political, economic and cultural structures of a city are far too complex and all-embracing to become a manageable object. Instead, they are packed into a simplistic picture that is meant to facilitate strategies of certain material transformations.

Hence, and this forms a major argument of this research, *for becoming an agent of change in planning, culture needs to be reduced to a simplistic cognitive construct*. Powerful economic and political actors employ reductive interpretations of how "a culture" might support urban development to legitimize material strategies for their individual benefit. Yet, as there are many understandings of and approaches to the fuzzy concept of culture in the context of urban development, this needs further clarification.

"Which culture?" Critically reviewing the culturalization of urban space

Culture is a broad concept (Göschel & Kirchberg, 1998; Miles, 2007; Young, 2008). We are facing a number of definitions that are so dispersed among disciplines and over time that they cannot be comprehensively managed (Fohrbeck & Wiesand, 1989). Thus, one might easily end up asking, *"Which culture?"* What do we mean when we speak of culture? How is it conceptualized, and which role does it play in the development of cities?

Social science definitions tend to interchangeably speak of culture as an item or product, a distinct attribute of social groups, or as a dimension of social interaction (Lagendijk, 2004). In this research I define culture as all contextually produced difference. As in anthropology, human and cultural geography and sociology, this is meant to describe the entirety of a system and the specific ways in which it functions (Fohrbeck and Wiesand, 1989; Göschel and Kirchberg, 1998). For culture and city this generally implies that they are to be imagined as liberating counter-proposals to the constraints of nature (Göschel and Kirchberg, 1998). Yet as is recurrently criticized, in this regard culture has literally become *"everything and anything"* (Madgin, 2009: 60). But as Miles and Paddison (2005) emphasize, *"[...] culture needs to mean something, but it can and should not be expected to mean everything."* (ibid. 2005: 837)

The academic discourse distinguishes culture as "the arts", artistic practices and objects, and culture as the conglomerate of all social, religious and political trends, norms and values, which characterize a social group or territory. While culture as the arts is the narrow definition, which mostly implies high threshold cultural projects for urban elites, the broad definition also comprehends all urban ways-of-life and signifying practices of identity and difference (Hall, 1997; Young, 2008; Bauman, 2011). The second acknowledges the disappearance of a high-low distinction and the evolvement of a popular culture instead, which has in the meantime become common sense in social science research (Evans, 2001; Bloomfield & Bianchini, 2001; Lewitzky, 2005).

For this work, I divide these definitions into three categories. Together they describe what I termed above as contextually produced difference[4]: first, heritage and traditions, i.e. the references to a city's past and the modes of celebrating and representing norms, values, and beliefs that together form place-specific cul-

---

4   The definition of culture as introduced here builds on conceptualizations employed in Zukin (1995), Hall (1997), Göschel & Kirchberg (1998), Evans (2001), Miles (2007), and Young (2008).

tural identities; second, all artistic and creative practices that are collectively discussed as contributing essentially to social and economic innovation in cities after Fordism; and third, the diverse ways of life and distinct everyday practices of a local population that shape places and the picture of urban life in today's globally embedded cities.

But researching culture-led urban transformation would fail if it ignored the *"[...] strong criticism of culture in modern society, [where] a general view increased that only certain social groups could make use of cultural opportunities for their demand for freedom."* (Eckardt & Nyström, 2009: 12) The past decades have brought about a number of critical accounts of such an instrumental view of culture in different parts of the world, at all times revealing that culture is utilized as an add-on to individual planning projects – a tool safeguarding the facilitation of economic and hegemonic ideological strategies. Hence, I describe my research as *a critical review of the instrumentalizations of reductionist interpretations of culture*. The following is meant as a clarification of what this means in the context of this book.

Cultural processes are frequently brought into line with the economic process, consequently separating cultural production from cultural consumption. Bianchini (1993), for instance, refers to the creative economy as cultural production, while he subsumes all infrastructures, events, and images based upon cultural content under cultural consumption. This division already suggests what is largely being criticized by several authors – that culture is increasingly considered as a commodity to serve only the economic interests of an exclusive group of people. This trend cannot be denied in the past decades – particularly in the context of utilizations of culture in profit-oriented urban development (Scott, 1997, 2000; Garcia, 2004; Miles and Paddison, 2005; Young, 2008).

"[P]lace, culture and economy are highly symbiotic with one another, and in modern capitalism this symbiosis is re-emerging in powerful new forms as expressed in the cultural economies of certain key cities" (Scott, 1997: 325)

As a consequence of the growing instrumentalization of culture in capitalism, critical authors increasingly point to culture as a number of unique, contextual processes and their role as critical resource for societal progress and inclusion as counter-conceptualizations to economic exploitation (Miles et al., 2000; Stevenson, 2001; Moulaert et al., 2004; Eckardt & Nyström, 2009). These authors also acknowledge that there is anything but a stable or undisputed definition of culture within one place. Rather, culture is a contested concept that is constantly reframed, depending on underlying values, visions, and interpretations of the urban world (Zukin, 1995; Hall & Hubbard, 1996). This is in line with Gupta & Ferguson (1997a, 1997b), who call for speaking of *multiple urban cultures* instead of *one culture* to acknowledge the overlaying and competing identities and cultures of place.

The acknowledgement of such a multiplied conception of *cultures* shifted the interest in the politics of planning to everyday experiences and the practicalities of the lived social life as a new quality to build upon in urban development (Young, 2008). Approaches thus diversified and implied not only high cultural interventions for positive economic effects anymore, but started to consider also the specific urban ways-of-life, the identities of urban citizens, and the characteristic history and heritage of the city. Here, culture describes the whole of what is specific of a place: the norms and values, the traditions and heritage, the ways of life, and typical landscapes (Göschel & Kirchberg, 1998). Interpreted as a development context, culture is a substantive value of any city. It represents the spectrum of human achievements, which constitute a city in its current form (Mumford, 1970; Eckardt & Nyström, 2009). Cultural development, in this sense, is closely linked with any urban development. *"Cities are produced, then, according to cultural values."*, state Miles et al. (2000: 3). Yet, what needs to be repeated in this context: cities are produced upon a conglomerate of *competing* cultural values. Recent accounts of urban cultural development have all pointed to the cultural contestation over the city (Zukin, 1995; Gupta & Ferguson, 1997a, 1997b; Stevenson, 2001; De Frantz, 2005, 2011; Bauman, 2011). And it is also this research's endeavor to employ a conception of the city as determined by contesting cultural values and identities and, relatedly, competing definitions of culture and its role in urban development. Such a broadened interpretation of multiple cultures also demands reconsidering culture's general role in society.

"So the language of the modern period relegated culture to a sector of social life, rather than recognizing the cultural embedding of all social life." (Healey, 1997: 65)

The identification of the primary position of culture for urban processes is a central theoretical shift, termed as a *"cultural turn"* (Eade and Mele, 2002; Lagendijk, 2004; Berndt and Pütz, 2007). Consequently, the need for a *culturization* of planning is voiced in recent planning literature to meet the expectations of a new understanding of culturally grounded processes and to acknowledge difference in a culturally diverse urban environment (Young, 2006, 2008).

The above elaborations lead us to a conceptualization of culture in urban development that includes two opposed views (cf. Tab. 1). First, *culturalization*, which subsumes all approaches of planning the city with culture, meaning, the typical and often criticized instrumentalizations of cultural values, images, products, or ways-of-life for political and economic reasons, particularly their utilization for legitimizing power or residing in a *"global capitalist cultural economy"* (Scott, 1997: 324). Culturalization interprets culture as a sector of social life and primarily as an economic resource, an image or a unique selling proposition of places in interurban competition (Ward, 1998; Benneworth & Hospers, 2009; Hornig, 2011). Thus, the outcome is *one* commodity culture – a mainstreamed delineation, adapted to a globally common language that understands culture as a growth factor and ideological representation of consumable places (Zukin, 1995; Scott, 1997; Hall, 1998; Madanipour, 1999, 2003; Gottdiener, 2000; Evans, 2001, 2003; Young, 2006, 2008). In this understanding, *"Culture itself has become a key form of capital."* (Bloomfield & Bianchini, 2001: 101)

Culturization, then, is the opposing interpretation. It builds upon a cultural turn, which broadened the conception of culture, making it a useful analytical concept for revealing difference in planning (Eade & Mele, 2002; Young, 2008). Moving away from the notion of one local culture to a multiplicity of simultaneously existing cultures allows for seeing the varying developments, needs and potentials of these different cultures evolving in a city (Jacobs, 1998; Rojek, 2000; Bloomfield & Bianchini, 2001; Puype, 2004). It also unveils the contested nature of the city as the arena of cultural representation. Relatedly, a culturized view in planning is considered as the tool for seeing cultural difference and planning for cultural development. It endows planners with the ability to reveal niche-cultural expression and to support experimental cultures, empowerment, and cultural citizenship (Stevenson, 2001; Young, 2008; Eckardt & Nyström, 2009). Such a conception also allows to analytically approaching the antagonisms, commodifications, contestations and exclusions inherent in the discursive constructions of a commodity culture for facilitating political and economic strategies.

Of course, the latter is not uncritical either. Culture as contextually produced difference is also increasingly utilized in (re)urbanization processes for the benefit of individual political and economic interests. But in this regard, culture is again interpreted as a unique selling proposition and resource for economic profit only, pointing to *culturalization* and an approach of planning *with* culture. Hence, the distinguishing line I want to point at here is one between promoting individual political and economic benefits of gaining or maintaining power and creating profits upon the instrumentalization of cultural values and processes (=culturalization), and an inclusive process of planning for social and economic development upon the recognition of cultural diversity (=culturization).

Tab. 1: A culturized planning view. Critically reviewing the capitalist culturalization of the city

CULTURALIZATION	CULTURIZATION
= Planning *with* Culture	= Planning *for* Cultural Development
- Culture as sector of social life - Culture = arts & ways-of-life, economic resource / commodity - Culture as unique selling proposition (of products / places) - Agent of change	- Social life culturally embedded - Culture = contextually produced difference and critical resource - Culture as analytical concept (difference) - Concept for interpretations of cultural turn
→ **Fostering one commodity culture**	→ **Fostering many cultures**

This distinction opens up a broad spectrum of questions about the underlying values represented and pursued through supporting or instrumentalizing cultural activity. Literature offers a wide range of readings on the value tensions inherent in culture-led urban development (Bloomfield & Bianchini, 2001; Garcia, 2004; Jones & Wilks-Heeg, 2004, Kloostermann & van der Werff, 2009). It might either be a conflict of culture for aestheticization versus culture for society-building (Moulaert et al., 2004; Lewitzky, 2005), equity and inclusion versus efficiency and distinction (Evans, 2001; Gordon & Buck, 2005; Markusen & Gadwa, 2009), or the interpretation of culture as a critical versus an economic resource (Zukin, 1995; Eckardt & Nyström, 2009), which leads to such value tensions between actors involved. But in the end they all point to the above delineated distinction between culture as a planning tool in development strategies for the profit of few, and planning for a city of cultural diversity and the development of many.

Looking at culturalizations of the city through the lens of a culturized planning view hence allows to critically investigating culture-led processes of a city. Whether it is the interpretation of culture as an identity-forming factor, a resource of representing difference, a pillar of urban renewal, an economy, or an asset in inter-place competition – the critical question always is, who succeeds with pushing through their visions of a cultural city in the politics of planning. Presumably, the underlying values and principles of applying culture in planning, the ideologies and imaginations of a cultural city, collide in the discursive formation of space that constantly informs the materialization of culture-led processes. Explorations of the discursive construction of a rationale of planning the city with culture – the cultural imaginary – thus aim at disclosing the legitimation, stabilization and regulation of a certain material cultural city. Whether the imaginary rather leads to a mainstreamed commodity culture for capitalist accumulation, or supports a city of cultural difference (Fincher & Jacobs, 1998; Stevenson, 2001; Young, 2008) and a pluralist politics of planning (Mouffe, 2007), forms a central question then.

As was shown, the understandings of and reports on culture's role in urban development are manifold. Anyhow, the elaborations point to two general conceptualizations, which form the definition of culture to be employed in this research: first, culture and the arts as signifying practices and ways of life, expressions and representations of identity, and, relatedly, contextually produced difference; and second, an instrumental view of culture, where cultural processes and values are judged not by democratic principles, but promoted or excluded upon their assumed value for facilitating economic and ideological strategies.

Hence, an analysis of culture's role in urban development must take this divide serious and consider the antagonism of *culturization* and *culturalization*, of planning *for* cultural development and planning *with* culture, both as a theoretical and empirical foundation of urban research. As uncovering the dominant approaches to culture in planning aims at deconstructing a deeply political process, it further needs to combine the above antagonism with an analysis of power that is embedded in the belief that planning itself is a political process permeated by ideologies, values, beliefs, and power geometries. And finally these two pillars need to be grounded in a well-elaborated conceptualization of the city as both the arena where the politics of planning with culture are staged and as the material outcome of these processes.

Thematically embedding this research

As explained above already, there is no doubt that culture has reached a pivotal position in urban development today. This acknowledgement dates back to the early 20th century, when the Chicago School first stressed the notion of difference and cultural specificity in cities with its research on subcultures, migration and the city as melting-pot. Later, scholars such as Lewis Mumford heightened our perception of the particularities of urban economic and social life, urban architectural form and urbanity as such, brilliantly elucidating that all this needed to be understood as a unique culture of cities (Mumford, 1970). Yet, only in the early 1980s and after the experience of a wide-ranging urban crisis, scholars recognized new patterns of urban transformation that were distinctly "cultural" – not in Mumford's sense of an urban culture, but as artistic and cultural practices and products spurring urban change. Sharon Zukin is maybe the most prominent scholar in this regard. In her research she found that artists as specific cultural actors had a significant role to play in the visible makeover and economic regeneration of formerly run-down, de-industrialized urban quarters in New York (Zukin, 1989). It was back then that literature also recognized the evolvement of a "cultural society" ousting the industrial urban paradigm. Research based on the West-European context revealed tendencies of a turn to culture as the new signifying element of urban economies after industrial decline (Fohrbeck & Wiesand, 1989). Most obviously, culture had entered the center stage of political debate and planning practice (ibid.).

The advent of research on culture-led regeneration then came in the early 1990s. Bianchini and Parkinson (1993) collected a number of European examples of huge urban restructurings based upon culture. Thereby, they drew the picture of cities that found their confidence again after Fordist decline, establishing a new mode of planning, i.e. active regeneration through culture-led urban transformation. Simultaneously, a row of critical accounts of utilizations of culture for economic strategies and ideological projects appeared. Kearns & Philo (1993) highlighted the multiple instrumentalizations of a city's past and its cultural specificities as political instruments, stressing particularly their use and precise framing for a new form of outward-oriented, entrepreneurial policy that implies the selling of places. With reference to Mumford, Sharon Zukin published *"The cultures of cities"* in 1995, criticizing the gap between an obvious diversity of cultures to be found in cities and the one culture persistently reproduced in planning. She refers to this phenomenon as a symbolic economy, thereby creating a valuable concept that points at the contest over the city in cultural terms (Zukin, 1995, 1996, 1998). Zukin's influential concept resonated in a number of subsequent critical accounts of how cultural symbols are utilized in planning to represent power and a certain worldview of what the urban sphere should be like (cf. the contributions in Gupta & Ferguson, 1997a, 1997b, and in Göschel & Kirchberg, 1998). Together, these contributions set off a critical discussion about the multiple utilizations of culture as a tool in urban development. From accounts of cultural exclusion (Kearns, 1993; Zukin, 1995; Hall & Hubbard, 1996; Madanipour, 1998, 1999), to more recent instrumentalizations of artistic creativity (Scott, 1997, 2000; Mattl, 2009; Stalder, 2009), the spectrum covers a huge variety of critical views on how culture is employed by political and economic elites to develop contemporary cities into wished-for directions.

At the turn of the millennium, when the urban renaissance was in full swing, research reflected on two decades of culture-led regeneration. The result was two lines of interpretation of how culture could help solving recurrent urban crises. One attempted to establish a new form of *"cultural planning"*, claiming an integration of all urban political spheres into a cultural perspective to support civic empowerment, pave the way for the development of cultural difference, and thereby cherish democratic principles (Evans, 2001; Stevenson, 2001). The other was an array of sometimes overly positive strategies and handbooks for urban policymakers on how to capitalize on their local cultures. Most widely known among these are the creative industry strategies promoted by Charles Landry (2000) and Richard Florida (2002), advocating urban economic regeneration based upon creative innovation and knowledge-intensive industries. These experienced a true hype, although they were subject to sometimes harsh critique (Peck, 2005; Göschel, 2009). Nevertheless, both strands of theory largely influence the politics of planning with culture still today.

These approaches are already by and large influenced by a widened interpretation of the concept of culture as not only a form of high-brow artistic production, but as the specific ways of life, practices, products, identities and images that as well influence the constitution and perception of place. In social science research, such a cultural turn allowed for extending the criticism of how culture is recently utilized in capitalism for legitimizing urban change and securing surplus value (Harvey, 1990; Jameson, 1991, 1998; Scott, 1997, 2000; Gottdiener, 2000). Referring to it as the *culturalization* of urban economies and cities' physical appearance upon the commodification of cultures points at the currently dominant form of culture-led regeneration (Young, 2008). Here, the conditions of an increasingly globalized economy structure the context of urban development. The underlying principle of inter-place competition for all forms of capital makes culture the versatile tool to construct distinct places and products that, at the same time, speak a global cultural language. Hence, current culture-led transformation often largely builds upon the notion of global visibility through culture's appeal and image value (Harvey, 2002; Evans, 2003, 2006; Lagendijk, 2004; Monclùs & Guardia, 2006; Young, 2006, 2008; Miles, 2007; Eckardt & Nyström, 2009; Benneworth & Hospers, 2009; Sassen, 2011).

As can be seen, academic accounts of culture-led urban development practice are informed by a general critique of narrow interpretations of culture and elitist modes of governing urban change. This work builds upon a similar critique by adopting a political-economic understanding of urban development. The book's aim of unveiling discursive cultural imaginaries as legitimations of urban transformations is based on theoretical considerations from CPE. CPE is described as an adaptation of urban political economy that seeks to go beyond the notion of the cultural, economic and political spheres as unequal variables. Instead, it considers all three as interdependent:

"[...] moving from a one-sided emphasis on either the cultural constitution of political economy, or on the political economy of culture, towards a critical cultural political economy of social processes. This means that culture cannot be reduced to the economic and vice versa. Social processes are co-constituted by cultural, political and economic processes." (Ribera-Fumaz, 2009: 457)

CPE conflates state theory, the regulation approach and institutional economics with recent interpretations of a cultural turn (Jessop, 2004, 2008; Ribera-Fumaz, 2009; van Heur, 2010a; 2010b). Thereby, it sheds light on the influence of culture (interpreted as identity, difference, meaning, and practices) on the specific political-economic constitution of territories, and at the same time, on instrumentalizations of culture(s) in political economy (Best & Paterson, 2010). It is thus interested in both, questions of classic political economy, i.e. crisis tendencies in capitalism and related modes of stabilizing accumulation regimes, and questions acknowledging postmodern thought, i.e. semiosis and handling difference (Jessop, 2004, 2008; Jessop & Oosterlynck, 2008; Ribera-Fumaz, 2009). As it would be an overambitious endeavor to attempt to uncover all of these layers of research in the framework of this book, *this work focuses a distinct form of discursively constructed imaginaries as framings of a certain mode of planning*. While this doesn't mean to ignore the comprehensive framework of CPE, it emphasizes one layer as being of particular significance to the concept of Cultural Imagineering: the regulation approach.

In short, the regulationist approach proclaims that building regimes of accumulation for the creation of wealth in capitalist economies demands an equally strong construct of state regulations to avert the crisis tendencies inherent in capitalism. Regulation in this sense means the stabilization of the related modes of production and consumption, social relations and institutional forms, yet, not merely as legal, juridical, but as well as discursive regulations (Boyer & Saillard, 2002; Jessop & Sum, 2006). The regulation approach seeks to reveal the role of certain institutions and practices in securing accumulation strategies. It does so by analyzing political economy, civil society and the state to draw a comprehensive picture of how accumulation strategies are being governed (Jessop & Sum, 2006). While most regulationist research engages in answering rather big questions of comprehensive, somewhat paradigmatic regime transformation in this regard – most popularly that from Fordism to post-Fordism (Jessop, 1993) – my concern is of comparably smaller size. The regulation-accumulation-coupling as I conceptualize it for Cultural Imagineering demands a cultural imaginary to discursively regulate and stabilize a regime of culture-led accumulation, i.e. capitalization upon culturalization.

But this research seeks to enrich critical reviews of capitalist instrumentalizations of culture with an equally important perspective. Although acknowledging the centrality of culture in accumulation strategies upon urban development, it emphasizes a multi-faceted contest over urban space that extends beyond economic antagonisms. With regard to the definition of culture as a *"signifying practice"* in Cultural Theory (Hall, 1997; du Gay & Pryke, 2013), urban space also becomes the contested arena of cultural representation. Here, culture serves as the material expression of values and identities, often with no direct consideration of their economic capitalization, but as a symbol of ideological power or cultural difference (Jones, 2006; Bieling, 2006a; Schulz, 2006; Bauman, 2011). Hence, in conceptualizing Cultural Imagineering, I merge two strategic principles of employing culture in planning: accumulation and representation.

As the specificity of goods, ways of life and places, culture has become an indispensable economic resource. On global markets determined by similarity, cultural specificity is the unique labeling to attract resources and thereby secure capitalization – both upon material culture-led transformation and discursive culture-led reconfigurations of space. As Bauman (2011: 17) summarizes in this regard, *"The function of culture is not to satisfy existing needs, but to create new ones."* As a representational process, culture serves identity formation and the expression of difference of the diverse identities inherent in a city (Hall, 1997; Baumann, 2011; du Gay & Pryke, 2013). Here, cultural processes are to symbolize values and ideologies of cities characterized by cultural pluralism (Stevenson, 2001; Bloomfield & Bianchini, 2001; Young, 2008). At the same time, cultural signifying practices are instruments of social control and representations of hegemonic power (Jones, 2006; Bieling, 2006a; Göschel, 2009). The decisive element, though, lies between capitalization and representation processes in urban space. It defines the material and discursive regulation of both strategic principles tackled in the analysis of Cultural Imagineering. Hence, this work is particularly interested in the imaginaries that form the *discursive regulation* of culture-led representation and accumulation strategies; the imaginaries legitimizing certain materializations of conceptualizations of culture in urban space, thereby fostering the establishment and stabilization of hegemonic power over space and power over planning.

Research Approach

Contemporary planning practice increasingly incorporates communicative modes of guiding development and negotiating about potential urban futures in its approaches (Healey, 1992; Helbrecht, 1994). It applies new methods of constructing meaning and image of places to attract a transnational capitalist class of investors, high-skilled workforce and visitors (Harvey, 1989; Jameson, 1991, 1998; Hall & Hubbard, 1996; Jessop, 1997; Hall, 1998). And it is here that culture has become a thematic pillar to the politics of planning. Producing exceptional image value, culture-led processes have the ability of boosting political status and the economic value of place (Zukin, 1995, 1996, 1998; Springer, 2007; Best & Paterson, 2010). As culturalizations, they instrumentalize the distinct character of cultural processes and products to re-shape city space in favor of elitist economic and political interests, while the diversity of cultures of a city is marginalized by being excluded from representation and the economic process (Zukin, 1995; Gupta & Ferguson, 1997a, 1997b; Scott, 1997, 2000; Madanipour, 1998, 1999; Harvey, 2002; Miles, 2007). Which interpretation of culture is to be materialized in urban space and for what purpose, is hence a highly contested process.

In this regard, the basic assumption that power is unequally distributed among actors of the city becomes central, particularly if we consider power over space and power over planning not just as materially mediated, but also as discursively fought out (Torfing, 1999; Scott, 2001). Building upon the notion that discourse can produce meaning and unquestioned knowledge, the processes of meaning-making must be interpreted as powerful tools to steer urban development (Flyvbjerg, 2000, 2002, 2003; Jessop, 2004, 2008). This immediately brings a crucial question to the fore. What if meaning and image are not just discursive representations of the cultural artifacts of a city? If we conceptualize the mutual relation between materiality and meaning in the production of space as a process with constant feedbacks between the two, a discursive construct of the cultural city might not just be the outcome of a material practice serving marketing reasons and ideological representation. It might as well be considered as a targeted attempt of individual powerful actors to steer future urban development into a desired direction with no consideration of cultural diversity.

So, this research makes the two-way link between materiality and meaning its basic framework, bearing in mind that both are questions of power at the same time. Yet, it attempts to go beyond the widely-known critical accounts of instrumentalizations of cultural processes for establishing accumulation or representation strategies (Zukin, 1995, 1996, 1998; Hall & Hubbard, 1996; Kirchberg,

1998). While it is obvious to us that the distinct cultures of a city are sometimes ruthlessly exploited by powerful actors for economic capitalization and ideological representation, we often seem to consider the material cultural processes and the distinct local practices of cultural expression as randomly evolving or predetermined. Yet, by acknowledging the interdependence of the material city and its interpretive layer, we need to recognize the influence of discursive meaning-making on material processes of the city as well.

Thus, this work emphasizes a so far under-investigated process in cultural planning research, i.e. the influence of discursive framings of culture on material practice. By turning to this view, the formation of the material cultural processes of a city takes on a political dimension. The local culture(s), upon which accumulation and representation strategies are established, cannot be interpreted as detached from the politics of planning any longer. The culture(s) of place are not anymore – if they ever had been – arbitrarily evolving local processes. Instead, the culture-led development of a city must be understood as a contested process that is influenced by discursively constructed cultural imaginaries.

Fig. 2: Conceptualizing the process of Cultural Imagineering

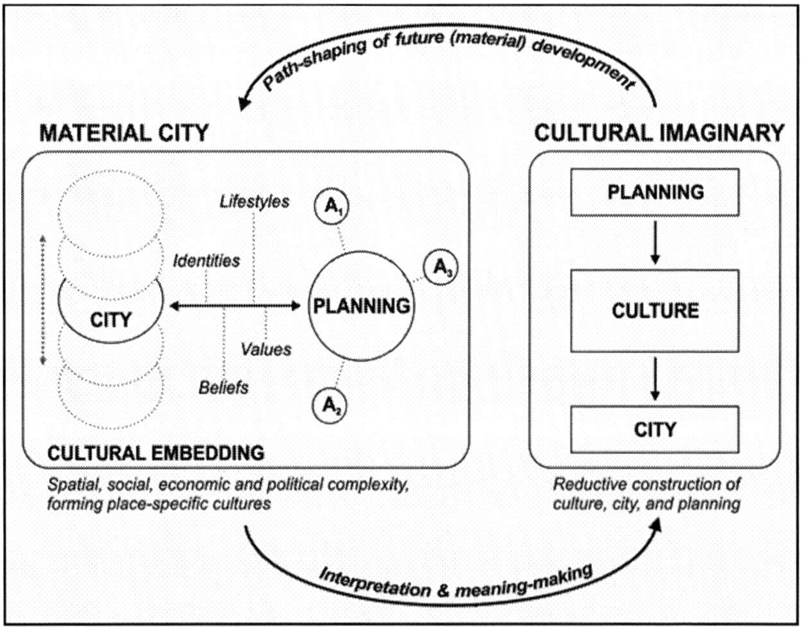

As Fig. 2 illustrates, the material city is conceptualized as a complex set of intermingled scales, where diverse actors intervene in planning to shape the city's form. They are all influenced by certain identities, value sets, lifestyles and beliefs that altogether form the place-specific cultures of a city. The cultural imaginary is the discursively simplified interpretation of how these variables should interact and develop to form a certain urban future. It is the objectified regime of truth of how planning can reasonably utilize a particularly defined culture to impose change on the city. The underlying assumption is that the imaginary frames the development of the material relation between culture, city and planning, while it is also made obvious that the materialities of urban space shape the cultural imaginary. Hence, I conceptualize a cycle, in which materiality and meaning mutually interact. Material development and urban practice, history and institutions, social formation, space and place influence the symbolic and cognitive layer of space to the same extent that discursive constructs determine material urban futures. For the cultural imaginary this means that it is a discursive regulation of a certain form of planning, legitimizing accumulation and representation upon urban culture-led transformation.

The concept of Cultural Imagineering focuses the discursive construction of a simplistic cultural development vision as a legitimation, regulation and stabilization of elitist culture-led accumulation and representation strategies. By discursively reducing the complex concepts of culture, city, and planning to a simple relation, powerful actors construct an argument for the materialization of a certain cultural vision instead of many others. Herewith they facilitate the realization of individual economic and ideological projects in urban development that do not serve a public interest, but secure only their benefit. In this sense, Cultural Imagineering is the regulation of hegemonic projects in planning upon a dominant and unquestioned interpretation of culture and its role in urban development. These unquestioned cognitive ideas are the cultural imaginaries that establish a rationale of planning the city with culture via discourse. They influence a cultural planning reality, thereby re-formulating the limits to what is possible and what is not in the development of a city. Hence, the pivotal question to be posed here is, *"Which and whose cultural imaginaries succeed to influence the materializations in culture-led place transformation, and who benefits from the so-created material cultural places?"*

Approaching the concept of discourse in analyses of the politics of planning

Cultural Imagineering wants to shed light on the so far under-investigated path-shaping of material culture-led development through discursive constructions of culture. Its analysis attempts to disclose how actors engage in discursively promoting arguments for or against certain forms of planning to push through the materialization of their economic or ideological project. It therefore applies the theoretical concept of imaginary. To reveal the cultural imaginary empirically, discourse analysis is employed as the primary method of investigation. As discourse is a fuzzy concept though, it needs to be clearly defined for this work.

In its simplest, discourse means "text". This implies not only written (or spoken) language, but also the process of meaning-making and interpretation that take all sorts of signs into consideration (Jessop, 2008; Wodak, 2008). In fact, it can subsume anything from traffic signs, pictograms or brand logos, to our surrounding physical environment of streets, squares and buildings – as long as it transports significant meaning. It thus determines the relationship between form and function. (Wodak, 2008) *"A discourse is a differentiated ensemble of signifying sequences in which meaning is constantly renegotiated."* (Torfing, 1999: 85) This research largely refers to political economy influenced Critical Discourse Analysis and its prevailing discourse definition. Here discourse refers to the cognitive, symbolic layer of space, which constructs meaning to co-constitute the material city. It is regarded as an essential factor in stabilizing social order, objectifying knowledge, and legitimizing arguments for or against certain forms of planning.

"Discourses, then, can be interpreted as attempts to stabilize meanings and interpretations of material objects and processes, aiming at the institutionalization of a certain knowledge order" (Keller, 2011: 8, author's translation).

Theories of discourse are always interested in the relation of power and knowledge as two key factors determining urban politics and social life. Two quite different conceptualizations of the role of power and knowledge in discourse are recurrently debated in the context of urban planning research. One derives from German philosopher Jürgen Habermas, who, based on a theory of communicative action, elaborated on discourse ethics. He envisions an ideal-speech act, where power is equally distributed among actors, hierarchies are neutralized and decisions only made upon the rationally best argument. Thus, validity of discourses would derive from consensus and consequently allow for the democratization of urban society, he claims (Flyvbjerg, 1998, 2000; Torfing, 1999; Keller, 2011). In this conceptualization, discourse is a neutral ground. Equal distribution of power among actors facilitates the rationally best solution (Torfing, 1999; Scott, 2001).

Although the interpretation of power as fluctuating among actors is similar to both approaches, it is here that the second notion differs from the Habermasian approach. Here, power is understood as a means to construct knowledge and a dominating discourse. This notion is most prominently represented by French historian and philosopher Michel Foucault. Like Habermas, Foucault was trying to depict the process of validation of opinions. Yet, he did not believe in a similar ideal as the Habermasian consensus-oriented *"homo democraticus"* (Flyvbjerg, 1998). Instead, he was keen on revealing processes that let one discourse become dominant among a number of competing discourses. Thus, underlying power structures play a central part in Foucault's discourse theory as producers of universal knowledge (Mills, 2007; Keller, 2011) – a so-called *"regime of truth"* (Lees, 2004). Flyvbjerg (2000) aptly describes the difference between the two, leaving no doubt about him feeling closer to Foucault's discourse theory and conceptualization of power/knowledge:

"The value of Habermas' approach is that it contains a clear picture of what Habermas understands by 'democratic process', and what preconditions must be fulfilled for a decision to be termed 'democratic' [...] The value of Foucault's approach is his emphasis on the dynamics of power [...] and how these might be influenced and changed in a specific political or administrative context." (Flyvbjerg, 2000: 14)

Political philosophers utter a similarly situated critique on Habermas' discourse ethics. Mouffe (2007) strongly disagrees with the concept of deliberative politics and rational discourses. Pointing at Habermas, she criticizes his notion of rationality, which considers the existence of some kind of universal truth. Zizek as well is opposed to this conception, insisting that the practice of communication is not comparable with the envisioned ideal-speech situation (Torfing, 1999).

Although adopting a narrower discourse definition than that applied in Foucault's work, this research employs the Foucaultian discourse theoretical considerations and conceptions of power/knowledge regimes. It builds upon the basic assumption of unequally distributed power in planning and the idea that these power structures decisively influence the construction of unquestioned knowledge and meaning through discourse. The attempt of identifying a dominant discourse of planning with culture makes it an appropriate theory to ground this piece of work. If discourses are interpreted as producers of meaning and objective regimes of truth, they must be considered as powerful tools influencing urban planning realities. Thus, the analysis of discourses is one source for analyzing the politics of planning with culture empirically (Glasze & Mattissek, 2009; Schipper, 2012).

CPE and critical semiotic analysis

The research engages in revealing potential instrumentalizations and exclusions of cultural processes, stressing the notion of culture as a contested arena. The various conceptions and differing roles of culture ask for an altered research approach, which combines the political economy of urban development with the acknowledgement of a cultural turn. Relatedly, Young (2008) advocates a culturization of planning to open our eyes to the multiplicity of competing cultures, and to understand the various shades of how culture is used, e.g. for state legitimation, community development, or marketing. In recent years, the concept of CPE has entered urban research, tackling just this issue of how cultural specificity is used in capitalist approaches to urban development, and how political economy itself needs to be seen as culturally influenced in the ways it functions (Jessop, 2004; Harrison, 2009; Ribera-Fumaz, 2009; Best & Paterson, 2010). In the meantime, critical accounts of CPE are manifold. Van Heur (2010a, 2010b), for instance, analyzes the cultural economy of electronic music production in London and Berlin as a culturally determined political economy of aesthetic production. Best & Paterson (2010) critically investigate the advertisements of HBSC in London as an example of how cultural difference is increasingly exploited in global economic marketing. And only recently, Jessop (2013) depicted the mechanisms of how the global financial crisis and the potential recoveries from it are being discursively constructed. In all these studies, *"critical semiotic analysis"* (Jessop, 2004) is a central empirical research method. Hence, for depicting the Cultural Imagineering of place transformation, I follow the call for critically investigating constructed meaning to detect the paths of a CPE of planning with culture in contemporary cities.

To be more exact, considering the arguments that power to produce and reproduce urban space is discursively and institutionally mediated (Jessop and Oosterlynck, 2008), and that mediatic permeation of literally all spheres of urban development is the current condition (Lundby, 2009; Friesen & Hug, 2009), I put my empirical research focus on the analysis of strategic and mediatic discourses. The need for integrating such analyses in recent urban studies is uttered by several scholars. Eade and Mele (2002), for instance, rate the exploration of urban discourses and the role of imaginaries in the production of urban space among the most important fields of contemporary research. Smith (2002) further explicates the important role of mass media in framing space production and urban development in general. The analysis of political and mediatic discourses has two parallel effects. Not only does it inform about the role(s) attributed to culture in urban development, it furthermore reveals who the discourse-producing actors are. Hence, discourse analysis explicates who has power over such discourses and therefore can exert power over urban cultural development (Flyvbjerg, 2004; Mills, 2007).

Anyhow, discourse analysis is often criticized for blinding out extra-discursive concerns, such as path-dependencies, institutional frameworks, or material practice (Torfing, 1999; Jessop, 2008). In a radical constructivist perspective this seems plausible as any of these concerns is considered to be determined by discourse only (cf. for instance Berger & Luckmann, 1980). Yet, as was prominently elaborated, the understanding of the city as a dialectic relationship between materiality and meaning draws me to a different understanding. I apply a CPE approach, where urban phenomena are understood as being influenced by discursive features, while emerging from and again resulting in materialities (Jessop, 2004, 2008; Ribera-Fumaz, 2009; Harrison, 2009; van Heur, 2010a, 2010b). In this sense, CPE goes beyond Critical Discourse Analysis, as it is not only interested in reconstructing discourses, but also in depicting material change (Jessop, 2008; Ribera-Fumaz, 2009). Such an understanding of urban development considers the materiality of space as the ultimate objective of accumulation strategies and ideological projects, making it a second layer of empirical investigation, in which discourse is embedded as a presumably influential factor, yet not as an end in itself.

From imaginary to Imagineering:
Confronting discourse with material practice

Pointing to Bayart, Jessop (2004: 24) clarifies, *"Indeed, there is no [...] imaginary without materiality."*, emphasizing that the city represents a dialectical relation of discursively constructed meaning and the materially existent social formation, institutional and physical structures. The city houses processes, which always produce both material and discursively formed realities (Hofmann, 2011), meaning, the cultural imaginary is central for the culture-led transformation of the materialities of space, but not the only influencing factor. *"Extra-semiotic factors"*, as Jessop (2004) terms them, are equally important development characteristics. These material factors of place transformation subsume history, as well as a distinct socio-economic development context, a particular institutional framework and adjacent legal regulations, and all forms of path-dependencies resulting from these materialities. So while it is a stated objective of this research to explicitly analyze the discursive formation of a simplified cognitive construct of culture-led urban planning as a *regulation* and *legitimation* of distinct processes of capitalist urbanization and hegemonic ideological representation, the analysis as well takes into account the material preconditions of place transformation. It analyzes the distinct development history of each case study site, the planning-political, institutional, and socio-economic, as well as the material cultural context of place as its materiality.

This is where the third layer of analysis comes into play. It is based on a review of the material practice of local place transformation, i.e. the documentation of significant material alterations. This includes physical transformations, institutional changes, and newly evolved or vanished processes, and is meant to uncover the transformed materialities of place. Reflecting the approach employed in policy analyses (cf. for instance Hajer, 2003; Hajer & Wagenaar, 2003; Healey et al., 2003), findings on the transformed materialities of place are to be confronted with the analysis of discourse in order to depict potential moments of Imagineering. This aims at revealing whether the instrumental use of culture in imaginaries of urban transformation can actually be linked to the material transformations of place, or whether they remain on a discursive level.

Empirical research object: Culture-led place transformation in Vienna

For empirically analyzing processes of Cultural Imagineering, this research makes the city of Vienna its research object. It chooses the city for it being an exceptional case of intense planning-political interest in cultural affairs and the common sense that its development is characterized by a path that is distinctly "cultural". Vienna forms a typical example of the European city and combines structural, architectural, and institutional characteristics from diverse periods of history, which very much influence its planning still today. Its outward image is largely determined by the powerful subject of a heritage culture from the times of the Austro-Hungarian monarchy and meant to attract cultural tourism, while its self-perception is somewhat torn between traditional value constructs and growing lifestyle diversity through increasing metropolisation (Mattl, 2000; Maderthaner, 2006; Bihl, 2006; Meißl, 2006; Musner, 2006; Steinert, 2009; ESPON, 2012). In public discourse and planning practice these interpretations of the city's contextual culture are always involved in any development considerations, hence making Vienna a good case for analyzing potential hegemonic and counter-hegemonic constructions of culture as influential factors of material planning practice.

As an analysis of the city's cultural transformation as a whole would neither be feasible, nor senseful considering its diversity in places, cultures, and planning preconditions, the analysis turns to three recent sites of culture-led place transformation, making them the units of empirical analysis within the case study of Vienna (cf. Yin, 2009 for a detailed taxonomy of case study research designs). This potentially generates a wider range of results on different processes of Cultural Imagineering, while simultaneously allowing for obtaining potential similar patterns within Vienna's cultural planning practice when conducting cross-case synthesis (ibid.). The three case study sites are: Karlsplatz, an inner city public space, Brunnenviertel, an urban neighborhood in transition, and Seestadt Aspern, an urban expansion project in the city's periphery. In all three, culture is discursively and materially introduced as a factor of transformation recently. Also, the units of analysis cover three different parts of the city, i.e. central and peripheral, in order to unhide potentially different approaches to cultural development and planning with culture in different locations. Furthermore, the case studies also constitute processes at varying stages of place transformation to include this factor in the analysis as well. Ultimately they also cover three determinant thematic fields of Vienna's planning culture: high-cultural institutions, ethnic diversity and soft urban renewal, and public infrastructure provision and social housing. Hence, they represent three different preconditions for Vienna's urban and cultural development. The following introduces the case studies in short.

Karlsplatz is a large central public space of Vienna with a long development history. Its transformation within the past century includes manifold physical regeneration projects of a place that was ever since criticized for being unfinished and lacking a clear concept (Geschäftsgruppe Stadtplanung, 1981). Today, it hosts a number of important urban functions as it is a central hub for public transport, car traffic and pedestrians, and houses large cultural institutions, from the University of Technology to federal and municipal museums, a theater, concert hall, school, and the architecturally outstanding St. Charles Church. The density of art institutions and its close vicinity to the inner city and the Ringstraße make it a very much pre-determined space in cultural terms. Its recent transformation is thus also dictated by a politically promoted regeneration project, which aims at turning Karlsplatz from an undefined traffic hub into an aestheticized, representational art space of the city. The empirical analysis thus asks, whether the anyway dominant approach of promoting high culture for capitalizing on tourism is further consolidated through Karlsplatz transformation, or if the potential of a so far undefined central public space for a metropolis in the making is recognized to materialize in a new agora of Vienna.

The second case study site is Seestadt Aspern. The project located in the Northeast of Vienna currently constitutes one of Europe's biggest planning projects, and it is a novice in the city's planning cultural tradition. Forming a state-induced urban expansion project, it not only breaks with the long tradition of solely promoting renewal and inner transformation in Vienna's development, but it forms a symbol of a declared political belief in urban growth and metropolisation. Yet, the urbanization project is not just remarkable due to its size, but also as concerns the governance structure, which facilitates state-related, yet profit-oriented agencies with decision-making power in planning. This is reflected also by the planning approach, which turns to entrepreneurial modes of place branding as a development strategy. In this context, cultural interventions come into play to promote and legitimize the development project. Although its realization only recently began, Seestadt Aspern's planning was soon accompanied by an intense strategic and mediatic debate on the distinct culture of place, its identity, and its role in Vienna's development path (Tovatt Architects & Planners & Projektteam Flugfeld Aspern, 2007; Municipal Department 18, 2005, 2012a). Hence, the question to be posed here is, whether, first, early materializations point to the influence of processes of Imagineering at all, and if, second, the transformed materialities of place are able to combine the utilization of certain cultures for a profit-oriented urbanization project with the expectations of the many cultures to be accommodated there in the future.

The third case study unit is Brunnenviertel, a densely populated urban neighborhood in transition. It is located in the northwestern part of Vienna, in Ottakring, the city's 16th district. Brunnenviertel is determined by a large street market, which constitutes the neighborhood's social and economic backbone, and the urban pattern of Gründerzeit housing structures, which were erected due to the city's rapid growth in the 19th century and characterize the area structurally still today. It shows a unique urban character due to high densities and a mix of urban functions, while the low quality housing stock is a recognized challenge since long. Hence, the neighborhood is part of the city's soft urban renewal program since the 1970s. Its socio-cultural conditions are shaped by an above average share of a migrant population, which started to become apparent mostly in a transforming local economy in the 1990s, and which was recurrently problematized in public discourse (Rode et al., 2010; Municipal Department 21A, n.d.). More recently though, it has attracted public attention for another reason, as with "Soho In Ottakring" a self-determined, local art-led project evolved that turned out to be an image factor for an otherwise problematized urban quarter (Rode et al., 2010; Suitner, 2010). Soho became a role model of art-led urban renewal in Vienna, which established both the arts and different lifestyles in place-specific discourse, but also increased the development pressure on Brunnenviertel upon its new cultural image. Hence, the empirical analysis considers Brunnenviertel as a contested neighborhood in transition, where state, market, and civil society interests collide both in discourse and materially. The important question to be dealt with is, whether discursively informed materializations can be regarded as the sequel to a well-functioning bottom-up neighborhood development for a diverse population, or if individual interests succeed upon the materialization of different cultural imaginaries.

Fig. 3: Locating case studies of culture-led transformation in Vienna

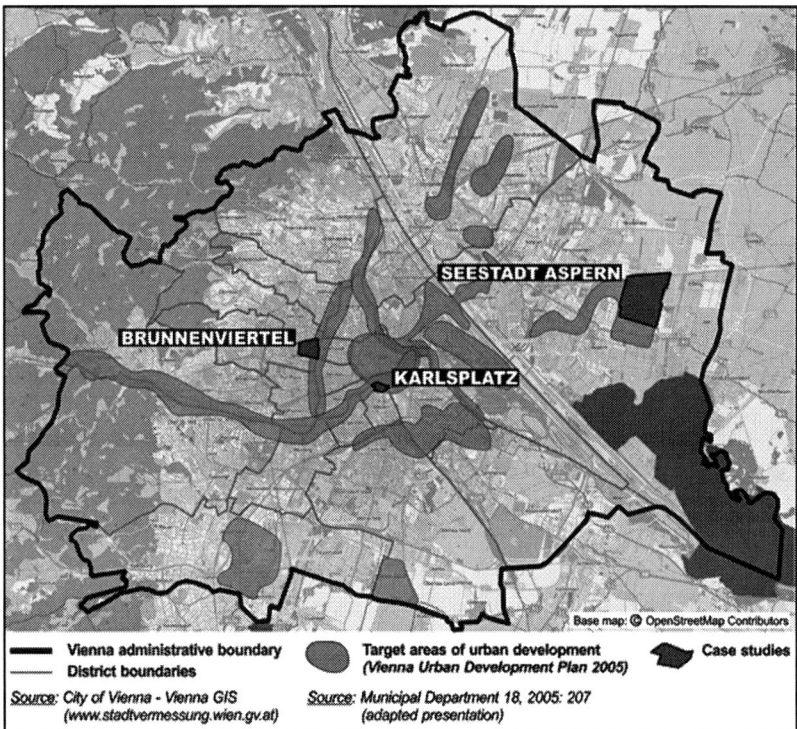

Structure of the book

The first chapters are dedicated to theoretical elaborations on the concepts of culture, city, and planning, and their deep links as conceptualized in Cultural Imagineering. I start with the major transformations of cities within the past decades, introducing the spatial turn and consequent acknowledgement of a duality of urban space. The shift from static object to constant process is the beginning to the story of multiform urban complexity in economic, social, political, and cultural terms that planning faces today. Thus, the new modes of governing urban development are being discussed then, pointing at accumulation and representation as the two principles permeating the politics of planning in contemporary cities and resulting in contests over the future use of urban space. With this in mind, the concept of culture is being introduced as the all-embracing concept in urban development today. Referring to recent scientific discourses on culture and planning, the salient narratives of culture as an agent of change are outlined. These reveal the variety of utilizations of culture in accumulation strategies and ideological representations. Theorizing the concept of Cultural Imagineering concludes the theory section of the book. It is pointed out that discursive constructions of culture in planning can become powerful regulations and legitimations for accumulation and representation strategies in the politics of planning.

Following, the empirical analysis of Vienna's Cultural Imagineering is presented by an introduction of empirical research design and methods applied. To contextualize the case study, I start with the material urban development trajectory of the city. It embeds the case study in the specificities of a local planning culture and serves as an analytical background for assessing distinct discursive constructions and material processes. Following, the three Viennese case study sites are being investigated to unveil the Cultural Imagineering of place transformation. In the next section, the three are being conjoined to draw a comprehensive picture of the rationales and hegemonic practices influencing recent cultural planning in Vienna. Referring to the transformed materialities analyzed before, it points to a number of critical implications as concerns culture-led place transformation and Vienna's cultural development as such.

I conclude on the empirical findings then, not only to sum up this piece of work, but to accentuate those results that are considered momentous for Vienna's cultural development. It recommends necessary steps for Vienna's cultural planning in particular and for planning *for* cultural development at large, and finishes with indicating further research needs in the context of analyzing processes of Imagineering.

Contextualizing urban development
Cities between materiality and meaning

The city is a process. The spatial turn in social sciences clarifies that *"[...] space is made not by underlying structures but by diverse social, economic, cultural and physical processes."* (Davoudi & Strange, 2009: 14). In this line of reasoning cities must be understood as the outcome of *"complex associative life"* (Mumford, 1970: 482) – the diverse connections of political, social, economic and cultural actions that refer to the urban sphere (Berndt & Pütz, 2007; Jung, 2010).

Thus, space is not a pre-given thing. As Soja (2008) explains, we must think of space as an active and political process. And as Gupta and Ferguson (1997a) clarify, the social and political processes of place-making are the vital ingredients to the production of the spaces we inhabit. In this conceptualization space can constantly be de- and re-constructed. The resulting new urban realities – the physical structures, the uses of urban space, and the meanings attached to it – must all be considered as socially, politically, economically, and culturally produced (Sadler, 1993; Pratt, 1998; Soja, 2008; Glasze & Mattissek, 2009; Jung, 2010).

Yet, if the city is a process, it cannot be viewed as merely being a material object anymore. And the notion of discrete moments of interfering in this static urban space to bring it to another end-state must ultimately be dismissed. Instead, the development of the city and its parts needs to be considered as a continuous process of constant bargaining, where actors advocate their own ideologies, identities, values, and visions of how their urban environment should be constituted (Helbrecht, 1994; Healey et al., 1999; Albrechts, 2004).

A SPATIAL TURN: THE CITY AS DISCURSIVE PROCESS?

> "[I]t is increasingly apparent that the forms of discourse used to describe, analyze, and construct the city are central to social, cultural, political, and economic processes that produce the city and occur within it."
>
> EADE & MELE, 2002: 6

Considering urban space as a variable thing urges us to deal with the question how it is being produced. In all social, political, economic, or cultural terms, discourses are considered as decisive elements affecting the (re-)formation of place, as the above statement makes clear. Hence, the making of contemporary cities needs to be understood as being heavily influenced by public discourse. This notion of discursive space production follows the arguments from discourse theory that discourses can construct a common understanding of how social processes function (Torfing, 1999; Taylor, 2004; Mills, 2007). Yet, discourse is more than a representation of a certain truth. In accordance with definitions of discourses as processes of meaning-making (Torfing, 1999; Jessop, 2008; Wodak, 2008), the discursive production of urban space must be considered as a process of attaching space with meaning. *"People do not live in a framework of geometric relationships but a world of meaning."* (Hubbard et al., 2004, cited in Davoudi & Strange, 2009: 26) Accordingly, Cresswell (2004) explains that what we perceive as place is *"a meaningful location"*, pointing to the differentiation between space and place in social sciences after the spatial turn. I want to refer to this process of discursive production of space as a process of *construction*, as to me it best suits the fact that powerful actors can intentionally influence discourses to *"construct"* the immaterial layer of urban space and the objectified truths that influence urban futures (Torfing, 1999; Jessop, 2004, 2008; Mills, 2007).

It is evident that the discursive construction of the city follows certain regularities of how power and knowledge interact (Torfing, 1999; Flyvbjerg, 2003; Mills, 2007). Yet, the ever specific contexts of a certain place obviously frame the process of meaning-making, as *"every society and every mode of production produces its own space"* (Davoudi & Strange, 2009: 28). In a similar vein, it would thus be too reductive to not consider any material aspects in the conceptualization of a city and its processes of meaning-making, as, of course, space also becomes attached with meaning through the material processes happening there (Springer, 2007). And, in this broader understanding it must be more than the discursive construction that shapes our impressions. Jung (2010), for instance, emphasizes the importance of a physical environment, legal and regulated structures and symbols as other distinct characteristics of the spatial structure, which all influence the conception and perception of the city and how it is politically approached.

Urban geography today emphasizes a duality of conceptualizing urban space, which consists of an immaterial layer of imagined or discursively constructed space, and a material layer including the built environment and all material processes (Soja, 2008). Thus, urban space can be considered as a conflation of *"real and imagined assemblages"*, (Davoudi & Strange, 2009: 35) where material and discursive realities interact and mutually influence each other to construct space and place (Cresswell, 2004; Davoudi & Strange, 2009). This mutual influence of space as discursive product and space as a material reality is highlighted by other authors as well. Referring to seminal sociologist Henri Lefebvre, Miles (2007) states that for the field of culture and the city we must comprehend the built urban world as being interrupted by *"a dimension of constantly remade meanings and associations"* (Miles, 2007: 17). Also considering Lefebvre's and Doreen Massey's oeuvre on the production of space, Martin et al. (2003) clarify the interrelations between space as social product and its related material reality. Mumford (1970) also stressed the importance of the material urban environment in shaping the culture of cities already more than four decades ago. He discussed urban architecture as a symbolic representation of urbanity and civilization and, thus, as an expression of power in planning (ibid.). More recently, Hannemann and Sewing (1998) state that architecture still is vital to staging the contemporary city in global images. And, as Schroer (2008) explains, we should not dismiss the notion of urban space as socially produced, but we need to consider the co-determination of discourses by a material reality as well. And although space is constantly being re-produced through social interaction, these constructs do reach a certain "end-state" as well – in the political, institutional and physical reality of the city (ibid.).

These first elaborations already highlight the complexity of the city as a research object. The spatial turn in social sciences calls for the acknowledgement of the processual character of the city – its constant re-making through social interaction and discourse. Yet, it doesn't ignore the significance of a material urban reality as a determinant of envisioning urban futures. This is the contextualization to all urban development. As Gupta and Ferguson (1997b: 40) put it: *"Places, after all, are always imagined in the context of political-economic determinations that have a logic of their own"*

So, to better understand these contexts, the following sections describe the recent spatial, societal and economic constitution of contemporary cities. This is supposed to explicate why processes of Imagineering play such an important role in today's urban world and why culture takes such an important place in both the discursive and material determination of the contemporary city.

THE MULTI-SCALAR CITY: BETWEEN LOCAL AND GLOBAL

> "Cities [...] are supposed to link up the local and the global. But this is exactly where the problems start, since these are two conflicting logics that have torn cities from the inside when they try to respond to both simultaneously."
> CASTELLS, 2005: 49

The embedding of cities in global urban networks is not new to planning. Much has been said on its effects and how it puts cities into a new context of increased transnational interconnection and competition (Sieverts, 1990; Dicken, 1998; Turok, 2005; Giffinger & Wimmer, 2005). As a result, cities perform a tightrope walk. For one thing, they often try to adapt to a competitive context by employing new, mainstreamed modes of planning for a transnational capitalist class. At the same time, they try to avoid the pitfall of sameness and homogenization by establishing distinct narratives and pictures of the livable city (Evans, 2001; Fessler Vaz & Berenstein Jacques, 2006; Young, 2006; Miles, 2007). Anyhow, we, as planners, must be aware of the fact that as framers and co-designers of urban life we have to take this new multiplicity of controversial spatial and political orientations of how to direct urban futures serious (Swyngedouw, 1997; Castells, 1998).

Writing about the multi-scalar character of today's cities, urges for introducing globalization – a phenomenon that has received major attention in Urban Studies in the past two decades. When we speak of globalization, we speak of very abstract transnational relations and a world economy (Friedmann, 1986; Sassen, 2001). But what is implicitly subsumed, are very specific processes of intertwining on a worldwide scale, of which some have tremendously increased over time. This is particularly the case for economic factors, such as foreign direct investments and international trade, which have multiplied within the last decades (Gunter & van der Hoeven, 2004). But such quantitative shifts, impressing as they may be, refer rather to an intensified internationalization of economic interaction – a major characteristic of recent globalization, but only one aspect among a greater variety (Kelly, 1999; Marcuse & van Kempen, 2000).

Friedmann (1986) first provides an explicit hypothesis of cities being nodes in a worldwide network. He emphasizes the notion that urban agglomerations need to be analyzed in a broader context, and that the world economy is such an instance. He points to the fact that specific functions make what is called a *world city*: corporate headquarters, global transport and communications, and sites of information, news, and entertainment among others (ibid.). Yet, what the numerous typologies of cities in a world economy to be found in literature actually present (cf. Friedmann, 1986, Sassen, 2001; Smith & Timberlake, 2001 to name just a few) is the significant shift of scope of present-day urban conurbations. Evidently, cities now find themselves embedded in global networks, which not only uncover a city's position and economic power, but, more generally, represent a new geography of urban interaction. And this interaction is not merely of an economic nature. The apparent social, political, and cultural interrelations point to the thematic multiplicity of processes of globalization (Friedmann, 2011).

We all know about the conspicuous shifts in global politics. Regions and nation states increasingly team up in supra-national bodies to be less vulnerable to the newly emerging, world-spanning challenges: democracy and human rights, climate change, economic crises (Held et al., 1999; Gunter & van der Hoeven, 2004; Gordon & Buck, 2005; United Nations, 2012; Jessop, 2013). Relatedly, economic transformations caused a total makeover of local economic structures. Cities began to widen their area of interest in economic terms far beyond their surrounding regions (Goodwin, 1993; Harrison, 2009). Consequently, economic interactions started to shift from internal to global, intensifying international relations between urban economies, and blurring also the boundaries of the city at least in terms of trade and other economic ties (Turok, 2005). Capital, goods, people, and information face an erosion of the barriers of mobility and are able to move more freely (Dicken, 1998; Kelly, 1999; Marcuse & van Kempen, 2000; Gottdiener & Budd, 2005). These preconditions allow for the connection of global centers of economy, politics and culture – sometimes regardless of where they are actually located. Industrial production all too often drifts away, and knowledge-based businesses appear, although they are hardly able to replace the loss of industry and often go along with intensified social inequalities (Hall, 1998; Sassen, 2001). And on another front, globalization as the process of diminishing boundaries allows for the appearance of a transnational social space, in which a global culture emerges to serve a dominant social class (Sklair, 2006). In this context, entertainment, shopping and all patterns of consumption are relocated – either to peripheral areas regionally, or to centers of mass tourism globally (Zukin, 1995; Gottdiener, 2000; Rojek, 2000; Oh & Arditi, 2000). The access to massive flows of information provides a whole new diversity of choice with global extents, and the abovementioned transport opportunities cause that culture, leisure, and tourism go global and seem to become one (Castells, 1998; Gottdiener, 2000; Rojek, 2000) – allowing for the evolvement of what is recently called a global capitalist cultural economy (Scott, 1997, 2000).

So, it already gets clear why globalizing cities of today must be considered as multi-scalar entities. To internalize these contextual changes even better, let's think back to the medieval city. We would picture a clearly delimitable entity, surrounded by city walls and constituting an economic, political and legal counterpart to its rural surroundings. In some parts this is still true for the industrial cities of the 19th century (Mumford, 1970). But only during the last hundred years (and with an increased velocity during the last few decades) this has decisively changed. The face of the city mutated to a fuzzy, border-crossing urban agglomeration, characterized by all sorts of relations with regional, national, and even global extent, regardless of size and location (Sassen, 2001; Albers, 2008; Schäfers, 2009). *"Cities are inserted into local, regional, national, supranational, and global fields"*, finds also Kofman (1998: 283) and identifies that cities cannot be reduced to their local administrative boundaries anymore. They are required to handle different tasks on different spatial scales with ever-varying contexts.

In such a blurry geographic setting of borderless interaction, cities are increasingly challenged to cope with numerous external shifts, causing changed preconditions for their development. Planning interventions that once had local, regional or at best national impacts now need to be considered in front of a multitude of influential layers of world-spanning networks (Heineberg, 2005). This new context provokes a modified behavior of cities and different ways of planning. The functionally intensified and spatially extensified interconnections between cities in the world and the increased interdependencies of economy, politics, societies and cultures call for new approaches to cities and how they are being planned (Amin & Graham, 1997; Sassen, 2001; Smith, 2002; Albrechts, 2004). And it is common ground to consider this as a constant, on-going process, which calls for adaptations and adaptable approaches in planning as we are confronted with a world that is in a state of flux (Schneider, 1997; Healey et al., 1999; Albrechts, 2004). So, for the object of the city, we are witnessing a pluralization of scales that are relevant for its development, while at the same time these scales ever more intensely intersect (Swyngedouw, 1997; Swyngedouw & Kaika, 2003). Urban scholars today are aware that considering the city as an entity fails, if the various levels of interconnectedness on different spatial scales – from the very local to the all-embracing global – are not taken into account. And it would also be too easy in this regard to conclude that the global simply replaced the local. Instead, we have to consider the city as a multi-scalar entity, where processes and actors can also be situated on more than one spatial scale at a time (Castells, 1998, 2000, 2005), which not only increases the level of complexity again, but leads to new challenges in terms of power and inequality (Harvey, 1990).

Another differentiation to be made is that different scholars have meanwhile explained why not all cities encounter the same *kind* of globalization (cf. for instance Marcuse & van Kempen, 2000). Not all are affected by it in the same positive or negative way. So should we conclude from globalization to homogenization? At least, in the heydays of the globalization debate, some writers argued that the new common context, the universal framework of a borderless, globalized world would cause global homogenization in the functions and behavior of cities, but even more in their look-and-feel (Koolhaas, 1995; Gunter & van der Hoeven, 2004: 7). And, the conception of globalization with its new hierarchies, networks and interdependencies was often proclaimed to be an irreversible endstate (cf. Kelly, 1999). But soon a huge counter-discourse emerged in reaction to the *"death of geography"* reports of the late 1990s, proclaiming the high significance of cities in the globalized world (Kelly, 1999; Morgan, 2004). Orum and Chen (2003), for instance, stress that global contexts should be considered in planning and research, but that they do not produce any kind of sameness. Writers as Swyngedouw strongly oppose the view of a globalized world where local qualities don't play any role. Instead he introduces the term "glocalization", giving recognition to the fact that urban development must be steered considering a global *and* a still existing local context (Swyngedouw, 1997; Swyngedouw and Kaika, 2003). Yeung (1998: 292) argues from a similar point of view, recognizing globalization, *"[...] as a dialectical process between homogenization and differentiation"*, and qualifying the borderless world argument as simply wrong.

These elaborations show that the process of globalization and the following intersection of scales lead to a new significance of place (Döring & Thielmann, 2008). The mere fact that cities have become the centers of a world economy and the arenas of global political decision-making under globalization assigns them with an undeniable symbolic role (Bahn et al., 2003; Orum & Chen, 2003). *"Cities are containers of the world; they are where the world, the global, becomes localized and rooted."* (Swyngedouw & Kaika, 2003: 15) The new global political and economic hierarchies and functions associated with them can be counted in for sure when it is about to reveal the key characteristics and roles of globalizing cities in the world (Marcuse & van Kempen, 2000). But in the end, it is the cultures of cities and the cultures of how urban societies deal with contexts such as globalization that play the decisive role in defining the new significance of place (Mumford, 1970; Sieverts, 1990; Evans, 2001; Sennett, 2008; Young, 2008).

One might now all too easily conclude that the local stands in strong opposition to the global. Yet, this dichotomy must be critically reviewed from case to case. Serious doubts exist about the strict dichotomization of "the global" and "the local" (Smith, 2002; Berking, 2006). Scholars suggest to rather speak of a global-local dialectic, where global forces are mediated locally (Hall, 1998). This term better fits the current picture of local politics and planning dealing with globally oriented actors and their networks within the micro-structures of the city (Lange, 2007). And it is in line with the notion that it is not the city, which is global, but only some of its inhabitants (Marcuse & van Kempen, 2000). Even more, regarding the process of a city's development in the world as a mutual relation between global and local allows for overcoming the God-given character of an inevitable globalization threat. Massey (2006) reminds us that the local scale still produces meaning and its own contexts. Hence, cities are not mere victims to a globalization produced elsewhere. Local action can influence the global at least to the same extent as the other way round (Smith, 2002). Cities are not merely spectators of an external globalization steamrolling all their efforts to shape their own future. As Doreen Massey puts it, "the global" is also locally produced. Cities are thus in power to construct their own global context (Massey, 2006).

This is being reflected not only in various counter-globalization discourses, but is considered as a main argument in discourses on planning culture and urban politics. Local differentiations of handling globalization and reacting to it appear in comparative studies and are even more apparent when investigating specific cases in depth (Faludi, 2005; Sanyal, 2005). Each locality on the global map and each city in the world has its own context of globalization, its own historical development paths, and its specific political and planning cultures, which effectuate in different globalization contexts from case to case (Suitner, 2014).

"Globalization, then, need not simply mean the globalization of a particular model of economic and social policy. If instead it is taken to be simply a process of extensification and intensification of social connectedness across space, rather than a normative and inevitable end-state, then it can be interpreted as either progressive or regressive (or somewhere in between), depending upon how such processes are harnessed and used." (Kelly, 1999: 385)

Thus, it would be wrong to speak of *the* globalization as if it was a transcendent master-narrative, disempowering any urban development. Instead, each place needs to be looked at separately concerning its approaches to, interactions with, and influences by globalization (Marcuse & van Kempen, 2000; Massey, 2006). So, if we agree with Massey and others, we need to regard the global and the local as imagined entities – as socially produced constructs that serve the goal of making "here and there" and "us and the others" a tangible thing (Kearns and Philo, 1993; Anderson & O'Dowd, 1999; van Houtum, 2011). Or to put it with John Friedmann: *"Localization and globalization are cultural processes like any other ones."* (Friedmann, 1990, cited in Peters, 1997: 86).

So while evidence seems to exist, which allows negating the idea of a dichotomy between local and global, it cannot be denied – and this is important to be stated – that processes of bordering are constantly initiated, trying to discursively produce such a dichotomy for political, cultural, or economic reasons (Scott, 2012). Hence, the fact whether we face a dichotomy or dialectic between the global and local spheres of urban development depends on how these scales are introduced into discourses about the city's past, presence and future (McCann, 2003). *"[W]e might well say that globalization is always experienced (and constructed) from highly local situations [...]"* (Elliott, 2001: 58).

Thus, it can be concluded that the proclamation of a borderless world is by far an exaggeration. Yet, an intensification of economic, social, cultural and political relations beyond the boundaries of a local urban sphere is as evident. The loss of political significance of the nation state and the simultaneous evolvement of supra-national entities only complicates these new geographies that surround our contemporary cities. Yet, this complication and fuzziness doesn't weaken the importance of the city as anchoring point in the world. Quite the opposite is true. Cities are more than ever places of political power, economic and social innovation and cultural evolution. Thus, it would also be wrong to outline them as disempowered spectators of a globalization happening elsewhere. They are themselves producing it and should therefore consider it as just a change of context. But the ways in which these contexts are discussed and thus reflected need to be looked at closely from case to case. In the end, it is the local planning cultures, histories, institutions, path-dependencies and discourses that determine how this phenomenon is perceived and approached.

URBAN ECONOMIES IN TRANSITION: FROM PRODUCTION TO CONSUMPTION

> "In the industrialization period, the city underwent a radical transformation, adapting itself to its new condition as a material production center. At present, in the post-industrial economy, new transformations are under way: non-material production obliges cities once again to transform themselves."
>
> FESSLER VAZ & BERENSTEIN JACQUES, 2006: 241

Since its earliest days the city is attributed with economic power. Whether we think of Jane Jacobs' imagined New Obsidian or ancient Rome – cities ever since accommodated the production of goods, particularly those crafted goods distinct from the rural agricultural ones. And the towns and cities of that time hosted the first markets for their exchange, herewith signifying the rising division of labor in urban economies (Jacobs, 1969; Sennett, 2008). Later on, cities almost perfected their role as hosts of economic life. In medieval towns, the producers of goods were affiliated with guilds that represented the craftsmen, and markets had become the foundation, the backbone of any flourishing place (Mumford, 1970; Sennett, 2008). Renaissance and baroque brought about conspicuous transformations of artistic production, namely its emancipation from crafts and the rise of the artist as genius. Yet, this change should not become significant for urban economic development before the modern era (Mumford, 1970; Springer, 2007; Sennett, 2008).

What changed the economic constitution at least of European cities most radically, though, was industrialization. This process implies not only the replacement of manufactured goods by industrially fabricated products. It also signifies the appearance of urban factories for mass production of goods – a circumstance that completely changed the nature, look and functioning of cities. Rich employment opportunities started to attract people from almost everywhere to live and work in the industrial towns, which let cities grow like never before. Relatedly, the baroque picture of the bourgeois urban citizen got more and more replaced by the working-class man, who from then on symbolized the new economic strength and independence of the city (Mumford, 1970; Sennett, 2008; Schäfers, 2009).

For urban economies this meant just another transformation, which it had already experienced several times throughout history – but never within such a short period of time, and never with such wide-ranging effects on urban structure and the organization of economic and social life. Settlements soon crossed the cities' earlier boundaries, factories were implanted literally everywhere, and the required redevelopments were implemented without showing any courtesy to existing social and cultural structures (Mumford, 1970).

Only in the 1970s the praised model of the Fordist city, the industrially characterized urban economy, was confronted with a severe break (Hall, 1998; Albrechts, 2004). The projection of on-going growth in demographic and economic terms proved to be wrong. The consequence was that cities experiencing growth since long had to witness severe decline for the first time in centuries (Hall, 1998; Ward, 1998; Albers, 2008). Typical urban industries declined as approved modes of production were replaced by new, less labor-intensive ones. The industrial sector withdrew from Western cities to move to those places with low labor costs and liberal laws of production (Goodwin, 1993; Hall & Hubbard, 1996; Hall, 1998; Sassen, 2001).

Facing the decline of Fordist urban economies, cities understandably craved for a different source of economic activity, a new foundation of success. The arrival of new technologies since the 1970s, the global restructurings of the following decades, and the fact that today cities are at center stage in these newly evolving environments, allow for the advancement of a new economic culture. Contextual changes and the recognition that cities are huge pools of valuable human and economic capital re-invent urban economies, making cities what they are today: centers of a post-industrial, consumption-oriented economy (Hall, 1998; Ward, 1998; Sassen, 2001, 2011). Urban development discourses explain in detail how cities reacted to the shift from Fordism to post-Fordism in the 1980s and 1990s, illustrating how they tried to attract industries that fit their reconfigured urban economic paradigm or tried to push the development of new ones (Jewson & MacGregor, 1997; Hall, 1998; Orum & Chen, 2003; Häußermann et al., 2008). This re-orientation is particularly characteristic for its turn to immaterial production and consumption upon the construction, reinterpretation and commodification of values, identities and places (Scott, 1997, 2000; Hall, 1998; Gottdiener, 2000; Bloomfield & Bianchini, 2001; Lagendijk, 2004; Young, 2008).

Urban economic re-orientation implies several paths of transformation. Jessop (1993), for instance, points at the paradigmatic shift from Fordism to post-Fordism, i.e. from productive to service economies in Western cities. He and others highlight the ideological change in economic policies towards supply-oriented approaches that is linked to such a shift (Harvey, 1989, 1990, 1997; Jessop, 1993). While it occurs that the attraction of economic actors to the city increased in general, attracting firms is now largely accompanied by strategies for attracting highly-skilled people (Turok, 2005). In a setting of globally intertwined urban agglomerations, economic differentiation and the attraction of external capital resources become central goals of action. Thus, theorists also speak of a transformation from Fordist economies of scale to economies of scope that aim at flexible accumulation (Harvey, 1990; Turok, 2005; van Heur, 2010a, 2010b).

Very soon it became clear that it was the distinct immaterial qualities of place – namely lifestyle, culture, identity and image – that would give cities back their economic power (Harvey, 1990; Helbrecht, 1993; Bloomfield & Bianchini, 2001; Eade & Mele, 2002). And there are several reasons for cities to set their focus on these resources of immaterial and symbolic production. First, urban economies as such have increasingly become abstract spheres of immateriality. Instead of producing tangible goods, most cities' economies today are based on information and communication technologies, dealing with consulting of all kinds, stock exchange, capital transaction, and financial services (Göschel & Kirchberg, 1998; Sassen, 2001; Fessler Vaz & Berenstein Jacques, 2006). Second, the view on the essential characteristics of cities changed among economic actors. While land and labor still play a role in the productive sector, soft locational factors have clearly outraced them in the sought-after economic segments. Place-image, reputation and regulations are the new decisive criteria for actor's investments (Helbrecht, 1993; Hall, 1998; Knierbein, 2010). Thus, cities logically focus on *"[...] spectacle and image rather than on the substance of economic and social problems"* (Harvey, 1989: 16). If we believe the proclamation that, *"[e]xperiences are replacing goods and services"* (Florida, 2002: 168) it becomes clear why so much effort is nowadays put into the production of place-specific symbols. They are the new means of attracting economic actors and have even become a substantial pillar of urban economic production (Eade & Mele, 2002; Ermann, 2007).

So, in some regard urban economies have shifted their main focus from the production of goods to the consumption of places. Whether this is being labeled as a process of commodification of all urban life (Gottdiener, 2000), or described by the example of the mutation of cities into theme parks (Zukin, 1995, 1998) – the consumption of immaterial goods now forms a central part of the new urban economy. Scholars pronounce the comprehensiveness of this transformative process. Urban consumption exists since long but only in the past few decades became so pervasive. And just as production moved beyond national borders, also consumption became a global phenomenon through online shopping and global tourism (Sassen, 1994, 2011; Zukin, 1998; Gottdiener, 2000; Orum & Chen, 2003; Gotham, 2005).

This shows how place and territory have moved to the center of attention in urban development again. The individual qualities of place are the pivotal ingredient to urban economic success after Fordism, as the distinct identities, ways-of-life and values attached to the city are commodified to make them the consumable goods of a re-oriented economy. In this sense, whole places can become consumable goods – a chief conception in post-industrial economies (Zukin, 1995, 1998; Hall, 1998; Gottdiener, 2000; Gottdiener & Budd, 2005; Schmid, 2007).

To sum this up, urban economies undergo a triple transformation on their way from an industrial to a post-industrial constitution. First, typical production of industrial goods is largely replaced by the service sector. Second, the remaining productive segment experiences a paradigmatic shift and changes its focus on the production of distinct symbolic goods and the (re-)interpretation of cultural meaning. And third, the reduced productive function of the city is compensated by promoting all kinds of consumptive patterns – from shopping and tourism to spectacular events – aiming at the commodification of urban environments as the new urban distinctiveness.

PLURALIZATION, FRAGMENTATION, AND AN URBAN REVIVAL IN A POSTMODERN AGE

> "Cities hit hard by a long-term decline in middle-class residents and the erosion of commitment by business elites have gradually begun to view the diversity of 'urban lifestyles' as a source of cultural vitality and economic renewal."
> ZUKIN, 1998: 836

Profound structural transformations are characteristic of the development of cities and their societies over the past decades. Not only do they fluctuate in terms of size, leading to simultaneous de- and re-urbanization trends around the globe. Also, they have massively altered concerning their functional organization within small spatial units. Even more, the patterns of work, leisure, housing, and mobility have not changed along a common line. They have developed into different directions, sometimes even leading to opposing lifestyle models, and in general leading to a diversification of *the* urban society into a conglomerate of *multiple* lifestyle milieus (Spiegel, 1990; Zukin, 1998; Schulze, 2005; Bauman, 2011).

One might oppose to this statement now, emphasizing that diversity is not new to the city. *"Cities are – and have always been – highly differentiated spaces expressive of heterogeneity, [and] diversity of activity."* (Swyngedouw & Kaika, 2003; 5) Yet current societal diversity exceeds earlier conceptions by lengths. First, at least European cities have changed in terms of their demographic structure, thus heavily changing the demands towards the city and its infrastructures. Birth rates decrease due to lifestyle changes, making in-migration a vital part to population development. Consequently, different cultures and lifestyles of young and old, foreign and native meet in the city, letting fusions appear and new models of urban life grow (Spiegel, 1990; Sackmann et al., 2008). Second, new counter-models to male and female prototype biographies evolved. For instance, young urban professionals entered the scene of urban life in the 1980s. These highly-skilled, financially independent individuals became central actors in processes of urban regeneration and gentrification of that time – not only in U.S. cities. And they established a new urban lifestyle of conspicuous consumption and urban living to accumulate cultural capital (Zukin, 1998). Yet traditional family models didn't disappear. Instead, they revived by the end of 20th century as cities offered them a serious alternative to themed suburban life again. Thus, they co-exist now with yuppies, dinks, immigrants, ethnic and sexual minorities to form a socio-culturally diverse postmodern societal conglomerate (Kofman, 1998; Fincher & Jacobs, 1998; Zukin, 1998). Third, work-life cycles changed dramatically in the past decades, which greatly owes to the more general economic transformations of cities after Fordism. The claim for workers' flexibility, increasing specialization in post-industrial production, and rising service economies constructed a diverse world of urban employment, where the male factory worker symbolic of the industrial city got replaced by a mélange of different models – from the untrained 9-to-5 employee to the highly-skilled, ultra-mobile, global manager (Spiegel, 1990; Harvey, 1990; Heineberg, 2005).

Yet, the more striking social transformation I want to point to is a fundamental change concerning societal value sets. It is considered central for the turn of planning to culture and the changed politics of planning (Schneider, 1997; Brühl et al., 2005). The twentieth century has seen the rise of a secular society. Religion – once a major resource of common identities – has today resolved into a society of both nonspiritual individuals and believers of any confession (Spiegel, 1990; Evans, 2001; Taylor, 2004). Relatedly, once stable value systems underwent a sea change. Hedonism, pleasure and personal development have come to the fore and more worldly concerns, such as ecological awareness, a demand for communication, health and a greater focus on alternative cultures are at the center of attention now (Schäflein, 1994; Bauman, 2011). Furthermore, leisure in general wins over employment as the central element of identification. What we do in our spare time, where, how and with whom we do it, is a vital ingredient to the construction of personal and group identities. And consumptive practices have in this regard taken a particularly decisive position (Schäflein, 1994; Schneider, 1997; Gottdiener, 2000).

These value shifts cause not only a pluralization of urban societies in terms of identities and local milieus, but also a whole new variety concerning demands, needs and wishes of citizens towards their city. Mumford (1970) perceived the *"disappearance of the uniform"* in the city in societal terms more than four decades ago, advising planners to be aware of the challenges arising from social diversification (ibid.: 448). Nowadays, this diversity is evident and materializes in cities in form of socio-cultural fragmentation, economic polarization, or segregation (Sassen, 1994, 2001; Madanipour, 1998; Swyngedouw & Kaika, 2003). The resulting challenges for planning the future of these urban environments are obvious. Several cultures, lifestyles, values, and norms overlay each other in one place (Schroer, 2008). It seems as if modernity's project of identity building has failed. Thus, 21st century cities characterized by fragmentation and liquidated identities recently try to celebrate heterogeneity and difference as their new characteristic qualities (Jacobs, 1998; Marcuse & van Kempen, 2000; Elliott, 2001). But the mere marketing of these perceived changes as a place identity seems to be a rather superficial approach to handling a multiform urban society. Instead, as Helbrecht (2001) reminds us, cities must truly accommodate to this individualized society to stay alive. This means that urban politics and planning must find ways to integrate this variety into processes of governing urban change, having in mind that diversity implies an intensified contest over the use of and representation in urban space.

This reconceptualization of urban societies as a kaleidoscope of lifestyles, values and visions is reflected by the concept of postmodernity (Harvey, 1990; Jameson, 1991, 1998; Heineberg, 2005). Although not being a clearly delimited and thus rather controversial concept, the characteristics of postmodernity make an important argument of the close relation between social change and the revival of the city after Fordism (Appignanesi, 2003; Davoudi and Strange, 2009). Postmodernism has three distinct definitions. First, it describes a philosophy – one that denies the master-narratives of modernist rationality, as Davoudi and Strange (2009) explain. In this understanding, it blurs the boundary lines between scientific disciplines, spheres of life and cultures, giving the phrase *"Any-*

thing goes!" by Paul Feyerabend world-class recognition (Appignanesi, 2003). Also, postmodernism is sometimes used as a term covering the characteristics of a new political culture of governing cities after Fordist modernity (Harvey, 1990; Häußermann et al., 2008). In this sense, it subsumes flexible accumulation and market-oriented services, strategic and laissez-faire approaches in planning, and the heralding of spectacle, mass events and consumption (Harvey, 1990; Jessop, 1993; Heineberg, 2005; Häußermann et al., 2008). Most often, though, postmodernism is referred to as a style, originating from deconstructivist critique on modernity. It is particularly being related to architecture, and thus having a strong influence on the physical structure of contemporary cities. In this concern, it also stands for the aestheticization and commodification of the city, and thus needs to be viewed in close vicinity to a global capitalist culture (Harvey, 1990; Hannemann and Sewing, 1998; Heineberg, 2005).

It is under these newly given circumstances that actors of the city heavily engage in celebrating the new-found values of aesthetics, arbitrariness and a global culture in urban development to appeal to a postmodern society cherishing the same ideals. Hence, they advocate the most promising economic motors of knowledge and creativity, consumption, tourism, heritage and culture (Harvey, 1989; Hall, 1998; Evans, 2001; Florida, 2002; Smith, 2005; Young, 2008; Davoudi and Strange, 2009). Ultimately, this paves the way for the often-cited "urban renaissance" – the revival of the city after the setback of the Fordist rationale (Harvey, 1990; Hall, 1998; Evans, 2001; Sennett, 2008).

To suit the new rationales of a post-Fordist economy and a postmodern urban society, the process of active re-arrangement tackles the removal or at least the re-use of an industrial urban fabric that has become obsolete. To better fit the demands of a re-oriented economy and society, city centers are sometimes radically renewed, as they have become *the* target area of new businesses and the stage to best theme culture, heritage and shopping for postmodern tourism and events (Hall, 1998; Hannemann and Sewing, 1998; Evans, 2001; Gotham, 2005). Even more, cities also revive as residential locations. Due to the intense restructurings, the unpleasant picture of the polluted, unsanitary and crime-contaminated industrial town is replaced by that of a vibrant, secure and livable city. In that sense, the urban sphere has something to offer again – for visitors, investors and inhabitants (Sieverts, 1990; Hall, 1998; Brühl et al., 2005; Albers, 2008). This revival of the city since the 1980s is a well-debated fact (Harvey, 1989; Hubbard and Hall, 1996; Hall, 1998; Zukin, 1995, 1998; Evans, 2001; Moulaert et al., 2004). By considering the eye-catching changes in social organization and identity formation that became subject of wide-ranging discourses at that time, it gets evident why cities are now popular again. Meaning and image-value have clearly outraced the use-value of both products and places, which perfectly fits the logic of developing cities upon image, identity, culture and other immaterial factors of society building (Eade and Mele, 2002; Springer, 2007; Hornig, 2011).

The striking commonality is that both, modern city and urban society, struggled with a severe problem of a loss of common identity due to the economic and cultural restructurings introduced above. The decreasing importance of the nation-state, global shifts of economic and political relations and the ended dream of infinite growth under Fordist welfare regimes all sucked the life out of traditional modernist urban values. Simultaneously, secularization, increasing diversity of milieus and lifestyles, and a related fragmentation of demands and wishes of urban populations led to a similar break with approved uniform social identities and associated values. As Pratt (1998) and Pott (2007) remind us, identities have long been imagined as uniform and clearly delimitable. Today we consider them as socially produced instead and thus as fluid, unstable and overlapping. Elliott (2001) also explicitly marks this turning point by distinguishing modernity's project of building "the one" identity from postmodernity's celebration of (constructed) heterogeneity (Elliott, 2001). Although these elaborations only seem to complicate the connection between contemporary city and society, it is exactly here that we can uncover the link to the new-found popularity of urbanity. The link is culture and identity. The moment we recover the definition of cities as projections of values and ideologies (Hall, 1998), as materialities representing memories and shared meanings (Bloomfield and Bianchini, 2001), we find that cities are inseparably connected with culture represented in identity.

The importance of places as anchors of meaning gets clear just from these short elaborations. Under conditions of severe economic and social transformation, cities and the people inhabiting them face an identity crisis. The new approaches of fostering post-industrial economies and establishing postmodern, spectacular urban environments, try to tackle just this crisis. Hence, cities are today again perceived as the places where meaning and identity arise, where knowledge and creativity meet, and where symbols and images are created (Orum and Chen, 2003). This re-interpretation is not only distinct within the paths of history, but it explains why cities witness such a revival. And it reveals the most ground-breaking difference to earlier conceptions of urban economies, as they are now producing *places* – materially, as physical structures and everyday life, and immaterially, as meanings, identities, and images (Gupta and Ferguson, 1997a; Orum and Chen, 2003; Morgan, 2004; Davoudi and Strange, 2009).

The contested politics of planning
Ideology and power, accumulation and representation

The above chapter has clearly shown that preconditions to guiding the contemporary city are tough. Urban agglomerations need to be considered as complex processes in many terms. They interact and compete on various spatial scales for diverse scarce resources and are characterized by value-diversity, fragmented identities and social imbalances. Reasonably, the planning discipline started to re-arrange its approaches of how to guide and direct urban development under such circumstances of constant change and uncertainty. These new political and planning logics not only changed the set of approaches for adapting urban environments and related patterns of decision-making. They further transformed the objectives and goals of planning, letting new rationales in urban development occur (Amin & Graham, 1997; Davoudi & Strange, 2009; Marcuse, 2011). The most important strands of these prevailing theories of planning and their consequences are outlined and discussed in the following chapters.

I start by discussing the consequences of multiform urban complexity, which is a diffusion of power in planning, where negotiations about potential urban futures are not always part of formal decision-making processes, but of overt agenda setting, particularly through media and discursive practices. I then give an overview to the new planning principles that arrived in reaction to recent transformations, where communicative, as well as entrepreneurial approaches prevail. The section emphasizes that these modes of planning are increasingly determined by only a few powerful actors, their ideologies and development interests. Thus, the final section debates the city as contested terrain, pointing to the political in planning as a basic, yet essential fact. It shows that analyses of power in planning are essential for understanding decision-making processes and the paths taken by a city. Here, the chapter refers to political economy and discloses capitalist accumulation and ideological representation as the two major interests that actors attempt to enforce in the politics of planning today.

THE CHANGED FACE OF THE STATE: NEW COALITIONS, NEW DEVELOPMENT GOALS

Imagining someone "doing" planning, we might sketch in our minds the picture of a person in the midst of a variety of people – from politicians to residents, from artists to managers, and from shopkeepers to developers. The planner is a central node in an actor network hard to overlook, a communicator and catalyzer of ideas and sometimes averse visions in a decision-making process about a possible urban future (Schneider, 1997; Albers, 2008). And the planner represents just one position among many. This is what makes the political complexity of the urban sphere today. As Gualini (2005) explicates, the local state as the once stable entity of top-down decision-making for all has massively changed. The new policy challenges are those of multiform complexity and contestation when it comes to deciding about urban development. Flexibility, networking, problem-solving and strategic competition – these are the new characteristics of the local state (Rhodes, 1996; Gualini, 2005). And they condense in an altered form of governing the city: urban governance (Harvey, 1989; Rhodes, 1996; Hall & Hubbard, 1996; Stoker, 1998; Pierre, 1999).

The role of the city as a place of change is not new. Throughout urban history, political decisions, technological innovation and societal change were always linked to the city (Jacobs, 1969; Hall, 1998; Orum and Chen, 2003; Sennett, 2008; Hofmann, 2011). But what is new is that the acknowledgement of the complex character of the urban sphere makes attempts of steering these processes of change a difficult endeavor. Not only has the contemporary city adopted global systemworlds to become a mélange of various spatial scales (Lagendijk, 2004). Also, its functioning is now more complicated than before, as the spectrum of actors and the underlying social values, demands and wishes of social groups have multiplied (Hall & Hubbard, 1996; Hall, 1998). This multiform urban sphere needs some form of targeted steering – of governing – to set the scene for organized community life, the pursuit of politically defined goals and social and economic innovation (Schneider, 1997; Albers, 2008; Jessop, 2008).

Yet, in places where actors from different fields, representing the most unbound, global interests and the very local identities meet to negotiate on possible urban futures, this seems a hardly achievable goal. Thus, contemporary cities must be considered as constantly transforming political processes, where the local state tries to manage complexity and deal with uncertainty to maintain the capability of steering development (Marcuse and van Kempen, 2000; Gottdiener, 2000). The most significant of these changes is the often-cited shift from government to governance as a new mode of steering development processes of the city (Harvey, 1989; Rhodes, 1996). Two major arguments explain why state actors are increasingly drawn to applying governance approaches in planning.

First, politics and planning face increasing actor multiplicity within state, market, and civil society, who all have a specific stake in planning (McGuigan, 2001). Overall, urban politics is today permeated by a broad and ever changing constellation of actors, who all pursue varying interests based on the value pluralism characteristic of urban societies (Hajer & Wagenaar, 2003). And claims for citizen participation in decision-making processes widely replaced top-down-imposed planning. Instead, a variety of actors are today involved in deciding about the outcome of any process of urban development (Schneider, 1997).

Second, due to resource scarcity after industrial decline, the call for efficiency changed the typical actor constellation in the politics of planning (Rhodes, 1996). As typical ingredients to prosperity and economic growth became scarce, increasing internationalization and globalization involved cities in competition for investment and human capital (McCann, 2003; Giffinger & Wimmer, 2005), and shrinking budgets asked for cooperative efforts of state and market actors in planning to maintain the capability to act (Rhodes, 1996; Stoker, 1998). Resource scarcity led to an even more comprehensive transformation of the urban regime. Regulated mechanisms of state-initiated planning under a Keynesian welfare-paradigm were widely dismissed for the sake of efficiency, the proclaimed new goal under a Schumpeterian workfare rationale (Jessop, 1993). Planning itself changed from adjusting and arranging urban space due to evolving contextual challenges to a discipline engaged in active development, focusing locational attractiveness and marketable images as two central concerns of urban development (Bloomfield & Bianchini, 2001; Kühn & Fischer, 2010). Consequently, planning actors bowed out of solely framing urban development. The new actor constellations – adapted to the ever specific processual contexts and permeated by multiple, often opposing interests – is what makes the political complexity of the contemporary city.

Even more, the increasing interference of market and civil society actors in political processes of urban development leads to the blurring of boundaries between actor groups and thus effects in a changed face of the state (Scott, 2001; Jessop, 2008).[1] Analyses of the politics of planning thus need to take the state in-

---

1   Jessop (2008) refers to the state as all spatial, temporal and functional organization of a territory, thus being a function, not a subject. He explains that the state is constituted of an ensemble of power centers – a conglomerate of multiple social forces competing for power that looks different in each case, depending on history, social formation, place and objectives.

to account as an important research variable. Relatedly, the common sense goals pursued by state intervention and its legitimacy changed within the past decades. The turn from a Keynesian to a Schumpeterian rationale, from *"wealth, welfare and social harmony"* (Torfing, 1999: 327) to *"[...] innovation and structural competitiveness in economic policy and flexibility and competitiveness in the field of social policy"* (Jessop, 1993: 18), became a paradigmatic shift that influences both urban economic production and the whole organization of the city still today (Harvey, 1989, 1996). A severe transformation appeared in the principal development goals of the city and its related political organization. While the Keynesian regimes of the 1960s and 1970s were primarily interested in maintaining welfare and full employment, Schumpeterian regimes now try to foster competitiveness due to the awareness of a new economic context: the evolvement of transnational markets and a global capitalist economy (Harvey, 1989, 1990; Lagendijk, 2004; Heywood, 2013; Martinelli & Novy, 2013). While postwar economic regimes were by and large characterized by the *"development-planning-state-nation"* quadruplet (Martinelli & Novy, 2013), the current paradigm subsumes *"competitiveness-market-firms-glocal"* as the signifying variables (ibid.). Supply-side measures are considered as sufficient methods to come up to a new economic paradigm of transnational interaction and global competition, which is thus referred to as the *"new conventional wisdom"* (Gordon & Buck, 2005) guiding the politics of planning to a great extent (Harvey, 1989; Jessop, 1993; Hall, 1998). Calls for growth-orientation foster the adoption of policies letting for more liberal, market-oriented strategies of urban development, which signify a new public management and an entrepreneurial turn in urban politics in general (Harvey, 1989; Jessop, 1993; Rhodes, 1996; Hubbard and Hall, 1996). Most obviously, this shift effectuates in a reformation of the state, leading to new political complexity when it comes to steering urban development. Its *"hollowing out"* due to calls for efficiency (Jessop, 1993; Rhodes, 1996) is only one result, which, in consequence, diminishes the power of planners to steer the city and hands the solution of development problems over to other actors.

The other is an entrepreneurial turn in urban planning. It is argued that due to the exposure of cities to global market competition, the local state had to rearrange its manner of governing urban economies and adopt entrepreneurial characteristics (Orum & Chen, 2003). Harvey explains that, due to Fordist crisis and the need for economic restructuring, *"[...] the 'managerial' approach so typical of the 1960s has steadily given way to initiatory and 'entrepreneurial' forms of action in the 1970s and 1980s."* (Harvey, 1989: 4) The essential belief that began to prevail was, that, *"[...] cities can benefit not only from 'conventional' wel-*

fare measures or land-use planning but also by mobilizing local resources in the scramble for rewards in an increasingly competitive free market." (Hall & Hubbard, 1996: 154) This implies a reorientation of typical modes of governing to partnership, where actors to coalesce with are chosen by their *"capacity to act"* (ibid.: 156). The fact that this is often to be equated with a chase after private investment with no consideration of long-term development goals and social concerns is one central point of critique (Hall & Hubbard, 1996; Miles et al., 2000; Swyngedouw & Kaika, 2003). Attracting private investment and promoting urban growth are two central concerns of entrepreneurial urban politics (Harvey, 1989; Jessop, 1997; Ward, 2003, 2006).

These are also reflected in the concept of governance that was long praised as *the* solution to cities and regions that had lost their capability to act under Fordist crisis and increasing globalization. Governance approaches adopted the ideals of cooperative and entrepreneurial politics, perfectly fitting the post-Fordist context of blurred boundaries between scales, networks, identities and cultures (Stoker, 1998). In fact, governance networks were established literally everywhere to pool investment capital, know-how, and decision-making power for the (re-)development of cities (Harvey, 1989; Hall & Hubbard, 1996). The argumentation for governance seems rather simple: planning needs to engage in cooperative action to maintain the power to act in a context of uncertainty, resource scarcity and complex challenges (Salet & Faludi, 2000). Although urban governments as central state actors hold decision-making power, the post-Fordist, Schumpeterian rationale requires creative knowledge for innovation and investment capital for efficiency as indispensable planning resources as well. The alliance of public governments with private capital is a major characteristic of the new urban governance (Hall & Hubbard, 1996; Bahn et al., 2003; Harding, 2005). For maintaining the power to act, state actors cooperate with economically flexible actors – rentiers, media, business- and utility groups, as Hall & Hubbard (1996) elucidate.

Consequently, local actor constellations in strategic planning processes change dramatically, putting the corporate sector at center stage. And all too often, these actors push through their development goals, making them part of a political elite of decision-makers at the same time (Logan & Molotch, 1987; Harvey, 2002; Bahn et al., 2003). The shift from government to governance is thus often criticized for not seriously enough taking into account central ethic principles of planning under a democratic, communicative and participatory city paradigm (Goodwin, 1993; Hall & Hubbard, 1996; Rhodes, 1996). Even more, political theorists sound a cautionary note about the arbitrariness in the constant intermingling of actor spheres and related value re-orientations, as it would lead to a loss of ideological commitment in the politics of planning (Scott, 2001; Mouffe, 2007). The debate about post-politics and post-democracy has emphasized well enough that the new governance in planning must be viewed from a critical perspective, as it favors economically powerful and ideologically dominant actors in decision-making processes, and tends to reduce urban politics to solving technical problems, neglecting the politically relevant ideological questions (Crouch, 2004; Mouffe, 2007). So, obviously the intense interference of state actors, who hold decision-making power, with knowledge- and capital-rich actors from other spheres is critical. Apparently it excludes minorities, marginalized groups and others affected by state interventions but without a strong stake in planning, creating and conserving undemocratic planning regimes and planning results (Molotch, 1976; Logan & Molotch, 1987; Harvey, 1989; Rhodes, 1996; Hall & Hubbard, 1996).

Nevertheless, classic state actors and planning administrations still play a significant role in the politics of planning. It would be wrong to conclude from the above elaborations that the state lost all its importance and power. Although it is now sharing its decision-making power with actors from other spheres to maintain the capacity to act, local and national governments are still central actors in steering urban development and guiding urban politics (Albers, 2008; Häußermann et al., 2008). New actor constellations merely changed the *role* of the local state (Castells, 1998, 2000; Sassen, 2001). As Castells argues, in a networked society where centralized power typical of the state can easily be bypassed, the state itself becomes a networked entity. It becomes a node in a network of shared power where typical state organizations and institutions fail to exercise theirs (Castells, 2000). Thus, the local state has not disappeared (Kelly, 1999). Only its form has changed, as it is now constituted of actors from all spheres and scales, and is characterized by conflictive values and visions that are fought out in the politics of planning. The state has become even more central to processes of urban development today, as it shapes the regulation-accumulation regimes of a city, which are the framework to any urban development (Gualini, 2005; Jessop, 1993, 2008, 2011; van Heur, 2010a, 2010b).

These first findings on the contested politics of planning call for taking the underlying ideologies of powerful actors engaged in planning into account, as these ideologies constitute the taken-for-granted, objectified contexts of where, how and what to plan. And it calls for investigating the allocation of power in processes of urban development to reveal whose values and visions are being realized and who actually has the power to plan (Gupta & Ferguson, 1997a; Scott, 2001; Martin et al., 2003; Flyvbjerg, 2004) – a notion that is also stressed by Pierre (1999), who clarifies that, contrary to the general assumption, no governance model is actually value-free. Instead, all planning coalitions are permeated by individual objectives and values. The formerly stable values and principles that guided urban politics are now all too easily replaced by the discursively constructed goals of a "here and now" (Grubbauer, 2011a, 2011b; Hofmann, 2011). Consequently, contexts, problems, space and time, and the normative goals of planning are often enough framed by individual interests of powerful actors (McCann, 2003, 2004; Schipper, 2012).

NEW MODES OF PLANNING: CONSTRUCTING IDENTITY AND DIFFERENCE

The city hasn't lost any of its importance as the terrain for the forming forces of society to interact. But recent development trends and constant contextual transformations have massively influenced the stability of urban systems. Approved modes of planning could neither guarantee serving the common good of a general citizenry anymore, nor secure prosperity and future growth (Schneider, 1997; Albrechts, 2004; Albers, 2008). Popular modes of planning were thus modified or replaced by new ones to fit the as well transformed political objectives of a restructured state that has adopted entrepreneurial principles (Goodwin, 1993; Jessop, 1993; Gualini, 2005; Harding, 2005; Turok, 2005).

Considering this change in all its bearings, one needs to go back to the 1970s, when the harsh criticism of rationality and universalist top-down planning was for the first time put into practice via participatory approaches (Lindblom, 1959; Davidoff, 1965). Calls for explicating values and taking notice of the political in planning soon enforced more open and democratic approaches in postwar urban politics (Sennett, 2008). Citizens desired empowerment to self-determine *their* city and express their values and identities without top-down imposition of how to lead their lives. The right to be different and for involvement in decision-making was uttered, letting a new understanding of civil society and citizenship evolve (Torfing, 1999; Stevenson, 2001; Eckardt & Nyström, 2009; Bauman, 2011). Due to increasing societal diversification, secularization and value diversity, "allowing for difference" slowly but surely became a central goal in urban development planning – particularly in more recent years (Gupta & Ferguson, 1997a, 1997b; Young, 2008). Adopting the notion of *"planning through debate"* (Healey, 1992) increasingly made urban planning negotiative and communicative (Healey et al., 1999) and allowed for participation of those affected by planning and for bottom-up approaches to local transformation (Küpper, 1990; Schneider, 1997; Albers, 2008; Davoudi and Strange, 2009).

Consequently, it became a significant aim of a new communicative planning practice to advocate empowerment and diversity and serve the political ideals of equity and justice (Marcuse, 2011).

Planning practitioners reacted on social change by refocusing on the local and neighborhood scale to better confront the particularities of place and their specific development challenges. Top-down master planning approaches were largely dismissed in European cities and planning practice encountered a shift to urban renewal as the prevailing form of urban change for at least three reasons. First, increased value- and ideological diversity made it almost impossible for political leaders to push through all-encompassing plans and visions for big cities. Second, the acknowledgement of uncertainty and unpredictable futures made long-term urban visions as transported through urban master plans seem obsolete as well. And third, claims to nurture citizen's participation in decision-making asked for smaller-scale approaches to urban development – with first attempts of bottom-up planning and decision-making occurring (Küpper, 1990; Fassbinder, 1993; Schneider, 1997; Albers, 2008; Häußermann et al., 2008).

However, this rationale not only implied a broadened involvement of local populations. It also started to complicate planning processes in terms of decision-making and thus led to uncertainty concerning both contexts and outcomes (Amin & Graham, 1997; Hajer & Wagenaar, 2003). Multiform urban transformations and the economic upheaval in particular effected in further inner fragmentation of cities and the evolvement of new inequalities despite the changed form of planning (Molotch, 1976; Molotch & Logan, 1987; Harvey, 1989; Sassen, 1994, 2001; Swyngedouw & Kaika, 2003).

Consequently, the general ideological shift to more market-led development brought about another turn in planning in the 1980s: the development of big projects: events, huge infrastructures and heritage planning, implemented to "get things going" in cities by taking private capital on board (Schneider, 1997; Hall, 1998). City administrations started to compete for mobile capital, unbound production and tourism on an increasingly globalized market. By exploiting local advantages for appealing to global audiences and intensifying consumption through tourism and global events, the new scope of action of cities began to encompass literally all parts of the world. Cities began to invest huge sums in supply-oriented policies and spectacular projects to attract the masses – within and beyond city limits (Harvey, 1989; Sieverts, 1990; Ward, 1998; Orum & Chen, 2003; Benneworth & Hospers, 2009). Although this shift from public to public-private (or even fully private) planning is more linked to the 1980's Anglo-Saxon politics of Thatcher and Reagan, similar tendencies of market-led planning through big projects occurred as well in other European cities, even recently

(Häußermann & Siebel, 1993; Novy et al., 2001; Martinelli & Novy, 2013). At the same time, practices of urban renewal did not disappear. They still co-exist with approaches of planning through big projects, yet with a minor welfare orientation (Marcuse & van Kempen, 2000).

Another emblematic change in directing urban development is the apparent focus on inner city areas. The makeover of city centers is an often cited exemplar of the new modes of planning. As unique representational spaces of cities, they are used both as powerful representations of political, cultural and business elites, and as drivers of an urban renaissance to attract a new middle class of tourists and well-off dwellers (Zukin, 1998; Evans, 2001; Füller & Marquardt, 2009). Relatedly, imaging of place and the reconfiguration of meaning attached to spaces are characteristic of the new face of planning, pointing at the popular recognition of an interplay between materiality and meaning. The notion that the city is both a physical representation of a past, present and future, and a mental construction and image of a certain way of living, is incorporated into recent planning approaches. Thus, the targeted place promotion to inward and outward audiences has as well become a typical feature of the new politics of planning (Ward, 1998; Ward, 2003, 2006; Häußermann et al., 2008).

Also recently, and with a greater focus on European cities, planning makes attempts to confront a global market economy and inter-place competition via strategic planning (Fassbinder, 1993; Salet & Faludi, 2000; Kühn & Fischer, 2010). Although there is no definite delineation, "strategic planning" mostly refers to the targeted exploitation of place-specific potentials for making them distinct assets of a territory in urban competition (Fassbinder, 1993). Putting it simple, Albrechts (2004) explains that "strategic" means to define what is more important than something else. Hence, in urban planning it means to set priorities – for development aims, spaces of the city to be renewed, social groups to be favored, or actors to be involved (Healey et al., 1999; Albrechts, 2004). Arguments for strategic planning are manifold: first, the recognition that comprehensive planning is an illusionary task, second, the agreement upon economic competition on transnational markets, and third, the evident scarcity of local budgets as a claim for strategic partnership (Albrechts, 2004; Kühn & Fischer, 2010). Thus, it doesn't come as a surprise that strategic planning is the recent continuation of the transformation of urban planning practice from comprehensive to project-based development (Cataldo, 2009; Kühn & Fischer, 2010).

Importantly, strategic approaches differ from entrepreneurial, i.e. liberal, business-oriented development models – at least in theory. First, strategic planning is based upon a general vision of a city's future development, which needn't necessarily be of a laissez faire, market-led nature (Cataldo, 2009). Second, strategic projects to be realized are meant to be in harmony with this general vision (Albrechts, 2004; Kühn & Fischer, 2010). And third, broad participation of stakeholders and feedback loops are intended to allow re-considerations of paths taken and less exclusive decisions (Healey et al., 1999; Albrechts, 2004). Critical points seem to be similar to those on entrepreneurial urban politics, though. The balance between top-down-imposed decisions towards transnational markets and bottom-up approaches of local planning is hard to achieve (Cataldo, 2009). Political leadership is necessary, yet hard to combine with constant participation in decision-making processes (Kühn & Fischer, 2010). And, short-term actions and big projects are still at center stage. Not only do such projects need liberal rules and huge investments to be realized, they often tempt political leaders to adapt strategic visions to project needs and force decision-makers to resign to powerful actor's interests (Häußermann & Siebel, 1993; Häußermann et al., 2008).

Yet another strand of theory introduces spectacular planning as a particular characteristic of recent urban development practice. Urban spectacle implies projects consisting of eye-catching architecture and urban design, extravagant events, commodified places for consumable experience and symbolic images (Heineberg, 2005; Häußermann et al., 2008). The prevailing postmodern conception of urban seems to demand planning to employ postmodernist approaches of theming urban space, constructing meaning via intense imaging and a focus on lifestyles, milieus, values and quality of life (Harvey, 1990; Zukin, 1995, 1998; Häußermann et al., 2008; Young, 2008). Urban spectacle, thus, refers to a diverse array of approaches in planning that take these particularities of postmodern societies into account – always aiming at visibility, distinction and creating added value (Schmid, 2007). Although an increasing dominance of *"symbolic politics"* over distributive approaches was recognized already some decades ago (Molotch, 1976), spectacular planning with its wide-ranging shift to symbolic projects is a recent phenomenon (Hall & Hubbard, 1996; Swyngedouw & Kaika, 2003; Gotham, 2005). The production of urban spectacle in planning can be read as the continuation of attempts to aestheticize urban environments for an urban renaissance upon new lifestyle diversity and place consumption (Zukin, 1998; Gotham, 2005). It thus fits the supply-oriented rationale of the new urban politics and their fixation on inter-place competition and takes into account the postmodern conception of society as fascinated by spectacle, distinct images and consumable cultural values.

These new modes of planning point at two general development objectives: identity formation in fragmented cities, and the celebration of difference. Whether it is increased citizen participation for place identification, or attempts to aestheticize urban environments via lifestyle-led and image-value-saturated renewal approaches – the construction of place and place identity is a central concern to the new form of planning (Zukin, 1995, 1996, 1998; Gupta & Ferguson, 1997a, 1997b). On the other hand, emancipatory politics and empowerment are the result of claims for "allowing for difference" in diversifying cities. This difference is also central to spectacular urbanism – the attempt to celebrate the distinctiveness of place to achieve greater global visibility in inter-urban competition. And only recently, strategic planning has become a widely implemented planning approach to bridge the gap between identity formation upon common urban visions and the celebration of difference upon spectacular projects.

Still there is one more strand to the new modes of planning that deserves extra attention, as it reflects the spatial turn and the acknowledged importance of a immaterial layer of the city: the construction of image. Within the evolution of urban planning, marketing and imaging gained practitioners' broad attention in the past two decades only. Although the "selling" of places is as old as the planning discipline itself (Goodwin, 1993; Hall & Hubbard, 1996; Ward, 1998), cities and their local places are being marketed heavily only since the turn to the new rationales of entrepreneurial development (Schneider, 1997; Giffinger & Wimmer, 2005). In a planning context that asks for uniqueness, cities are doing everything they can to appear as distinct. Supply-oriented planning approaches all incorporate a belief that place qualities need to be sold to specific target groups. Thus, cities celebrate and market their local qualities to inward and outward audiences (Jessop, 1997; Ward, 1998; Smith, 2005). This boosterism is considered a necessary precondition to creating global visibility in an attention-saturated, postmodern society and economic growth in contested transnational economies (Harvey, 1989; Goodwin, 1993; Helbrecht, 1993). The increasing invasion of planning by an economic logic let image planning appear as a potential instrument to accommodate to a new political-economic environment (Sadler, 1993; Monclùs, 2006). The attraction of investment and tourism became a guiding principle in processes of planning that were largely dominated by discourses of interurban competition for all forms of capital (Jewson & MacGregor, 1997; Ward, 2003; Smith, 2005; Lee, 2009). And advertising places was as well seen as a reasonable approach to counter all sorts of decline after Fordism (Ward, 1998).

Adopting a communicative rationale (Healey, 1992) and the notion of an attention economy (Franck, 1998; Knierbein, 2010) planning added marketing and imaging to its repertoire of approaches to not only do planning, but to advertise it as well. Thus the selling of places and the discursive production of urban images soon became usual practice in urban development approaches (Jacobs, 1969;

Ward, 1998). Image planning was even considered the cure to the planning crisis after the end of master planning. To some it seemed as if all-encompassing development visions had become possible again as vibrant images would drive a new enthusiasm for common efforts in planning (Helbrecht, 1993). At the same time, place images were considered producers of uniqueness through non-conformity (Ermann, 2007; Mattl, 2009) and the *"small differences"* that would appeal to capitalist markets (Molotch, 1998). It is this dichotomy of coherence and distinction, of identity and difference that these modes of planning are able to combine, making them seem so versatile and attractive to planning practitioners.

But of course, these are not viewed uncritically. Criticism arises due to the often stereotypical character of imaging approaches and their one-dimensional orientation towards a global capitalist market (Ward, 1998; Jones & Wilks-Heeg, 2004; De Frantz, 2011). What is portrayed are pictures of aestheticized urban lifeworlds, while urban problems are usually hidden (Hall, 1998; Jones & Wilks-Heeg, 2004). All too often these place images do not allow for the representation of genuine place qualities and local specificities, but stage a constructed spectacle for an urban renaissance (Miles & Paddison, 2005; Fessler Vaz & Berenstein Jacques, 2006). Even more, imaging activities are often nothing but the continuation of entrepreneurial urban politics, with the city being considered as an enterprise – a product that needs to be sold and consumed (Helbrecht, 1993; Swyngedouw & Kaika, 2003; Madgin, 2009), or to cite Landry (2000: 31): *"Cities are brands and they need glamour, style and fizz."* Thus, the claim in constructing discursive representations is to cover a sense of place (Comunian, 2009), to consider local identity instead of global patterns and entrepreneurial strategies (Mattl, 2009), and to think about modes of celebrating difference without falling into reactionary politics of top-down imposed planning or nationalist ideologies (Harvey, 1989; Bassett et al., 2005).

But this overview unhides an important antagonism in current planning. While supply-oriented strategies attempt to construct distinct places for a globalized capitalist economy, local neighborhood planning aims at fostering the city of difference as an expression of urban citizenship (Stevenson, 2001). This *"twin process of global homogeneity and local heterogeneity"* (Gotham, 2005: 226) is reflected not only in the opposition of diverse urban societies and the logic of staging them in a clear-cut place image. It becomes manifest in the cleavage of equity and efficiency as planning objectives, or, as Dahl (1994: 23) puts it, the *"democratic dilemma [of] system effectiveness versus citizen participation".* This antagonism is a perennial challenge to planning. Be it the competitiveness-cohesion dualism (Gordon & Buck, 2005), the equity-efficiency opposition

(Schneider, 1997), or the often cited global-local dichotomy described above; the political balancing act of achieving a state of coherence, i.e. identity, while not forgetting about the increased complexity of an urban world of difference is, in fact, one of the biggest challenges to urban planning today (Stevenson, 2001; Stäheli, 2006; Mouffe, 2007; Bauman, 2011). And it indicates what has recurrently been mentioned within this piece of work: that planning is political – a basic fact, which deserves special mention. Hence, we need to unravel the political in planning, i.e. the influence of power in decision-making and the recurrent contest over space in both economic and ideological terms.

THE POLITICAL IN PLANNING: CONTESTS OVER ACCUMULATION AND REPRESENTATION

> "[C]ommand over space is a fundamental and all-pervasive source of social power in and over everyday life."
> HARVEY, 1990: 226

Urban politics notably shape the social fabric – the organization of urban societies, their hierarchies and the chance of individuals to achieve fulfillment. As Torfing's quote tells us, politics need to be understood as ultimately having primacy over the social. Consequently, the politics of planning as well need to be understood as determinant of how individuals can lead their lives in the habitat of the city, what they can reasonably achieve, and what visions can plausibly be realized.

It is unquestioned that urban development is permeated by values, attitudes and the envisioned futures of different actors, who want their interests to be heard and their ideas to be realized. Decisions about urban development are based on value commitments, privileging one development path at the expense of excluding other positions, actors and demands (Mouffe, 2007). As urban planning is a major sphere of making such urban development decisions, the planning discipline must be considered a political sphere itself (Helbrecht, 1993; Schneider, 1997, Healey et al., 1999). The crucial question of democratic politics, *"who gets what, where and how"* (Barnett, 2008: 1639), must then be posed in planning as well. But more than that, the ideological question, who *should* or *should not* get something must be at the center of our attention (ibid.). As planning processes are about *"[...] taking the constitutive decisions in an undecidable terrain"* (Torfing, 1999: 67), they must be understood as the path-shapers of an ideologically determined urban future. For understanding why our urban surroundings – material and immaterial – are constituted the way they are, we must thus unravel the political in planning. After all, the unmistakably political dimension in active urban development is central for understanding how planning is actively shaped and our urban environments steered by powerful actors.

In fact, planning was ever since shaped by fights over power and allocation, with planners being the mediators of contesting expectations towards a city (Bahn et al., 2003; Albers, 2008). But with the turn to governance, with boundaries between state and non-state actors blurring, it has more than ever become a question of *who has power* to push through his or her visions and by what means (Hajer & Wagenaar, 2003; Davoudi & Strange, 2009). Of course, the wide-ranging shift from government to governance threatens the democratic principles of planning. For state actors, *"[...] practical needs drive the development of co-operative effects among new constellations of actors"* (Hajer & Wagenaar, 2003: 2). Yet, knowledge and investment capital are typically held by actors from other spheres than the public, most notably those unbound private institutions that function in the logic of capitalist accumulation (Harvey, 1989, 1990, 2002; Goodwin, 1993; Jessop, 1993). Hence, urban development is becoming more and more influenced by the visions of a few selected actors from different spheres and with different spatial, social and ideological orientation (Harvey, 1989; Hall and Hubbard, 1996). The most striking change is the obvious handover of a number of former public tasks and decision-making power in urban development processes to private actors, leading to the establishment of dispersed and often non-transparent networks of business-driven governance, endowed with the power to plan (Harvey, 1989; Goodwin, 1993; Hall & Hubbard, 1996).

Harvey stressed already in 1989 that it was obvious that power in urban development was dispersed in *"[...] broader coalitions of forces, within which urban government and administration have only a facilitative and coordinating role to play."* (Harvey, 1989: 6) And although governing regimes sometimes aim at inclusive goals of promoting territorial identity or economic and educational opportunities for the poor (Healey et al., 1999; Mossberger, 2009), recent research shows that they are all too often driven by the corporate sector's will to construct image and identity for capital accumulation only (Mossberger, 2009; Best & Paterson, 2010). The mere fact that flows of capital, power and knowledge determine urban life today (Castells, 1998, 2000), excludes those actors and groups, who are weak in one or all of these categories (McCann, 2004). Recurrently, growth interests of powerful non-place-bound elites are privileged over the social needs of a local urban society (Beazley et al., 1997; Swyngedouw & Kaika, 2003). And the past contextual transformations and resulting turn to post-Fordist modes of regulation made the discourse of global competition and the need for market-oriented policies prevalent – at the price of openness, fairness and social concerns (Healey et al., 1999).

These short elaborations point at the need to understand planning as a highly political sphere, where decisions made for the good of some always affect others negatively; that the politics of planning are ultimately confronted with taking ideological decisions (Torfing, 1999; Stäheli, 2006; Mouffe, 2007); and that for the critical planning researcher it must thus be a principal interest to investigate *how* these decisions are taken and argued for (Flyvbjerg, 2004). And these decisions are dependent on underlying constructions of knowledge, truth, rationalities, and power (ibid.). In this regard we return to Foucault's power/knowledge regimes, where knowledge production and power relations are inseparably linked, and power is ultimately a result of discursively constructed knowledge (Torfing, 1999; Flyvbjerg, 2000, 2002; Mills, 2007).

"Knowledge and power, truth and power, rationality and power are analytically inseparable from each other; power produces knowledge and knowledge produces power." (Flyvbjerg, 2004: 293)

In the same way, this also holds true for space as a discursive construct and explains to us why urban development needs to be considered as being determined by power/knowledge and certain regimes of truth. Powerful actors are able of constructing an objectified knowledge base for pushing through their will in processes of urban development. This basic conception is of high significance for comprehending the political in planning. Helbrecht (1993), then, reminds us that it is the city where power is actually exercised and that the decisions made ultimately become manifest as material representations in the urban environment. Hence, the city must be interpreted as the material manifestation of power relations (Marcuse & van Kempen, 2000), of which the built environment is the most apparent (Grubbauer, 2011a, 2011b). Thus, power in planning must be understood as the decisive factor in the material representation of certain values and identities in urban space. It is essential in the discursive construction of meaning in today's cities (Stevenson, 2001), and is thus both, a facilitator of certain cultural or ideological value representations in space, and an essential ingredient to the legitimation of hegemonic constructs and certain forms of planning.

While it seems reasonable in the first place to trace back such materializations in our urban environments to formal decision-making that constitutes the legally drawn up basis of planning, it is widely known that most often the political decisions taken are influenced by the less obvious, sometimes hidden processes of agenda-setting (Scott, 2001; Heywood, 2013). It is here that the new rationales of an open, communicative, cooperative and market-led planning become an arena of fights over power and allocation in planning. In reaction to an increased diversity and complexity of the city, planning processes have diversified as well. They have crossed the boundary lines between state and market, public and private, and individual and collective, with the aim of increasing democracy, efficiency and effectiveness – all at once (Rhodes, 1996; Stoker, 1998; Pierre, 1999). The once stable, formal top-down decisions in planning have by and large been replaced by cooperative models of bargaining and proactive approaches of self-determined development (Häußermann et al., 2008). Consequently, in the politics of planning, more than ever do varying interests and opposing visions collide, as more actors simply have a say in urban development decisions and underlying identities and ideologies have multiplied, leading to ever new antagonisms (Gupta & Ferguson, 1997a, 1997b; Elliott, 2001; Bieling, 2006a; Stäheli, 2006; Mouffe, 2007).

In this concern, it is only rational that actors equipped with innovative ideas, tacit knowledge, investment capital and the right to decide formally team up to become powerful enough to push through their development visions (Stoker, 1995, 1998). Actors engaged in the politics of planning sometimes form coalitions to collectively gain the capacity to act, meaning, to reach a certain goal in planning. The pursued aims seem to be clear in this regard. For one thing, actors form partnerships to gain political command or social control, i.e., *"[...] the active mobilization of resources (information, finance, reputation, knowledge) to achieve domination over other interests."* (Stoker, 1995: 65)

A distinct form of coalitions in the politics of planning is urban regimes. While it is not the aim to grapple with regime theory in-depth here, it is still important to delineate urban regimes as one particular form of coalitions aiming at intervening in urban development. Regimes are specific, because they are long-term coalitions. They are, *"[...] the result of a group of interests [...] to build a regime and achieve the capacity to govern"* (Stoker, 1995: 65) – the long-term goal being the establishment of dominance over the politics of planning to realize economic and ideological interests, the institutionalization of this regime, and the formation of hegemony (Hall & Hubbard, 1996; Scott, 2001; Bieling, 2006a; Keller, 2011). Thus, urban regimes are endowed with the power of social production (Stoker, 1995). Bahn et al. (2003) also emphasize that, besides the realization of specific projects in planning, particular goals of such long-term coalitions can be the maintenance of a status quo in the politics of planning and attempts to change ideologies upon symbolic urban politics. Although being a U.S.-based approach, which does not fit the political and institutional constellation of European cities all too well (Mossberger, 2009), the mere bearing in mind of the possibility of regime formation seems important at this point and for the empirical analysis that is to follow.

In parts the regime debate also reveals the arguments for actors to engage in the politics of planning that are of significance to this research. As was largely outlined before, within changed modes of governing, urban development, market and civil society actors are increasingly incorporated in the political sphere of decision-making in planning to ensure both efficiency and democratic decisions and to "keep things going" even under conditions of complexity and uncertainty. Only logically, individual interests of certain actors increasingly invade these processes.

As Soja (2008) so plausibly elaborates, these preconditions demand critical urban researchers to focus two directions of political contest over urban space that recurrently appear in this setting: first, a contest over the utilization of urban space for capitalist interests of commodification and capitalization, and second, its utilization for ideological and cultural representation. Thus, it is today a widely accepted notion that the city is a contested terrain, with the most diverse actors intervening in planning to re-interpret the meaning, image and identity of place as representations and to see their economic interests materialized. Of course, these fights for the capitalist utilization and the "prerogative of interpretation"[2] of urban space are highly political. They are a question of power relations between actors, of the construction and deployment of knowledge, truth and rationalities, and a clash of ideologies, identities and values (Torfing, 1999; Flyvbjerg, 2004; Stäheli, 2006; Mouffe, 2007). The outcomes of these struggles constitute our surrounding urban environments – from their most intense, physical appearance as built-in-stone planning results, to the institutional arrangements as expression of state visions, and the symbolic processes in and meanings attached to urban space. They all signify power over space, the triumphant actors of urban politics, and the dominant ideologies in planning (Jung, 2010). In this sense, *"Cities are not just collections of material artifacts, rather, they are also sites through which ideologies are projected, cultural values are expressed and power is exercised."* (Hall, 1998: 28)

Recent accounts of urban political economy and their critique of the local state provide a valuable basis to become aware of the underlying social antagonisms that lead to such contests over space (Molotch, 1976; Logan & Molotch, 1987; Harvey, 1985, 1989, 1997; Kirchberg, 1998; Allmendinger, 2002). The basic notion to this approach is that, *"[c]apital accumulation and the production*

---

2 "Deutungshoheit" (cf. Schulz, 2006).

of urbanization go hand in hand" (Harvey, 1989, cited in Allmendinger, 2002: 74). As Kirchberg (1998) explains, urban political economy is then a useful framework for understanding and explaining the political conflicts in processes of urban development. In its simplest, the concept builds upon a divide between two opposing interests of which would be the proper use of urban space. While profit-oriented market actors typically want their resources to be invested in growth-promising processes of urban development, civil society actors coin their opposing expectations towards other than the accumulation goals. The resulting dualism is that of use- and exchange value of urban space – two incompatible variables (Molotch, 1976; Harvey, 1985, 1989; Logan & Molotch, 1987; Kirchberg, 1998; Lewitzky, 2005). The inherent difference of urban political economy approaches to neoclassical conceptions of price formation is clarified explicitly by Logan and Molotch (1987: 1):

"Markets are not mere meetings between producers and consumers, whose relations are ordered by the impersonal 'laws' of supply and demand. For us, the fundamental attributes of all commodities [...] are the social contexts through which they are used and exchanged."

This view opens up another antagonism that goes beyond earlier, economistic political economy accounts (cf. Bieling, 2006a, 2006b; Stäheli, 2006). It points at an antagonism between the economic ideology of profit and accumulation upon planning that is embodied by (unbound) market actors, and a civil society of urban dwellers that wants to utilize the city in its own, non-profit-oriented ways (Kirchberg, 1998; Lewitzky, 2005; Jones, 2006). Since we know that urban societies are determined by lifestyle- and value diversity, post-structuralist thinkers enhanced the economically determined class antagonism of capital and labor with one that also respects politics, ideology, the state and cultural difference (Bieling, 2006a; Jones, 2006; Stäheli, 2006). This allowed to further distinguish the lines of conflict in urban politics to draw attention to a contest over the city in terms of different identities, cultural values, political ideologies, or opposing lifestyles – a contest over representation (Jones, 2006; Stäheli, 2006).

Representation is understood as the signifying practices that construct meaning upon language and symbols (Hall, 1997). In this conception, the process of representation involves both layers of space. On an immaterial layer, process and thing are attached with meaning to make them symbols, while materially these symbols are then representative of certain values, ideologies, identities and cultures (Du Gay & Pryke, 2013). In an extension of political economy, and by integrating the postmodern conception of society, Sharon Zukin intensely elaborates on the concept of a symbolic economy to interpret the ideology- and culture-driven fights for representation in urban space (Zukin, 1995, 1996, 1998). While political economy long dealt with approved modes of capitalist accumulation upon the material city only, Zukin's work enhances this view. She points at postmodern modes of planning that increasingly attempt to build spectacular representations upon the constructed identity and image of place. Thereby, a symbolic economy approach includes also the meaning attached to space as a contested thing (Zukin, 1995, 1996, 1998; Kirchberg, 1998). Yet, it is not only a second layer for constructing a regime of capitalist accumulation, for example upon images that speak a global cultural language. In a symbolic economy, urban space must be understood as the politically valuable arena of staging these symbols as representations of hegemonic power. Relatedly, it must also be considered as a political tool in the intended symbolic in- and exclusion of any counter-hegemonic processes from certain spaces of the city (Kearns & Philo, 1993; Zukin, 1995, 1996; Gupta & Ferguson, 1997b; Madanipour, 1998; Göschel & Kirchberg, 1998). Thus, the symbolic economy approach points to the need for exploring the constant struggles of the less powerful for expressing their identities, values, ideologies and cultures. Therefore, the concept considers the representational quality of space as a second important layer of contestation over the city (Zukin, 1996; Gupta & Ferguson, 1997b; Cresswell, 2004; Schulz, 2006).

Consequently, in the politics of planning we have to regard two major underlying principles of actors engaging in processes of decision-making in planning. First, as urban political economy teaches us, economic actors are driven by accumulation interests, while second, considering the logic of a symbolic economy, ideological representation is another objective. In both concepts, actors constantly struggle for utilizing urban space in their favored way. As Zukin (1998) finds, urban space is today signified by economic forces struggling for accumulation and political competition, which both condense in a discursive element of a public sphere. In the politics of planning, these plural antagonisms do collide. They result in conflicts over the representation of identities *in* urban space, capital accumulation *upon* urban space, and political power *through* urban space.

To conclude on the contested politics of planning, we need to bear in mind the increasing political complexity of steering urban development. It not only leads to dispersed powers between local and global, public and private, and capital and labor. Most importantly, it blurs the distinguishing line between formal and informal processes of planning. Thus, it is of importance to look beyond formal decision-making and focus the layer of overt discursive agenda setting to disclose who wins in the politics of planning. In this regard, we need to distinguish two lines of conflict. For one thing, we can understand processes of urbanization as attempts of capitalization upon the advantages of urbanity and the distinct qualities of place. Some actors in planning reasonably pursue accumulation interests upon both the material and immaterial layer of urban space. Then again, the city must be understood as an arena of representation, where the politics of planning decide about the materialization of certain identities and ideologies in urban space. While the first points to a contest in terms of the classic antagonism between use- and exchange-value, the second reveals multiple antagonistic lines between actors struggling for expressing their values and ideologies as statements of identity and difference. The economic and social antagonisms in urban development both reveal the political in planning, hinting at the important question of power and the ideological decisions taken in the contest over urban futures. Yet, only within the processes of active urban development these antagonisms become visible (Stäheli, 2006). Thus, in critical urban research we need to deconstruct these political processes to reveal the distinguishing lines between antagonistic interests. Only then we can widen our understanding of the politics of planning and attempt to change material practices upon altered approaches to urban development.

Linking culture, city, and planning
Entering a cultural era in urban development

The urban sphere has always been attached with a set of values. From the ancient Greek archetype of the democratic city to the industrial town as epitome of progress and prosperity, cities always stood for particular qualities (Hall, 1998; Evans, 2001; Schäfers, 2009). And they do so still today. Each city symbolizes a long tradition of values. They embody the visions and lifestyles of a certain zeitgeist. They are representations of specific people at specific times. And they all are materializations of this history, of values, identities, and power. Hence, cities express culture. And, cities *are* culture (Mumford, 1970; Scott, 1997; Schneider, 1997; Miles et al., 2000; Sennett, 2008; Eckardt and Nyström, 2009).

Indeed, culture has something to offer for urban development. It is the strong relationship between the formative forces of the urban sphere and the stimulus culture can have for economic and social innovation that became conscious only recently. Consequently, it was no surprise that culture was brought to the fore in the politics of planning, with the aim of utilizing the conglomerate of positive values and energies in development strategies. As the 20th century came to a close, this led to a true culture-hype in urban development (Zukin, 1995, 1998; Evans, 2001; Garcia, 2004). Regardless of specific contexts, culture is today considered as *the* tool to re-interpret urbanity (Fessler Vaz and Berenstein Jacques, 2006).

But why has culture entered planning agendas so intensely? How come actors of the city so vigorously turned to culture-led approaches? Many of the reasons for this planning practical shift lie in the multiform transformations of the city and the adjacent transformations of urban politics and planning. For one thing, the prevailing notion in planning research and practice of space as a material *and* discursive process explains why an awareness of the importance of culture in urban development evolved. If cultural influences are considered as determinants of constructing space, it gets clear why culture is now heavily employed in planning as a means of accumulation, representation and legitimation in development approaches across cities globally (Smith, 2002; Ribera-Fumaz, 2009; Davoudi & Strange, 2009; De Frantz, 2011). Furthermore, the decline of industrial cities after the breakdown of Fordism called for a reorientation of cities and their economic organization and development agendas. As discourses about the charisma of creative and artistic work emphasized and examples from industrially declining cities have shown, experimental culture has the potential to regenerate former industrial areas, run-down quarters and ruinous neighborhoods (Hall, 1998; Puype, 2004; Benneworth & Hospers, 2009). Particularly under tough economic conditions it is these open cultural interventions, which are able of reinterpreting urban environments that suffered from economic or identity crises (Albers, 2008; Sennett, 2008; Carp, 2009). Understandably, cities everywhere tried to copy these "best practices" via establishing similar culture-led interventions for the regeneration of almost any place, regardless of contextual preconditions, or, as Gibson and Stevenson would call it, a *"just add culture and stir"*-mentality (2004: 1).

This turn to the production of culturally signified places can be interpreted as a reaction to the post-Fordist claim of establishing economies of scope. The so-created culturally loaded places and images serve as distinct and thus competitive niches on transnational markets signified by intense contest over capital and visibility (Harvey, 1989, 1990, 1997; Sieverts, 1990; Hall & Hubbard, 1996; Hall, 1998; Kaufmann, 2009). Thus, in planning, culture is being attached to almost any strategic measures deployed in the global arena. Whether it is an architectural landmark or the next "city of culture" event – culture is utilized to symbolize the distinctiveness and vitality of cities in global competition via representations of quality of life, political power and economic competitiveness (Kearns & Philo, 1993; Häußermann & Siebel, 1993; Monclùs, 2006; Fessler Vaz & Berenstein Jacques, 2006; Ward, 2006; Schmid, 2007).

Such culture-led projects and the related commodification of local cultural processes also deeply integrate the new political rationales and altered modes of planning. Through intense place-making, city space becomes culturally signified. Urban neighborhoods experience sometimes massive makeovers to appeal to the aesthetics of a new middle-class, and the local cultural practices are mutated into urban lifestyle images to convert both the materiality and meaning of space into consumable goods of external capital (Göschel & Kirchberg, 1998; Evans, 2001, 2003; Springer, 2007). The resulting creativity strategies, culture-led mass events, beautified urban environments and spectacular place images mushrooming in cities in the past decades indicate what is termed a culturalization of the city – the application of cultural values to projects of urban change (Scott, 1997, 2000; Young, 2006, 2008).

As can be seen from these first elaborations, culture-led approaches to urban development utilize the positively connoted values and rich images of culture (defined in whatever sense) to re-interpret the city and its places (Springer, 2007; Miles, 2007). Reasonably, culture is employed not only as a means to urban regeneration, but also as a means to inclusion – a central aim for cities struggling with spatial and social fragmentation (Fohrbeck & Wiesand, 1989; Marcuse & van Kempen, 2000; Bloomfield & Bianchini, 2001). Relatedly, constructing urban identities upon cultural values becomes a wide-spread purpose in planning. In this respect, cities often turn to the historic roots of urbanization, cherishing the long-known values of urban culture – democracy, diversity, citizenship and individual freedom – as the principal maxims of urban development (Mumford, 1970; Evans, 2001; Stevenson, 2001; Bloomfield & Bianchini, 2001; Sennett, 2008; De Frantz, 2011). Yet, critical accounts emphasize the misuse of history, heritage and adjacent urban cultural values in this regard, as they are recurrently being instrumentalized for consolidating cultural and ideological hegemony (Kearns, 1993; Sadler, 1993; De Frantz, 2011).

This indicates the political relevance of the concept of culture in planning. It can serve two seemingly opposing ends concerning the multiple identity crises of the city after rational modernity: identity formation *and* the celebration of difference. For one thing, the construction of *"an urban culture"* can serve as the unifying element within the value-pluralism of a city (Fohrbeck & Wiesand, 1989; Evans, 2001). As planning success strongly depends on the integration of the most diverse actors and sometimes opposed aims and visions, the elastic concept of culture (Bassett et al., 2005) is framed in a way that those actors to be included find themselves represented in the constructed cultural planning vision (Kearns, 1993; Zukin, 1995; Kirchberg, 1998). On the other hand, when it comes to celebrating difference, the *"manifold urban cultures"* of a city are put at center stage to symbolize democracy, diversity, citizenship and freedom of choice as the sought after values of the cultural city (Zukin, 1998; Jacobs, 1998; Elliott, 2001; Young, 2006, 2008; Davoudi & Strange, 2009; Quenzel & Lottermann, 2009; Bauman, 2011). By contrast, and with a more positive prospect, culture as a representational resource is also considered as a valuable source of hope in a transforming urban world that is characterized by fragmentation, inequality and multiform complexity. Culture is by some even hailed as the special ingredient to a multifaceted, democratic city and the establishment of a cultural public as the basis for a true political public (Fohrbeck & Wiesand, 1989).

So it seems as if culture was the common thread, the answer to the manifold urban questions arising under new circumstances of urban development. This, of course, owes in particular to a turn recognized far beyond the boundaries of scientific disciplines: a cultural turn, which attests that we have surpassed the materially determined times of modernity and entered a culturally determined era (Fohrbeck & Wiesand, 1989; Harvey, 1990; Jameson, 1991, 1998; Zukin, 1995, 1998; Young, 2008). Wide-ranging social and political transformations and the end of *"a single correct mode of representation"* (Harvey, 1990: 27) undermined the foundation of the concept of modernity. The diminishing importance of the nation state as territory of political intervention and cultural identification, the turn to leisure and consumption as identity-forming forces and *"the rise of economic culturalization"* (Young, 2008: 15) all led to an increased awareness of the significance of the cultural in organizing urban life and steering the future of cities (Rojek, 2000, Gottdiener, 2000; Evans, 2001). This recognition has become an established notion in planning practice, where the cultural turn is reflected in the politics of difference and the acknowledgement of the discursive formation of cultural meaning and identity. Thus, culture is today considered as an essential element of urban development (Fincher & Jacobs, 1998; Eade & Mele, 2002; Jessop, 2004, 2008; Young, 2008; Ribera-Fumaz, 2009; Quenzel & Lottermann, 2009).

The important point to be added here is the thick relation of culture and place, which is ultimately referred to in culture-led planning and makes culture such a valuable concept for both economic capitalization and representation. As was mentioned earlier planning today deals with the use, development, re-arrangement and re-interpretation of urban space in its material and immaterial form. In this regard, culture plays an even more significant role, as it is always strongly associated with place and its constant material and immaterial makeover. This deep link is a widely debated fact for the case of the arts and a cultural economy (Scott, 1997, Bassett et al., 2005). Sennett (2008), for instance, explains how, during renaissance, art and place for the first time ever formed a symbiotic relationship. The ingenious artist's studio had become an exceptional place, producing distinct image-value. And this cultural image-value is transferable to space to be exploited economically (Bourdieu, 1986; Springer, 2007, Suitner, 2010). In an inquiry of recent urban development processes, Zukin intensely debates the regeneration of urban neighborhoods through artist's residence (Zukin, 1989). But immediately she turns to the political effects of such culture-led transformation, finding that culture is utilized by market actors as an attribute to increase profit and growth, and that it serves as an instrument to gain power over contested space and exclude other forms of cultural expression (Zukin, 1995, 1996; Kirchberg, 1998).

So, the focus on capitalization through culture-led planning is as evident as that of cultural processes as representational practices. Culture can be a means to making sense of place for any actor of the city that is powerful enough to succeed in the struggle for the prerogative of interpretation (Schulz, 2006). It might as well serve real estate developers for increasing rents, as it might be a tool of expressing difference for marginalized groups of the city. Either way, planning processes are permeated by such competing interests concerning the use and future development of urban space (Zukin, 1989; Garcia, 2004, Bassett et al., 2005; Göschel, 2009). *"Culture is always about identities and power."* (Scott, 1997: 335) Thus, it has moved to center stage as a decisive factor in the politics of planning (Bloomfield & Bianchini, 2001; De Frantz, 2005, 2011). Being able of attaching space with meaning and image-value, culture-led interventions allow for targeted place-making and the construction of favored urban images as the added value of space to be exploited economically. At the same time, cultural processes and culture-led planning projects are the representations of specific identities and urban visions. They are symbols of power over space and are thus essential for the consolidation of power in the politics of planning and in the establishment or contestation of hegemony. (Zukin, 1995; Hall & Hubbard, 1996; Hannemann & Sewing, 1998; Jones, 2006) Consequently, with its broad range of transported values and meanings, culture can as well serve as the neutral language to maintain power and stabilize hegemonic economic and ideological projects in a diverse urban world.

Referring to culture as the distinct characteristics of social groups, products and places that make these things meaningful, makes it both the central element of identification and dissociation from "the other" (Gupta & Ferguson, 1997a, 1997b; Stäheli, 2006; Berndt & Pütz, 2007; Young, 2008; Eckardt & Nyström, 2009). At the same time, it has become common sense that culture is able of bridging the gaps between typical urban dialectics – public and private, work and leisure, art and economy, or high and popular culture (Lange, 2007). Thus, it is often employed to build social cohesion between the fragments of the post-Fordist city, foster identity formation and provide socio-political critique (Markusen & Gadwa, 2009). So what we see is that culture is both an element of coherence and differentiation. In this regard, it has also become an important analytical concept for understanding contemporary urban societies (Young, 2008) and handling diversity in practice in the *"cities of difference"* (Fincher & Jacobs, 1998). It is here that culture is interpreted as a tool of political expression of sometimes marginalized social groups that ultimately comes down to a materialization symbolizing both identity and difference.

Throughout modernity, the politics of nation states already relied on this symbolic strength of culture to construct national identity, social order, a distinction between the political sphere and society and cultural and political hegemony

(Taylor, 2004; Jones, 2006; Jessop, 2008; Bauman, 2011). And with the arrival of a cultural turn in the politics of planning, processes of urban transformation were increasingly linked to culture to legitimize a certain form of planning and to construct territorial coherence (Kearns & Philo, 1993; De Frantz, 2011). In contemporary planning processes though, culture is largely employed for reshaping a city's look, image and identity, and regenerating its economy – all aiming at capital accumulation (Ribera-Fumaz, 2009; Best & Paterson, 2010). Such "culturalizations" reduce culture to its function as an *"agent of change"* (Zukin, 1995), meaning it is degraded to an add-on for securing economic capitalization upon urban development (Evans, 2001; Lagendijk, 2004; Young, 2008; Hornig, 2011). On the other hand, ideological representation and the conservation of political power still play a major role in culture-led urban transformation, as the following elaborations are still going to show. Consequently, at least in theory a clear distinction needs to be made between urban development processes building upon a culturized planning view that attempt to foster cultural activity as a means to the democratization of the city and the establishment of cultural pluralism (Evans, 2001; Stevenson, 2001; Young, 2008; Bauman, 2011), and culture as an agent of change that points to CPE and the construction of cultural and political hegemony (Zukin, 1995; Jessop, 2004, 2008; Jessop & Oosterlynck, 2008; Ribera-Fumaz, 2009).

So, what remains as an important argument from these elaborations is that the cultural turn in social sciences leaves us with two essential considerations to be taken serious. First, within urban development culture's critical force – questioning the status quo – has clearly diminished (Garcia, 2004). Instead, its role as an agent of change is prevailing in current planning practice, where culture has become an instrument of securing accumulation strategies upon culture's surplus value and a means of hegemonic representation (Zukin, 1995; Gupta & Ferguson, 1997b; Harvey, 2002; Jessop, 2004; Ribera-Fumaz, 2009; De Frantz, 2011; Grubbauer, 2011a, 2011b). Garcia (2004) stresses that the employment of culture in planning is increasingly characterized by contradictions between empowerment and a new urban political economy. Thus, and this is the second central concern, within planning research, culture should be considered as an analytical variable for critical reviews of the materializations of culture(s) in urban space. It must ask how culture is discursively referred to and materially applied in urban planning practice, and whether this is to foster democracy and pluralist cultural representation, or merely to legitimize and secure hegemonic practices.

AN AGENT OF CHANGE: THE SALIENT NARRATIVES OF CULTURALIZATION FOR CAPITALIZATION

> "[T]he city has always been a site where culture has been mobilized in the pursuit of profit"
> HALL & HUBBARD, 1996: 169

A specific notion of the relationship between culture and planning started to enter urban development strategies of all cities at the close of the millennium. Culture was and still is seemingly attached to any planning measure that attempts to solve one among the many urban crises of the post-industrial city. It thus became a savior, employed to overcome any social, economic or political problem (Gibson & Stevenson, 2004). Sennett (2008) notes that culture – however defined – is said of having the potential to develop something even in the worst seeming environments where all hope is normally gone. And in a similar vein, Evans (2001) elucidates that it is due to this notion that culture is so heavily employed in processes of urban change, as it adds value to all kinds of projects, regardless of actors, scales, contexts and the very problem to be tackled. So, reasons for employing culture in planning seem to be endless. Evidently, the cultures of cities are in all these projects utilized as the unique selling proposition, aesthetic distinction and "finishing touch" in the construction of place and its economic capitalization. These culturalization approaches make culture an agent of change. Urban researchers have made numerous attempts to distinguish the various culturalization approaches as they have appeared within the past decades. Miles & Paddison (2005), for instance, point towards three distinct areas of intervention where culture-led strategies in planning are recently deployed: the physical appearance of the city, i.e. the built form, the urban economy, and city images. Freestone & Gibson (2006) detect six models of promoting urban space through the utilization of cultural activity: cultural tourism, place marketing and city re-imaging, culture-led urban regeneration, cultural districts, cultural industries, and community-based cultural planning. And Reicher (2009), referring to Kunzmann, speaks of seven objectives in contemporary planning to be reasonably tackled via culture-led intervention, namely economic regeneration and employment, image production, urban regeneration, entertainment, education, creativity, and identity formation. To evade inevitable confusion in reproducing this broad array of classifications, I condense these diverse distinctions – valuable as they may be for analytically describing the culturalization of cities in detail – to three major narratives of why and how culture is applied as an agent of change in planning in today's cities.

The first is the rise of the creative industry model as a regenerator of urban economies after Fordism. As the Fordist logic of mass production and mass consumption as backbones of a functioning economy had largely failed, new economic niches to be exploited needed to be established. The cultural turn offered just this opportunity to add force to an urban economy after Fordism again – only this time upon cultural specificity as the foundation to new modes of production and consumption (Zukin, 1998; Lagendijk, 2004). Consequently, culture and economy began to intersect ever more, leading to both the culturalization of urban economies, i.e. the saturation of mass-produced goods with cultural value and adaptation of local industries to fit certain lifestyle models, and the commodification of culture, i.e. the integration of cultural products and processes into cycles of economic exploitation (Scott, 1997, 2000; Lagendijk, 2004; Young, 2008; Lange et al., 2009). Problematically, this intermingling of culture and economy forces cultural actors to operate in a more entrepreneurial manner, as cultural production turns into an industry following the market rules of profit-orientation, supply and demand, and competition for audiences (Glogner & Föhl, 2010). It also effectuates a general aestheticization of urban lifeworlds as argued within discourses on postmodern planning (Harvey, 1990; Heineberg, 2005; Häußermann et al., 2008; Davoudi & Strange, 2009). The well-promoted message established by economic geography was that a creative industry based upon a "creative class" could be a vital base to endogenous economic development and would, by its very nature, produce a powerful post-industrial image (Florida, 2002). This seemingly easy-to-adopt formula drew local planners and politicians to employ culture-as-creativity strategies almost everywhere, as the cultural or creative industries had become promising economic regenerators and growth engines (Bassett et al., 2005; Miles & Paddison, 2005; Madgin, 2009; Benneworth & Hospers, 2009). As Evans (2001) notes, to a large degree the turn to creative industries owes to the recognition that Western cities are today characterized by a small enterprise economy. And, as creative milieus need *urban* environments to function properly (Crevoisier, 2001) it makes them an attractive model for cities encountering economic decline and fragmentation. Through that, the creative city discourse initiated a paradigmatic shift in the organization of contemporary urban economies and the politics of planning with culture. The reinterpretation of the role of culture in cities from art and heritage to an economic asset with market value was a first step towards this economic change (Garcia, 2004). Relatedly, both the business sector and urban politics turned their backs on former notions of culture as a soft locational factor, as it had obviously become a hard economic development factor (Quenzel & Lottermann, 2009). Thereby, culture clearly replaced classic Fordist industries as the main business of cities (Zukin,

1995), and creativity has become the buzz-word to be coined in the context of any urban development concern (cf. Landry, 2000, Kunzmann, 2009). The origins of the creativity discourse can be traced back to the work of seminal authors some decades ago. Jacobs already describes in *"The Economy of Cities"* that creative efforts have the ability to give cities back their economic prosperity and independence, which they might have lost at some point in history (Jacobs, 1969). And Mumford (1970), by describing the guilds of the medieval city as some sort of economic and social "glue", hints at a central objective of recent creative city strategies: the establishment of creative and cultural milieus as the economic and social glue of the contemporary city. Here, culture, economy and place amalgamate to complete the culturalization of the city upon a new post-industrial, creative economy. Creative workers are imagined as producers of symbolic goods with unique cultural value. This value is tightly related to the places where these actors reside. The creative milieus and networks that evolve from fostering creative work are rich in social and symbolic capital that is as well able of reconstructing urban space and its meaning (Zukin, 1989; Springer, 2007; Lange et al., 2009). Therefore, culture industries are promoted in many urban strategies, as they are assumed of creating positive, place-specific images that can be capitalized subsequently – particularly as culture is an elastic concept and almost any urban industry can be branded "creative" (Bassett et al., 2005). Yet, the story of the creative industries being the backbone of a post-industrial economy must be doubtfully refused for several reasons. The contribution of culture as the arts to a regional economy is often negligible, even more as it is known for its globalist nature. The same goes true for mass media as another fraction of the creative industry that is known for consisting mostly of non-place-bound global actors, who touch down at only a handful of places (Krätke, 2003). But as creative city policies are typical supply-oriented strategies (Hall, 1998; Evans, 2001), they contribute heavily to the general shift in cultural policies from provision to competition (Kloostermann & van der Werff, 2009). One of the most popular criticisms is the related commodification of culture in favor of maximizing profit. Evans (2001), for instance, asks, whether strategies towards enforcing cultural industries of a city are truly about the genuine production of *culture*, or, instead, about the culture of *production*, i.e. the imperatives of a culturalized economy aiming at culture-based capitalization. Furthermore, the creativity discourse puts an accent on the attraction of skilled human capital as a must-have of any effective strategy (Landry, 2000; Florida, 2002). This, of course, marginalizes the potential of an existent diverse urban population. Thus, the danger of constructing exclusive urban environments through the hallowing of a new managerial class of creative minds is at hand. Yet, the most disarming critique focuses a basic hypothesis of the creative class argument, which is that cultural actors are to a large degree dependent on subsidies and cannot produce their jobs on their own by just "being creative" (Göschel, 2009). Thus, the creative city paradigm is also critically reviewed as a neoliberal economic strategy promoting *"[...] insecurity as the new freedom."* (Peck, 2005: 759)

The second narrative of culture being an agent of change focuses culture-led renewal upon identity and difference. As introduced before, altered urban contexts lead to a serious struggle between identity and difference as a duality of objectives in governing cities. For actors engaging in the politics of planning it thus makes sense to turn to culture when it comes to processes of urban renewal, where the meanings and identities attached to places of the city are in distress and can be reconstructed for capitalization. As planning shifted its focus to smaller scales of local urban quarters, state-initiated urban renewal has become a major tool for restoring cohesion and securing socially inclusive urban development (Albers, 2008; Häußermann et al., 2008). But besides equity planning, urban renewal is today also oriented at re-facilitating urban quarters with specific cultural meaning and identity for economic reasons. This already points to the before mentioned duality inherent in culture-led urban renewal. In current planning, culture has become a means to different ends. As Moulaert et al. (2004) describe, culture-led renewal should serve deprived or marginalized citizens as well as the wealthy elites. Thus, it is utilized to construct both coherent urban environments that convey belonging and secure social order, as well as places representing distinct lifestyles and cultural exclusiveness for economic profits (ibid.). However, the turn to culture in urban renewal since the 1980s proved to be successful particularly in economic terms, as many examples of urban regeneration upon culture showed (Zukin, 1989, 1995, 1998; Hall & Hubbard, 1996; Garcia, 2004; Miles & Paddison, 2005; Springer, 2007; Scott, 2011). It is here that culture serves as the symbol of a new urban quality of life via signifying a (constructed) coherent urban identity and, at the same time, the right amount of cultural difference within its fragments (Fohrbeck & Wiesand, 1989; Evans, 2001; Garcia, 2004). While Fordist mass production and mass consumption had largely deprived products of their cultural uniqueness and, thus, their value for identity formation, rational planning and a global capitalist culture did the same to urban places. They obscured the unique qualities, histories and cultural values attached to cities and their places, making their economic liveliness by and large dependent from external factors (Landry, 2000; Sennett, 2008). The culture-led renewal of local neighborhoods now is the logical reaction – the attempt to physically re-shape urban space upon culture and attach it with unique meaning and identity again. Thus, culture-led renewal can be a foundation to both the material and immaterial regeneration of less favored areas of the city in order to economically utilize them. In Landry's account on the creative city (2000), he describes this prevalent belief, explaining that cultural difference is able to add value to cities again that seem to look and feel alike. In this regard, driving the urban renaissance is the major objective of attaching culture to revitalization strategies (Hall, 1998; Puype, 2004; Häußermann et al., 2008). This implies the aestheticization of neighborhoods and urban quarters, and their attachment with cultural activity to suit the lifestyle of a well-off, creative clientele (Zukin, 1998). What is being constructed is the picture of an open, diverse and tolerant city – pronounced values of the contested class of capital-rich visitors and investors and highly skilled workforce (Florida, 2002). It is clear that cultural production and the distinct ways of life utilized in these culture-led approaches have the power to produce and re-produce aesthetics and the perception of products and places. They have the power to reshape meanings and thereby produce symbolic representations that are inseparably linked to urban space (Springer, 2007; Quenzel & Lottermann, 2009). Thus, they are valuable factors of a symbolic economy, where capital accumulation builds upon exploiting culture's image value and the creation of exclusive urban environments (Zukin, 1995, 1996, 1998; Lewitzky, 2005; Springer, 2007). The dualism in culture-led renewal of (mostly bottom-up) experimental, inclusive and cohesion-oriented projects on the one hand, and (mostly top-down) aesthetic, exclusive and profit-oriented regeneration on the other seems to be problematic. Yet, it perfectly supports the heavily promoted idea of building heterogeneous cities as seedbeds of innovation and prosperity in a post-Fordist economy. Thus, culture-led urban renewal is hailed for bridging the inherent gap of globalizing cities between the still relevant goal of building a spirit of belonging and common identity, while celebrating cosmopolitanism at the same time (Elliott, 2001; Beck, 2005). Of course, this notion is not free of critique. First, urban renewal as the process of pure aestheticization runs the risk of reinterpreting the city as a kaleidoscope of places of consumption, consequently constructing exclusive urban environments (Ward, 2003). As recent examples have shown, inclusion cannot be achieved upon the culturalization of areas suffering from decline or marginalization. Instead, it only guarantees the integration of those, who are anyway affiliated to the marketplace – who want to be consumers and are thus not dependent on equity and access as normative goals of cultural policy (Evans, 2001; Miles & Paddison, 2005). For culture-led renewal to reveal its true value, planners must adopt a culturized view (Young, 2006, 2008), safeguard balanced powers in the multi-level governance networks of cultural planning (Evans, 2001; Föhl, 2009), and allow for experimental and empowering cultures to unfold (Puype, 2004).

The third narrative, then, interprets culture as an agent for the politics of visibility in global inter-place competition. Of course, culture-led interventions have become powerful tools in the locational policies of cities when it comes to global competition between places. Cultural projects serve as the business card of a city. They represent economic strength, leadership and a set of values the city stands for (Grubbauer, 2011a, 2011b). Thus, culture transformed from a secondary component of urban development policies to a core element of sometimes aggressive place-promotion now. It has become the number one tool to sell places to global audiences as part of a greater strategy of competition for capital (Harvey, 1985, 1989, 1997; Zukin, 1995; Madgin, 2009; Quenzel & Lottermann, 2009; Benneworth & Hospers, 2009). As Bassett et al. (2005) describe, it has become common sense among planners, politicians and developers that culture is a competitive advantage. Target audiences typically are global tourists and capital-rich, unbound investors (Hall, 1998; Florida, 2002; Garcia, 2004; Ribera-Fumaz, 2009). Put simply, culture-led inter-place competition means culturalization for distinguishing the local from an increasingly homogenous global space (Landry, 2000; Springer, 2007). What makes this stream distinct is its straight-forward orientation towards capitalizing on culture, both economically and symbolically. It attempts to attract touristic consumption and unbound actor's capital investment by speaking a global cultural language of spectacular planning and capitalist urbanization (Harvey, 1985, 1997, 2002; Sklair, 2006; Grubbauer, 2011a, 2011b). This "culture for competition" is the most widely debated phenomenon within cultural planning discourses, holding also the best-known examples of planning the city with culture: from New York's MoMA to Bilbao's Guggenheim, from the many "European Capitals of Culture" to the spectacular EXPOs, sports events and other global cultural happenings (Evans, 2001; Monclùs & Guardia, 2006; Ward, 2006; Miles, 2007). It thus implies both the aestheticization of the urban environment through iconic buildings and the revitalization of the historic urban fabric. Furthermore, it includes processes of commodification of the arts, cultural processes and urban space, e.g. the celebration of traditions and heritage in huge events and spectacular planning projects, or the active support of popular leisure activities (Ward, 1998; Evans, 2001; Young, 2006, 2008; Miles, 2007). The general trend to an intensified movement of people, information and symbols opens up global arenas of cultural interaction and transnational markets of culture-led competition (Best & Paterson, 2010). Actors of the city observing this development, try to force their way into these markets by positioning cultural products, culturally loaded places, and culture-led images on these markets to tie just these people and the highly mobile investment capital to their places (Kirchberg, 1998; Evans, 2001; Best & Paterson, 2010). The sometimes aggressive employment of culture in such urban strategies builds upon the recognition of culture as a hard development factor; as an indispensable page in the urban portfolio to attract investment. And the prospect of *"monopoly rent"* (Harvey, 2002), i.e. profit upon unique, place-specific culture(s), has made it a key characteristic of cities' development strategies and a definitive locational factor (Lewitzky, 2005; Quenzel & Lottermann, 2009). *"The arts are crowd-pullers"*, states Miles (2007: 101), pointing at culture's appeal and its role as a unique selling proposition in capitalist culturalization in this regard. As an incomparable place quality, culture's image value is instrumentalized as a factor of global visibility and distinction (Springer, 2007; Kaufmann, 2009), and as a feature for increasing the surplus value of urban transformation (Harvey, 1985, 1997, 2002). Interestingly, the urban political economy of planning consolidates a narrow definition of culture in this regard (Kirchberg, 1998; Molotch, 1998). Employing culture in inter-urban competition, planning coalitions often search for the *"small differences"* (Molotch, 1998) in culture-led interventions to suit the taste of transnational cultural markets, while still constructing the picture of a unique place. Such strategies then try to combine tourism, consumption and new urban lifestyles (Zukin, 1995), advertising high art and heritage, thus constructing a very limited conception of culture for a very limited group of spectators and participants (Puhan-Schulz, 2005; Fessler Vaz & Berenstein Jacques, 2006). So, the role of culture in strategies towards inter-urban competition is clear. It is meant to serve the consumption of place (Evans, 2001), the aestheticization of urban (public and private) space (Jameson, 1991, 1998; Zukin, 1995, 1996, 1998; Ward, 1998) and the attraction of capital investment by appealing to a transnational capitalist class (Sklair, 2006; Ribera-Fumaz, 2009). By trying to attract attention and constructing investment-friendly urban environments upon the shoulders of culture, such distinction strategies too often ignore the local qualities and cultural identities of cities and the multiform realities of place (Hall, 1998; Ward, 1998; Evans, 2001; Fessler Vaz & Berenstein Jacques, 2006).

To conclude, in all three of the above narratives, the culture-for-economic-development claim has clearly outraced one of culture-for-democracy (Zukin, 1995). *"Heritage, tourism, tertiary and quaternary sector employment are heralded as the keys to a post-industrial future"* (Ward, 1998: 180), while the once rising notion of culture as a liberating force is currently diminishing (Eckardt & Nyström, 2009). The resulting challenges throughout recent culture-led projects are well known. A small number of actors decide about urban cultural development by market-oriented goals and with very little concern about local populations, cultural diversity and the cultural specificity of place (Hall & Hubbard, 1996; Beazley et al., 1997; Ward, 2003; Swyngedouw & Kaika, 2003; Markusen

& Gadwa, 2009). The goal is to appeal to a well-off, well-informed and educated class of globally acting, highly mobile individuals and powerful, capital-rich institutions to become part of transnational competition (Harvey, 1989, 1997, 2002; Zukin, 1995, 1998; Jewson & MacGregor, 1997). Cultural meaning is often generalized and mainstreamed to fit into a global popular culture of tourism, consumption and spectacle (Zukin, 1995, 1998; Evans, 2001, 2003, 2006; Gotham, 2005). And what is sold to these outward audiences are usually the culture industries and not the cultural practices and place-specific ways of life, i.e. a very narrow conception of what makes a city valuable in cultural terms (Miles, 2007). Furthermore, such interventions are critical for not being *authentic* (Kearns & Philo, 1993) and speaking a rather exclusive language. Differences in age, employment, income, knowledge or language are sometimes intentionally instrumentalized barriers of participation in urban cultural activity (Evans, 2001; Hornig, 2011). Thereby, interventions tend to focus small economic and cultural elites, while poorer people or minorities are hardly ever addressed (Puype, 2004). Thus, there is a strong tension developing between high-brow projects appealing to tourists and cultural elites, and those processes rooted in local cultural identity and production (Suitner, 2010), which counters democratic principles and can be assumed to further drive the polarization of urban societies (Gualini, 2005; Jones, 2006).

CULTURE FOR REPRESENTATION: BETWEEN HEGEMONY AND CULTURAL PLURALISM

As the above has shown, the attachment of certain cultural values to city space is often an intended construction to capitalize these values economically. Yet, culture is at least as much a representation to signify power over space and power in planning (Flyvbjerg, 2002). Its function in planning is often reduced to back promotional place constructs established by a political economic elite (Ward, 1998). Cultural policies all too often serve just the construction of state power and the legitimation and representation of a ruling regime (De Frantz, 2011). Thus, culture-led processes must as well be understood as ideological representations (Sadler, 1993; McCann, 2003). They are in this regard considered as either the tool for signifying difference among the many cultures of a city, or as the intended framing of urban space for stabilizing hegemonic regimes (Hall & Hubbard, 1996; Kirchberg, 1998; Bieling, 2006a; Jones, 2006; Schipper, 2012).

Culturalization, as introduced above, implies mostly powerful elite projects aiming at the consolidation of hegemony (Kearns & Philo, 1993; Hall & Hubbard, 1996; Evans, 2001; Young, 2008). Discussing culture as a liberating force though, subsumes those bottom-up, self-evolving processes of cultural intervention that try to (re)claim power and usually do not receive institutional guidance (Ermann, 2007). Regarding culture's role as a critical resource and symbol of difference, conspicuous cultural expression needs to be considered as an attempt to establish anti-poles to the existing power relations and counter-hegemony (Schulz, 2006; Jones, 2006). Thus, there is a serious reason to separate this strand of culture-led processes from the ones discussed before as culturalization-for-capitalization.

Only this allows uncovering whether culture is interpreted as a tool for fostering the empowerment of a city's marginalized niche cultures, or whether it is implicitly meant to recall heritage and traditions as a representation of a specific history (Kearns & Philo, 1993); whether "value representation" means to face the challenges of fragmentation and diversity by interpreting the postmodern city of difference as a chance for social innovation (Gupta & Ferguson, 1997a, 1997b; Fincher & Jacobs, 1998; Moulaert et al., 2004), or whether culture is utilized for matching a city with global markets to increase economic profit and strengthen political power (Jones & Wilks-Heeg, 2004; Miles & Paddison, 2005). Is culture, thus, a purely promotional construct, used for maintaining political power, or can it be an openly debated development goal to serve urban diversity, empowerment, and inclusion (Miles & Paddison, 2005)?

Culture is today often employed in urban renewal when it comes to cohesion purposes, such as local identity building, social inclusion, and the enforcement of social capital for empowerment (Bloomfield & Bianchini, 2001; Bassett et al., 2005; Suitner, 2010). It has become a central element of the empowerment of locals (Zukin, 1995; Marcuse, 2011). Binns (2005), for instance, proclaims a "third way" to cultural planning beyond the production- and consumption-motifs that are pursued for economic success and political leadership. He calls attention to community programmes that focus participation in cultural activity in order to achieve inclusion and broad cultural representation. Quenzel & Lottermann (2009) also emphasize the role of culture-based processes as a means to cultural representation – a spokesman of the wish and democratic right to participate in urban (economic) life. Puype (2004) further explains that experimental culture-based interventions particularly support cohesion, inclusion and democracy. Relatedly, working with marginalized groups of the city and the specific challenges of places and neighborhoods even became an artistic genre itself, namely "new genre public art" (Lewitzky, 2005). Apparently, social engagement, rehabilitation of the excluded and strengthening informal social networks have become the aims of a broad array of empowering strategies in culture-led social and community policies (Pratt, 2009).

Scientific discourses on culture-led planning convincingly show that recent approaches to planning the city with culture neglect the once so heavily uttered claim for achieving pluralism all too often. For one thing, the production and distribution of mass culture as seen in sports-, music-, film- or art events is typically controlled by just a few placeless actors. Thus, these popular events and spectacular happenings are nothing but the representation of a culture favored by those actors, who are in control to shape the processes, their content, and the related in- and exclusions (Kearns & Philo, 1993; Gupta & Ferguson, 1997a, 1997b). Culture is in this concern typically reduced to passive consumption, which is synonymous with a culturalization of the city for economic reasons. It constructs exclusive urban environments by employing a global popular culture as a driver of consumption and image. And, to counter critique, local governments and planning elites try to attach a sense of place to these processes of culturalization to construct authenticity (Göschel & Kirchberg, 1998; Bloomfield & Bianchini, 2001; Madgin, 2009; Füller & Marquardt, 2009). The discursive representation of diversity also seems to be an unmanageable demand, as scholars frequently emphasize. When packed into marketable images, the contextual culture of a city is abbreviated, simplified and mainstreamed, and thus incapable of standing in for the diverse cultures of the city (Schneider, 1997; Garcia, 2004; Evans, 2006). Hence, if culture is considered as a representation of hegemonic state power and motor of the entrepreneurial politics of selling places, then cultural pluralism is illusionary. Discursive representations cannot but construct stereotypical pictures of place culture and a mainstreamed, exclusive image (Schneider, 1997; Garcia, 2004). Yet, it is particularly this notion that makes culture-led approaches so appealing to powerful actors, as they allow framing the material and immaterial city for legitimizing, representing, and further stabilizing hegemonic regimes (Jones, 2006).

So it seems as if culture couldn't fulfill the hopes of becoming a resource of liberation and achieving inclusion and democracy in cities characterized by diversity, uncertainty and constant marginalization (Mumford, 1970; Jameson, 1998; Stevenson, 2001; Moulaert et al., 2004; Young, 2008). Critical research emphasizes that instead of empowering difference, culture-led urban development is today predominantly shaped by processes of instrumentalization for hegemonic representation. Even the *"city of difference"* (Jacobs & Fincher, 1998) is mutated into a cosmopolitan vision utilized for selling the picture of diversity to transnational markets (Zukin, 1998; Jacobs, 1998; Jones & Wilks-Heeg, 2004; Mouffe, 2007). Thus, a guiding question needs to be, whether culture-led processes are to represent and maintain hegemony, or if they signify the rise of pluralism through the representation of cultural and ideological difference.

This challenges urban researchers to engage in analyses of the construction and conservation of political hegemony upon the shoulders of culture. It demands the critical investigation of politically emphasized arguments for or against certain cultures to be the foundation of urban regeneration, place-making and marketing. It further provokes the exploration of niche cultural, self-evolving processes as counterpoints to these established modes of culture-led urban development. And it demands us to rethink the claim for cultural pluralism under the perspective of culture being a representation instrument. Because then, culture-led interventions can either be elitist representations, maintaining the status quo of cultural and political hegemony, or a path towards establishing counter-hegemony upon culture's critical and liberating force. Yet, these cannot exist side by side. This shows that the application of culture in urban development is highly political and that it can never become a sphere without domination, fights over power and representation. Following Mouffe (2007), we need to be aware that there is no *"beyond hegemony"*. Instead, the challenge is to find ways to pluralize hegemony upon applications of culture as a liberating force in urban development.

Taking the insurmountable opposition between cultural interventions as a tool pro-democracy and an instrument of hegemonic representation for granted, it seems crucial to reconsider Young's (2006, 2008) differentiation between culturalization and culturization, which illustrates just this antagonism. This and the acknowledgement that a world without hegemony is delusory, opens up an essential question. How can planning in a cultural era employ culturally distinct values, beliefs, expressions and lifestyles for socio-economic development without falling into the trap of culturalization, i.e. the cementation of a hegemony of culture-led entrepreneurial urbanism and exclusive policies? Can it come up to this expectation at all?

Cultures are not stable constructs. They are constantly developing and changing (Pratt, 2009). It is evident that niche cultures and critical cultural movements are constantly evolving in urban environments. And in this sense they function as seedbeds of economic and social innovation or political critique (Moulaert et al., 2004; Bauman, 2011). The many local cultural initiatives, grassroots movements and creative niches are expressions of difference or disapproval, thus being sometimes path-breaking initials to the establishment of counter-hegemony or even the reformulation of social systems (Bloomfield & Bianchini, 2001; Taylor, 2004). Yet, in recent years many of these critical movements have overtly been incorporated into the procedures of political economy and instrumentalized for economic purposes and political legitimation, such as the utilization of migrant cultures to sell the openness and tolerance of cities to the world (Jacobs, 1998), or the alienation of demonstrative critique on neoliberal practices during the financial crisis by ruling regimes (Jessop, 2013). Efforts of culture-led emancipation from top-down imposed cultural value-sets are often incorporated into strategies of ruling regimes to inhibit the potential loss of power over planning. Niche cultures attempting to take a swipe at hegemony are often integrated into established institutional cycles of culturalization (Young, 2008; Best & Paterson, 2010).

It doesn't seem as if culture as a critical resource would stand a chance to escape culturalization tendencies in the first place. Yet, there are ways towards establishing cultural pluralism. First, some authors are skeptical about the possibility of incorporating critical cultures into elitist cycles of economic and political exploitation in general, as these would lose authenticity, image- and market-value (Evans, 2001; Springer, 2007; Comunian, 2009). Second, as cultures change persistently, it is reasonable to assume that the modes of incorporating them into hegemonic regimes need to change, too. Ways of employing the new forms and processes of culture as an agent of change and mode of representation must be found by a ruling coalition, as approved approaches and networks might not be suitable or turn out to be ineffective. These new modes need to be tested and adapted to local contexts and conditions to construct authenticity and embed them in an existent regime. It is particularly at these crisis-like transitions that the break of dominant regimes and the establishment of pluralized hegemony seem possible in cultural urban development (Stoker, 1995; Scott, 2001; Bieling, 2006a, 2006b; Jones, 2006; Young, 2008; Jessop, 2013).

Hence, the claim for re-establishing culture as a critical resource and liberating force in urban development doesn't seem illusory. It simply demands planners to employ a culturized view on the city, its transformations, and the power relations inherent in culture-led planning practices to safeguard democratic development and reveal culture's potential as a society-building relation (Moulaert et al., 2004; Puype, 2004; Young, 2006, 2008; Eckardt & Nyström, 2009).

Theorizing Cultural Imagineering

Conceptualizing the discursive regulation
of culture-led place transformation

Above I have introduced strategic imaging as a new mode of planning for constructing both identity and difference in cities embedded in a global capitalist cultural economy. It was also made clear that in culture-led planning, strategic imaging has become a regular exercise. The distinct character of cultural products and practices and their links with urban space endow places with particular image value. Thus, imaging is now a common tool of selling places to specific audiences all over the world and representing a framed picture of the cultural qualities of urbanity that are considered valuable in the politics of visibility. Increased urban image construction is at the same time an expression of a wider turn in planning, which I refer to twice in this book: first, as a spatial turn, acknowledging the duality of materiality and meaning inherent in urban space. The adjacent notion of space as discursively influenced has become a central argument in urban research. It regards the material city as co-constituted by another sphere of discursive meaning-making. And second, as a communicative turn, pointing at a significant re-orientation in recent planning practice towards more participatory and bottom-up approaches to do justice to claims for a democratization of planning and the recognition of urban diversity. In both, discourse has become a new layer of intervention in planning practice. And the strategic construction of images as discursive representations of place builds upon this altered focus heavily (Helbrecht, 1993, 1994).

Consequently, the discursive layer can be a powerful tool for coalition building and promoting certain planning visions (Healey et al., 1999; Salet & Faludi, 2000). It is the marketable reproduction of what is there in a city in material terms. Thus, the discursive constructions are considered as instruments for making material processes and things meaningful. The discursive layer of space represents them in a very particular manner in place images, marketing strategies and advertisements to determine how places and whole cities should be perceived in a globalized economy (Helbrecht, 1993; Sadler, 1993; Kavaratzis, 2004). It is not a groundbreaking reflection to point at the highly political character of the process of constructing these framed discursive representations. First, they are restricted to powerful urban elites who decide about the discursive representations (Zukin, 1995; Hall & Hubbard, 1996; De Frantz, 2005), while second, the representations themselves are the most extreme abstractions and alienations of the material city. They are framings of what *should* be represented of the city in immaterial terms, excluding the many cultures of place (Kearns & Philo, 1993; Gupta & Ferguson, 1997a, 1997b). In debates on the entrepreneurial city, this notion has become a widely accepted argument. Not without reason, Harvey's feeling a long time ago was that in most cities image had won over substance (Harvey, 1989). Hall and Hubbard (1996), in a similar line of reasoning, emphasize that apparently urban images have become at least as important as traditional, material concerns of urban development. More recently, Ward (2003: 117) points at the undeniable *"[...] importance of discourse, imaginations, narrative and representation in the performance of entrepreneurial urbanism."* And Kavaratzis (2004) finds that imaging, marketing and branding have all eventually become central planning agendas.

In this regard, discourse is by and large understood as an arena of meaning-making for the representation of the material city in a global capitalist cultural economy of consumers and investors. Here, place images are deployed in discourse to sell cities and their places to certain audiences. They frame the picture of what the city actually is in material terms by (over)emphasizing the distinct and thus potentially well-selling fragments of the urban world. But what if the immaterial layer serves not only as a framed representation of the material, but if it also has the ability to influence future material development?

Considering strategic imaging as a discursive practice of immaterially representing a framed picture of the city and its places on transnational markets is a well-known fact in urban research. Exhaustive critical inquiries of the past quarter century urban politics taught us that powerful actors of the city can influence the processes of meaning-making. They are able of manipulating discourse to determine, which qualities of urban space are representative of a city and which are not, thereby framing the pictures of urban culture, history and identity (Kearns & Philo, 1993; Kearns, 1993; Sadler, 1993; Zukin, 1995; Gupta & Ferguson, 1997a, 1997b; Göschel & Kirchberg, 1998). Yet, it would be a shortcoming to ignore that these manipulations also influence the material city in the long run. This has also largely been acknowledged by actors engaging in the politics of planning in the meantime (Hajer & Versteeg, 2005). The immaterial layer is not just a framing of what is materially there, intended to represent a certain extract to appeal to certain audiences. It is a discursive legitimation and objectification of a city's prospects, thereby influencing material urban futures (Lees, 2004; Jacobs, 2006; Glasze & Mattissek, 2009). This is where I move from imaging to Imagineering – from the representation of material cultural artifacts in strategic images to discursive meaning-making as a discursive construct influencing the material development of the city.

The immaterial layer permeates the material. It can legitimize planning strategies and their materialization in planning processes. Thereby, discourse can influence conceptions of truth, power and knowledge in planning (Flyvbjerg, 2002, 2003, 2004; Mills, 2007). It can establish hegemonic regimes upon discursively constructed rationalities and symbols that have become unquestioned realities (Sadler, 1993). Several scholars remind us about the influential character of discourses on material urban development. Two decades ago, Stoker (1995) already emphasized that policy outcomes are decisively framed by the negotiations and judgments about what is possible in urban politics and planning. And this, of course, is largely guided by the discursive element of urban space. Also the taken-for-granted planning contexts are discursively mediated, states Jessop (2008), pointing at findings from recent policy research. Their unquestioned implementation in strategies is an expression of hegemony stabilized through discursive power. Analyzing such political strategies and their discursive negotiation is thus considered relevant for revealing ideological principles and underlying values that frame urban development and establish hegemony in planning (Hajer & Versteeg, 2005; Barnett, 2008).

Furthermore, since we know that urban politics and planning are today intensely mediatized, we are certain that mediatic discourses are able of influencing the perception of the urban world. In fact, mediatic discourses co-shape our view of what is possible in urban development and what is reasonably not (Mautner, 2008; Lundby, 2009; Friesen & Hug, 2009). Discourse theory recurrently argues that the media are decisive for affecting social relations and material practices (Wodak, 2008; van Leeuwen, 2008; Keller, 2011). And this not only refers to newspapers, but as well to social media, TV, radio and film (Mautner, 2008; Gruber, 2008; Pollak, 2008). Hall (1998) highlights that place images are often unwillingly established through media coverage. Mattissek (2007), for instance, shows how identity and image of cities like Frankfurt are shaped by public discourses, drawing a clear picture of what the city *is* and *can be*. Thus, it is not enough to look at the formal planning processes to reveal how meaning is produced and attached to the materialities of the city. The informal practices that happen outside the formal political processes of active development and outside the formal modes of planning, particularly in mediatic discourses, need to be considered as equally important in this regard (Hall, 1998; Werlen, 2008). Knowing this, media are often instrumentalized by powerful actors to place their development visions, cultural values and beliefs in the public sphere, in order to influence or bias planning outcomes (Scott, 2001).

Apparently, political and mediatic discourses are decisive elements in the development of the city. They construct the narratives and "city myths" that have the power to push material transformations of the urban world into certain directions (Goodwin, 1993). They are the arena of actors mediating between power and knowledge, forming truth and rationalities, and establishing objectified planning realities. It is within the immaterial layer of urban space that meaning is constructed to inform future material development. For the case of planning the city with culture, it is important to re-emphasize that meaning-making plays a particularly important role. It is here that with culture, city, and planning three deeply linked, yet individually complex matters are combined to form a distinct mode of active urban development. Within discursive processes these spheres and their interrelations are being attached with meaning, while their complexity demands simplification to construct a cognitive picture of the urban world that is as intuitive as it is convincing. Their actual relationship is thus discursively reduced to make planning with culture a manageable object. The links among these spheres need to be made meaningful to allow for constructing a coherent picture of how they might reasonably interact, i.e. a cultural imaginary. The imaginary is assumed to be the dominant cognitive construct equipped with *"institutional power"* (Keller, 2011), able of decisively influencing material practices in what I refer to as processes of Cultural Imagineering.

Cultural Imagineering considers urban development as a process where discursive meaning-making functions as a legitimation and stabilization of certain material practices in planning. The concept argues that the imaginaries resulting from discursive meaning-making decisively influence the materialization of processes and projects in urban space. Imagineering denotes a term originally created by ALCOA, the Aluminum Company of America, who placed an advertisement in Time Magazine in 1942, stating, *"Imagineering is letting your imagination soar, and then engineering it down to earth."* (Time, 1942: 56) ALCOA's slogan unfolds this research's conceptualization of culture-led place transformation as a process influenced by Imagineering, where meaning-making forms an imaginary that is able of influencing the materialities of urban space. Of particular interest in this regard are the cultural imaginaries resulting from discourse. They articulate a reductionist idea of planning with culture, thereby preparing the ground for or against certain forms of urban development. This research engages in depicting these constructed imaginaries for places of the city that are tagged as "cultural". It reveals how interpretation and meaning-making legitimize distinct modes of planning for the realization of hegemonic economic and ideological projects. To achieve that empirically, the concept of Imagineering must first be theoretically grounded.

The concept of Cultural Imagineering basically refers to CPE. As a recent strand of classic political economy, CPE integrates the notion of a cultural turn to acknowledge both the increased culturalization of urban economies and their cultural specificity (Jessop, 2004, 2008; Jessop & Oosterlynck, 2008; Ribera-Fumaz, 2009; Best & Paterson, 2010; van Heur, 2010a, 2010b). Largely deriving from Bob Jessop's oeuvre, CPE is thus grounded in Marxist state theory and regulation theory, enriched with postmodern conceptions of a cultural turn. In this sense, CPE is interested in the complex relations between meaning and practices. It acknowledges that state power, i.e. power in planning, is both discursively and institutionally mediated; that imaginaries as the symbolic elements of space are as important as the material factors of history and institutions (Jessop, 2004, 2008; Jessop & Oosterlynck, 2008). As urban development and its constituent spheres, e.g. "the economy", "politics", or "culture", are way too complex to be comprehensively debated in state projects, powerful actors reduce this complexity by abstracting these spheres and their inherent qualities. Within discourse, these factors of urban development are simplified to a level that makes them manageable objects in planning, i.e. imaginaries (Jessop, 2004, 2008; Jessop & Oosterlynck, 2008). Thereby, imaginaries function as legitimizing arguments of certain state projects or forms of planning.

Here, regulation theory comes into play. As an approach to reveal how crisis tendencies in capitalist economies are averted and existing accumulation regimes stabilized, regulation theory became widely known in the 1970s and 80s for depicting these modes of regulation in the post-Fordist economic regime evolving after the crisis of Fordism. Several regulationist schools, most prominently the French schools evolving around Michel Aglietta's initial thesis of regulation (Aglietta, 1979), expressed their interest in *"[...] the inherent contradictions of the capitalist system [that] are ameliorated and stabilized by particular modes of social regulation"* (Hall & Hubbard, 1996: 160). Regulation theory thus aims at understanding the influential mechanisms that legitimize particular forms of production, consumption and the creation of wealth, i.e. predominant economic regimes (Aglietta, 1979; Jessop, 1990; Jessop, 2008). A central point is the instability of such regimes, which demands their constant reinforcement, stabilization and legitimation through active intervention (Hall & Hubbard, 1996). While initial regulation theory considered material factors, e.g. state institutional mediation, social formation, norms and history as the only interventions (Aglietta, 1979; Jessop, 1990), the recent integration of the concept in CPE enriches these modes of regulation with the notion of a spatial and cultural turn. Thereby, it allows considering the discursive processes of meaning-making as decisive nonmaterial elements in the regulation of accumulation regimes (Jessop, 2004, 2008; Jessop & Sum, 2006; Jessop & Oosterlynck, 2008). Jessop (2008) explains how discourses stabilize state regimes of capitalist accumulation. They legitimize state projects via political rhetoric, constructing a common interest, while actually they are strategic selections stabilizing hegemony (Jessop, 2008). In this regard, the discursively constructed imaginary can be understood as the discursive regulation securing accumulation strategies. As a cultural imaginary, it is then the discursive regulation to culturalization strategies in planning.

The concept of Cultural Imagineering integrates a third, distinct analytical layer besides the *"regulation-accumulation coupling"* (van Heur, 2010a). It attempts to go beyond CPE's focus on material and discursive regulations of hegemonic accumulation regimes upon the shoulders of culture by explicitly building upon culture's role as representation instrument as a second argument. While it is obvious that accumulation and representation strategies in urban development can hardly be distinguished, it is of importance for the theoretical concept of Cultural Imagineering to separate the two, as they point to different utilizations of culture and urban space in the politics of planning. Here, the neo-Gramscian understanding of multiple antagonistic relations inherent in urban societies plays a significant role. It widens the economistic view on urban development employed in political economy by stressing the importance of fights for representation as a further determinant of current political struggles. Cultural values, ideologies and identities thus become another line of conflict in the politics of planning with culture, yet, with no direct aim of economic capitalization, but of symbolic representation. These representations of social diversity and cultural difference in urban space collide with projects for hegemonic state representation in this concern (Jones, 2006; Bieling, 2006a; Stäheli, 2006). On the one hand, social groups claim their civic rights by attempting to signify their cultural identity and difference through material cultural processes in urban space (Stevenson, 2001; Bloomfield & Bianchini, 2001; Young, 2008; Bauman, 2011). On the other hand, powerful actors enforce the representation of *their* cultural values and ideologies to maintain the status quo and secure social control (Kearns & Philo, 1993; Zukin, 1995; Hall & Hubbard, 1996; De Frantz, 2005; Hornig, 2011). Referring to the work of Gramsci, representation strategies are thus another important element in establishing or maintaining cultural and political hegemony (Torfing, 1999; Scott, 2001; Jones, 2006; Stäheli, 2006; Keller, 2011).

The cultural imaginaries are influential factors of both accumulation and representation strategies in the concept of Cultural Imagineering and are thus placed in between. They function as discursive regulations of planning the city with culture by discursively framing a simplistic idea of why, how, and by whom this is to be done. Thereby, cultural imaginaries are assumed to decisively influence the materializations and non-materializations of certain strands of a cultural economy, cultural values, processes, and representations in urban space, which makes them pivotal to the process of Cultural Imagineering discussed in this book.

Tab. 2: Revisiting the regulation-accumulation-representation coupling of Cultural Imagineering in the duality of urban space

	MATERIALITY	**MEANING**
ACCUMULATION	Culturalization, spectacular urbanism and entrepreneurial planning (Harvey, 1985, 1990; Zukin, 1995; Hall & Hubbard, 1996; Scott, 1997, 2000; Landry, 2000; Florida, 2002; Ward, 2003, 2006; Gotham, 2005; Miles, 2007; Best & Paterson, 2010)	Culture-led place image and brand construction; advertising and selling urban lifestyles, cultural institutions and practices (Harvey, 1990, 2002; Helbrecht, 1993, 1994; Zukin, 1995, 1996, 1998; Jessop, 1997; Ward, 1998; Kavaratzis, 2004)
REGULATION	History, socio-economic development context, social formation, institutional framework, legal regulations, path-dependencies (Aglietta, 1979; Jones & Wilks-Heeg, 2004; Boyer & Saillard, 2002; Jessop, 2004, 2008; Jessop & Sum, 2006; Bieling, 2006b)	**Cultural imaginary as framing of planning with culture; complexity reduction for stabilizing and legitimizing a rationale of planning the city with culture** **(Taylor, 2004; Strauss, 2006; Jessop, 2004, 2008; Jessop & Sum, 2006; Jessop & Oosterlynck, 2008)**
REPRESENTATION	Material cultural processes as instruments of value, identity, and ideological representation; culture for expression of difference or hegemonic power (Zukin, 1995; Göschel & Kirchberg, 1998; Young, 2006, 2008; Bieling, 2006a, 2006b; Jones, 2006; Mouffe, 2007; Göschel, 2009; Eckardt & Nyström, 2009; Bauman, 2011)	Culture-led signifying practices, symbolic power, and prerogative of interpretation (Hall, 1997; Gupta & Ferguson, 1997a, 1997b; Schulz, 2006; Young, 2006, 2008; Markusen & Gadwa, 2009; Bauman, 2011)

Empirical research design
De- and reconstructing Cultural Imagineering in practice

The processes of meaning-making is embedded in discourse, which makes discourse analysis central to the empirical approach. But the production of meaning evolves from existing materialities as well to then shape the paths of a new, transformed materiality. Thus, empirical research demands taking into account the materialities of place as well in order to obtain the full picture of place transformation. Three layers of analysis shall thus be introduced here in short as the framework of methodological steps to be conducted.

The first layer comprises the city's urban development trajectory, i.e. a recap of its more recent development path in a historical perspective (Martinelli & Novy, 2013). It is meant as a multi-level contextualization of Vienna and a foundation of case study investigation. Herewith, it ensures the space- and history-sensitivity of the analysis (ibid.). In other words, the city's spatial, socio-economic, and planning-political analysis form the basis to appraise case-study-specific data and assess results on Cultural Imagineering in Vienna. Further, a basic cultural mapping shall point to the city's material cultural development preconditions (Evans, 2001). The general setting for cultural planning, the influence of existing cultural amenities and processes, and potential path-dependencies in Vienna's cultural politics and their influence on the city's urban development can be emphasized herewith (ibid.). Thus it builds the foundation for analyzing the three cases by providing a documentation of the local material cultural substance, i.e., the institutions and practices, the artifacts and activities that shape "the cultural" in material terms.

The second layer analyzes both strategic and mediatic discourses on the city's urban development and case study specific transformations as sources of the contested production of meaning. Following the methods applied in similar studies (cf. for instance Mattissek, 2007 and De Frantz, 2010), it analyzes relevant strategies that make distinct references to the case study transformation processes. As suggested by Mautner (2008), it investigates mass media discourses in this regard for being an important opinion-forming force in public discourse. The analysis of strategic and mass media discourses is meant to unhide the construction of dominant cultural imaginaries that potentially influence material place transformation and uncover the actors behind these discursive strategies to depict who has discursive power (Flyvbjerg, 2002).

The third layer then studies the material practice of local place transformation by documenting the significant materializations in terms of structural and functional organization, physical appearance, and evolving or vanishing processes. Therefore it creates case-study-specific chronologies of significant material transformations (Yin, 2009). By joining discourse with materiality, the potential path-shaping of material practice through interpretation and discusrive meaning-making can then be depicted for each case study site.

MATERIAL CONTEXT: VIENNA'S DEVELOPMENT TRAJECTORY

The empirical research begins with a contextualization of Vienna. As explained above, this is considered necessary for ensuring a place- and history-sensitive analysis (Martinelli & Novy, 2013). Yin (2009) explains that one method of case study analysis is to base it on case study documentation from secondary literature, as it provides useful information on the history of case development. This will be done for the contextualization of Cultural Vienna as well. It builds upon historical analyses of the city, research and planning reports on Vienna, and the analysis of strategic planning documents. Their structured wrap-up is meant to come up to the expectations of conducting multi-level analyses when reviewing urban development processes (McCann et al., 2003). At the same time it serves as an introduction to the city in structural, socio-economic, planning-political, and institutional terms. The multi-level approach shall draw a comprehensive picture of Vienna's material development trajectory. This will allow reflecting the process of meaning-making in discourse upon the city's material development path and will help to reveal and classify discursive strategies.

Yet, material development preconditions are not only of importance for the analysis of the whole city, but as well deserve attention when it comes to investigating the places of culture-led transformation. Thus, the material analysis will also use secondary literature on the distinct places, particularly research and planning reports and official planning-political publications dealing with them. As is going to be explained later on, conceived information will be underpinned with knowledge deriving from narrative interviews with actors involved in the place transformation process. This first material analysis covers the place-specific trajectories until 2005, as the analysis of processes of Imagineering covers the period from 2005 to 2013. Together these data will allow for a classification of the materialities of place by planning-relevant criteria, including urban structure, development history, socio-economic context, institutional and legal specificities, governance structures in local planning, material (cultural) practices, and place-based development potentials and challenges (Hajer, 2003; Martin et al., 2003; Grodach & Silver, 2013; Martinelli & Novy, 2013). This analysis of the materiality of place creates the ground for discourse analysis within the three case studies that is to be conducted in a next step.

THE CONSTRUCTION OF CULTURAL IMAGINARIES: CRITICAL DISCOURSE ANALYSIS

As exemplified in Hajer (2003), the analysis of policy discourse allows for uncovering three layers of information: first, active cognitive constructions of functional relations between distinct elements and their functioning that form the story lines, myths and metaphors of development, place, and society; second, the policy vocabularies that link processes and things – the objects of urban politics – to emotional categories, thereby consciously constructing conflict and steering the central themes of policy discourse; and third, epistemic figures – the underlying, unconscious references to how development functions that don't need any argumentation as they constitute an unquestioned knowledge of our time. Together they form what I refer to as an imaginary. The analysis of how such imaginaries come into being through the evolution of public planning-related discourse is central to this analysis, and is thus to be revealed via Critical Discourse Analysis (henceforth CDA). CDA wants to reveal the political intention of texts by conducting a problem-oriented analysis of how texts are put into context. Thereby, it wants to find out about hegemonic construals and actor coalitions, as well as issue framings, narrative structures and discursive exclusions of certain arguments. CDA on the dominant cultural imaginaries in place transformation is interested in revealing those texts and signs that have *"institutional power"* (Mills, 2007). Hence, the CDA on culture-led place transformation asks, *how* things are being said, in *which* context and by *whom* (Eade & Mele, 2002; Lees, 2004; Jacobs, 2006).

The text corpus to analyze the case studies empirically derives from mass media, or, to be more precise, from daily and weekly newspapers with a wide range of readers in Eastern Austria. This is justified by the fact that print media

"[...] very much reflect the social mainstream [...]. If you are interested in dominant discourses, rather than dissident or idiosyncratic voices, the major dailies and weeklies are obvious sources to turn to." (Mautner, 2008: 32) Texts derive from "wiso presse" database from the Austrian National Library. The covered period ranges from January 01, 2005 to May 13, 2013. This time frame is considered long enough to convey a big data corpus of useful texts for each case study and to recognize alterations and consolidations of certain dominant interpretations and discursive strategies throughout the years. With reference to methodological handbooks on CDA, articles are added to the collection if the case study's name appears in a text. It can be assumed then that the content, utterances, actor statements, and connotations have an influence on the reader, hence supporting the cognitive construction of a distinct place-related cultural imaginary (van Leeuwen, 2008; Wodak, 2008; Keller, 2011). As was explained above, only those texts with institutional power are useful for the analysis. Thus, the selection of texts is an iterative process, where the number of articles retrieved must constantly be reduced, widened, and reduced again to a workable amount of data that is still large enough to reveal dominant definitions, framings, and actors (Keller, 2011). The aim is to define text corpora of a minimum of a hundred texts for each case study with roughly the same number of texts per year to conceive results that are not biased by the dynamism of day-to-day politics and single events.

The completed data corpus is first analyzed with a basic quantitative approach, aiming at uncovering thematic tendencies and sketching the general orientation of discourses in the context of a specific project. This initial content analysis creates an overview to the emphasis that is given to particular contexts, projects, persons, or planning objects and the implicit or explicit role of culture in this regard (McCann, 2003; Mattissek, 2007; Mautner, 2008; Wodak, 2008; Keller, 2011; Schipper, 2012). For doing that I analyze word frequencies. Results are illustrated as word clouds to initially reveal the dominance of certain themes in the place-specific mediatic debate of the respective case study.

Following is qualitative analysis of the text corpus defined for each case study upon coding newspaper articles by relevant criteria. Qualitative coding is meant to support the depiction of dominant cognitive constructions, policy vocabularies, and epistemic figures that together form the dominant place-specific cultural imaginary. As is explained in Glasze et al. (2009), the structured coding of large text corpora allows depicting simplified constructions of relations between planning objects and fields of strategic intervention. For structuring, coding, and analyzing data I use MAXQDA, a software dedicated particularly to qualitative text analysis. Coding conflates a top-down and bottom-up approach.

The former builds on theoretical propositions of what is important to reveal potential cultural imaginaries. The latter refers to grounded theory. Here the definition of codes is based on the appearance of distinct events in analyzed texts that are of relevance to the analyzed topic. While they are not theoretically based in the first run, these codings constitute a potential indication to the enhancement of the analysis beyond initial hypotheses (Yin, 2009; Keller, 2011). The following variables form the spectrum of predetermined codes for structuring case study discourses:

Tab. 3: Analytical variables in Critical Discourse Analysis

VARIABLE	SPECIFICATION	SOURCE
Context & scaling	Which are the dominant scales and determinant preconditions that culture-led planning has to face?	Yeung, 1998; Kelly, 1999; Smith, 2002
Definition(s) of culture	How is culture defined? What counts as culture and what does not?	Göschel & Kirchberg, 1998; Eckardt & Nyström, 2009
Roles assigned to culture	How is culture interpreted in an urban development context?	Zukin, 1995; Evans, 2001; Miles, 2007
Actors "doing" culture	Who is typically connected with culture-led processes?	Rhodes, 1996; Hajer & Wagenaar, 2003
Audiences of culture	Who is typically targeted with culture-led initiatives?	Evans, 2001; Sklair, 2006; Miles, 2007
Imagineers of culture	Who is producing cultural imaginaries and "objectified knowledge" in discourse, and are these actors equipped with material decision-making power at the same time?	Kearns and Philo, 1993; Evans, 2003; Jessop, 2004; Binns, 2005

The next step focuses the distinct utterances of actors in discourse. It considers actor statements as having institutional power, hence being important for revealing who constructs power/knowledge regimes in planning (Flyvbjerg, 2000; Mattissek, 2009). Statements are grouped by planning-relevant thematic fields in a bottom-up manner, meaning, none of the thematic fields are predetermined. Instead they are defined upon the nature and orientation of distinct statements[1]. Actors making these statements are as well grouped concerning their affiliation.[2] This initial classification and a further differentiation of statements by the year of appearance uncover the chronology of discourse from 2005 to 2013. It further

---

1 Cf. ESPON, 2012 for a similar approach to defining fields of planning intervention upon actor statements.
2 Cf. Healey et al., 2003 for a similar classification of actor groups.

allows revealing relations between certain topics and actors, and distinct discursive strands, which deserve to be analyzed in more detail.[3]

The third step of CDA wants to reveal actor constellations in discourse. As Hajer (2003) claims, urban research should not only refer to discourse analysis to analyze the terms placed in and established through discourse, but also to reveal discourse coalitions upon shared story lines. This reveals which actors and actor groups jointly attempt to shape distinct imaginaries of culture to powerfully influence planning practice. Based on the thematic classifications of actor statements described above, actors are linked upon similarly oriented statements in the mediatic discourse. Results are then visualized as a discursive actor network that answers questions about the opinion leaders, powerful actors, and marginalized groups in discourse.[4] Potential actor coalitions can be uncovered to point to distinct power/knowledge regimes (Flyvbjerg, 2000, 2004) and potential particularities of a local planning culture (Suitner, 2014). Conflating this information with knowledge about who holds decision-making power in material planning indicates dominant actor coalitions in both discourse and material urban development. All this helps uncovering who has the prerogative of interpretation in Vienna's planning, culture debate, and culture-led transformation at large.

Practically, for each case study, actors and their relations are mapped as a simple *"who-to-whom network"* (Breiger, 2004). Linkages are based upon similarly oriented thematic utterances of actors in the relevant data corpus. It is assumed that actors uttering thematically similar statements within a defined timeframe herewith pronounce similar urban development interests (Mattissek, 2009). Hence, if two actors make similarly oriented statements on a thematic strand related to place transformation within one year, they are being linked in the graph. In this regard, each individual actor appearing in discourse is represented by a single node in the network. As actor affiliations are also considered as important for understanding the influence of individual social groups on culture-led place transformation, affiliations are indicated as well by node color. Node size depends on the number of links of an individual actor to others, thereby already uncovering opinion leaders in discourse. Edge thickness indicates the intensity of relations between two actors, thereby pointing at either loose ties or strong discourse coalitions. Furthermore, actors are clustered with reference to

---

3   Cf. Mattissek, 2009, for a detailed account of analyzing actor statements as a micromethod of discourse analysis.

4   Cf. Breiger, 2004, for a detailed overview to different modes of analyzing social networks.

their utterances to explicate potential hegemonic themes that dominate the place-transformation debate.

All graph visualizations are realized with *Gephi*, an open source network visualization and analysis tool. The algorithm used for mapping nodes and edges is "Force Atlas" (cf. Bastian et al., 2009, for a detailed introduction to the Gephi software and algorithms).

The final step of CDA, then, consists of an in-depth analysis of distinct utterances of actors in the project-specific discourse on planning with culture. It deconstructs each statement in terms of discursive regulations and legitimizing strategies of planning practice, distinct material processes, or interpretations of culture. This is what ultimately allows depicting dominant cognitive constructions of culture, city, and planning, and how they (should reasonably) interact. It further uncovers the evolvement of dominant discourse formations in terms of actor constellations, thematic foci, and cultural imaginaries.

TRIANGULATION AND HIDDEN INFORMATION: NARRATIVE INTERVIEWS

Yin (2009) explains that interviews are often considered a useful empirical tool in case study research, as they allow for a very specific focus on case study topics, hence revealing information that cannot be retrieved otherwise. In this research, interviews with actors involved in process of place transformation are considered an additional source of evidence. Following the approach of De Frantz (2010), I conflate discourse analysis with interviews in order to retrieve information that would otherwise stay hidden and cannot be retrieved from investigating public discourse. This includes significant material transformations as well as important actors and actor groups that might not be represented in public discourse. At the same time, interviews are meant for "testing" results of CDA. As we know that discourse analysis is an interpretative process (Keller, 2011), findings and interpretations deriving from CDA might be biased due to the researcher's individual perspective, positionality, and social embeddedness. Hence, this methodological strand helps uncovering lines of conflict that are not discursively represented, as well as antagonisms between constructed meaning and material practice (Stäheli, 2006; Mouffe, 2007).

I use focused interviews as the specific method in this regard. As described by Yin, *"[i]n such cases, the interviews may still remain open-ended and assume a conversational manner, but you are more likely to be following a certain set of questions"* (Yin, 2009: 107). Interview partners represent a set of actor groups for each case study, i.e. one actor in charge of the local planning agenda, one local cultural actor, one local market actor, and one representative of Vienna's institutional system of cultural planning. The material analyses of the trajectories of Vienna and the three case study sites might indicate specific actors to be interviewed already. Discourse analysis is also an important source pointing to local actors involved in or affected by place transformation. And, within interviews, references to other actors considered important might as well point to additional interview partners. This representational method was in a slightly different manner employed by Hunter (1983) in the power analyses of regional development. And despite the qualified criticism of this approach, it is considered helpful to widen the spectrum of information resources. After all, it is as well a pragmatic question which and how many actors are to be interviewed, as some are not willing to make any statements on the respective matter, are not available within a set time frame, or can simply not be contacted. For this analysis though, 8 focused interviews were conducted with 10 actors involved in the case study processes to form a useful source of information to conflate with the material and discursive analysis of place transformation.

CONFRONTING DISCOURSE WITH MATERIAL PRACTICE

The transformed materialities of place demand detailed investigation for being the layer to ultimately "mirror" the dominant cognitive constructions and important discursive moments. Only then can the influence of imaginaries on material practice in culture-led place transformation be revealed. This is practically achieved with three empirical methods. The first is the collection of information on recent important material transformations (since 2005) via secondary documentation, i.e. case-study-focused research and planning reports, including the widely known Workshop Reports published by the city's Urban Development Department, plus websites, blogs, and Facebook pages of local (collective) actors. The second method is to use field research. Gathering information upon focused on-site observations is considered a valuable resource. Although I do not aim at conducting detailed direct observations[5], field research is considered senseful for inspecting and document visible changes and conspicuous features in the material constitution of each place. And third, the above introduced focused interviews are conducted with actors involved in the respective culture-led

---

5   Cf. Yin, 2009, for an in-depth description of the pros and contras of direct observations as an empirical method.

place transformation process to get more insights into important material transformations. Information gathered from these three sources then serves as a basis to developing a descriptive chronology of material transformations within each case.[6]

These chronologies are then confronted with the findings from CDA to search for potential congruencies between important discursive moments and significant material transformations. Just as policy analysis analyzes policy discourse and its impact on and congruence with material planning (cf. for instance Hajer, 2003; Healey et al., 2003), this step aims at revealing answers to the ultimate question of this research: whether processes of Cultural Imagineering can be depicted in Vienna's culture-led transformation. This is meant to bring to light whether *"[...] the variation, selection, and retention of semiosis [...]"* (Jessop, 2004: 2) actually influences *"[...] practices in ordering, reproducing and transforming capitalist social formations"* (ibid.); whether discursive rationales actually shape the materialities of ideology representation (Torfing, 1999; Bieling, 2006a, 2006b; Mouffe, 2007); and whether material factors might have been equally important in determining place transformation (Aglietta, 1979; Jones & Wilks-Heeg, 2004; Hofmann, 2011).

Ultimately, a cross-case synthesis (Yin, 2009) is meant to retrieve results for the Cultural Imagineering of Vienna at large. Findings from each case study analysis are schematically compared by planning-relevant categories to draw a comprehensive picture of the politics of planning with culture, namely: definitions and utilizations of culture in place transformation, prevalent contextualizations and scalings, influential material regulations, audiences of and exclusions in place transformation, transformed material practice, and power over space and power over planning. This categorization conflates the congruent spectrum of features discussed in a number of other studies assessing (culture-led) place transformation across Europe[7], and concludes on the empirical analysis of Vienna as a place of Cultural Imagineering. Findings are then wrapped up in a conclusive chapter and serve as the basis to recommendations on future cultural planning.

---

6 Cf. Healey et al., 2003 for a practical application of a case study chronology.
7 Cf. for instance Evans, 2001, Healey et al., 2003, Ward, 2003, Binns, 2005, on UK case studies, and Hatz, 2009, Steinert, 2009, or De Frantz, 2010, as recent analyses of Vienna.

Contextualizing "Cultural Vienna"
Retracing the cultural development trajectory

MORPHOLOGY, URBAN STRUCTURES AND SPATIAL DEVELOPMENT

Vienna lived through an eventful history. Within the past 120 years, the city had been at the center of two World Wars, the capital of a European Empire with a population of fifty millions, home of a vibrant intellectual and academic elite, and the stage of political negotiations with global importance (Schorske, 1981; Mattl, 2000; Maderthaner, 2006; Bihl, 2006). Its younger historic development path begins with the city's almost complete physical makeover, which was initiated around 1850, only short after Franz Joseph I. had become Emperor of the Austro-Hungarian monarchy (Schorske, 19981; Maderthaner, 2006; Steinert, 2009). It is at that time that the Emperor induces the removal of the city walls running around the old city – they have become obsolete after the incorporation of the surrounding suburbs. He gives the order to construct the Ringstraße instead as a representational boulevard of the city's enormous importance as capital to an Empire of fifty million people. The whole Ringstraße, as Steinert puts it, is *"domination built in stone"* (Steinert, 2009: 280). It served as a symbol of Imperial supremacy over the bourgeois forces of that time (ibid.). The historicist monuments house important urban functions still today, such as the Parliament of the Federal Government, the Vienna University – Austria's biggest research and educational institution – and a number of cultural institutions with world recognition.

The Ringstraße is one of two rings that influence the city's morphology still today; the other is the Gürtel, Vienna's former outer fortification. These rings have favored a very typical spatial development path, making Vienna at least structurally a great example of the classic European city. It consists of an old city center that has hardly changed physically since the 19th century and is thus determinant of the city's architectural image (Hatz, 2009). Even today, Vienna is still organized as a monocentric agglomeration with densities decreasing at the boundaries (Posova & Sykora, 2011). At least within the Gürtel, the city is determined by mixed use and small-scale structural diversity, although modern (traffic) infrastructures have since the 1960s had massive influence on the cityscape (Pirhofer & Stimmer, 2007) – and so did skyscrapers as symbols of economic strength and cosmopolitanism since the 1990s (Grubbauer, 2001a, 2001b).

Particularities in urban design largely date back to the turn from the 19th to the 20th century, when two paradigmatic schools of urban planning and design evolved in Vienna that had massive influence on the European city and urban planning and design until today: Camillo Sitte's artistic view of the city as space of experience of individuals that would build upon everyday life and the range of movements of the walking citizen, therefore sketching detailed, small scale concepts of neighborhoods, always centering around the piazza, the square; and Otto Wagner's technocratic approach to the city as layers of different functions that had to be economically efficient and functioning at large. So, while Wagner designed large-scale plans for the city, leaving small-scale developments to the urban milieus, Sitte approached it the other way round. Although being diametrically opposed, both schools influenced Vienna's physical appearance at that time and still co-determine urban development visions and planning ideologies today (Schorske, 1981; Mattl, 2000).

The development of Vienna after WWI is determined by the city's search for a new identity. After the collapse of the Austro-Hungarian Empire it had become an inordinately huge metropolis missing an adequate hinterland. Its political power is now restricted to a comparably small national territory and political efforts largely aim at mitigating the negative effects of a world economic crisis. At that time, the huge public housing scheme initiated by the Social Democratic government is the biggest intervention in the city's spatial structure (Maderthaner, 2006; Novy, 2011).

The years after 1945 are shaped by the renovation of the massive material destruction caused by WWII. But this phase is soon followed by an economic boom that allows for more actively realizing urban development visions. Anyhow, Vienna finds itself in Europe's no-man's land due to the new geo-political conditions and is thus focusing largely on its inner development (Novy, 2011). Hence, the 1960s and 70s are determined by sometimes large infrastructural interventions within the city that follow the ideals of functional separation and the car-oriented city. Most notably, the flood protection at the Danube – which also produces the Danube Island, a central recreational area of the city – and the development of a dense underground network influence the morphology of the city at that time (Pirhofer &Stimmer, 2007). The underground construction is a particular success story in Vienna, as it is increasingly recognized as a driver of neighborhood development and, thus, a planning-political instrument in urban politics (Meißl, 2006). Even more, it has co-determined urban hierarchies and center-periphery structures within the agglomeration since the 1970s and is a substantive planning tool still today (Pirhofer & Stimmer, 2007).

Yet, economic growth and increasing prosperity have other structural effects for the city's spatial development as well. With the 1960s, first suburbanization tendencies appear that even reach a higher intensity in the 1970s and 80s. As inmigration and birth rates are stagnating, the city's population consequently decreases. On the other hand, though, the individual level of mobility is rising, which lets commuter flows between the city and its surroundings increase. While the city still is the unquestioned number one job center, it grows as an agglomeration and becomes more integrated due to a more dispersed distribution of its population (Pirhofer & Stimmer, 2007; Posova & Sykora, 2011).

Decision makers haven't even become aware of this dramatic transformation as another structural problem appears locally. Around 1970, experts increasingly point at the need of renewing the city's housing substance. More than half of the housing stock was built before 1919, most of it being under-facilitated and in generally bad condition. Out of this pressuring demand to act, Vienna's specific model of soft urban renewal is born. And in the late 1970s, the first neighborhoods are being regenerated upon the specifically issued law for urban renewal (Bihl, 2006). This state intervention in the local housing market is characteristic for two Social Democratic claims: first, the approach to providing amenities for the fundamental needs of citizens through the public sector, and second, the emphasis on equality as a guiding principle in urban development (Novy et al., 2001; Novy, 2011).

Vienna's intense efforts in fostering urban renewal are also connected to its ambivalent relation with urban expansion. With the take-off of the Austrian economy in the 1960s, the first expansion projects are realized. These are monofunctional housing structures such as "Großfeldsiedlung" that are soon being criticized for not functioning well. At about that time, *"urban renewal instead of urban expansion"* becomes a paradigmatic notion in Vienna's planning (Bihl, 2006).

Only in the 1980s Vienna starts considering itself a city embedded in a larger urban network again, with growth and expansion being actively approached. The increasing internationalization of trade and a beginning globalization discourse touch down in Vienna as well. But only with the fall of the Iron Curtain in 1989, the city sees a true chance to participate in transnational economic processes and push visions of the European metropolis. The geographic location of Vienna in the heart of Europe becomes a new contextual development potential for a greater outward orientation of Vienna in its planning efforts (Pirhofer & Stimmer, 2007). For the first time in the Second Austrian Republic, the Eastern Austrian region finds itself in the middle of Europe and begins to use its exceptional geographic location for positioning as a link between East and West. Its long cultural bonds with CEE and SEE regions of course serve as a motor for further promoting this attempt (Mattl, 2000).

The accession to the European Union in 1995 and the enlargement of the EU to the East of Europe in the 2000s position Vienna in a completely new geopolitical context that massively influences its strategic orientation in urban development today (Pirhofer & Stimmer, 2007). As seat of the United Nations and internationally renowned conference location Vienna has gained modern metropolitan functions and has thus become a hub between the East – which it is historically affiliated to through the Austro-Hungarian monarchy – and the West – which it was accounted to politically, economically and culturally in the years between 1945 and 1989 (Bihl, 2006; Meißl, 2006).

Fig. 4: Population development and forecast for Vienna and the Vienna urban region (1953-2030)

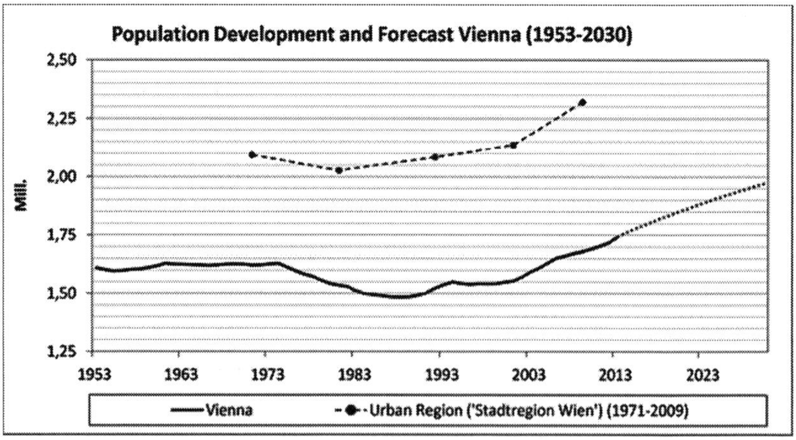

Data Source: Statistik Austria, author's illustration

On the micro-level, the city is today more than ever viewed as a conglomerate of centers housing distinct metropolitan functions and as the motor of a wider agglomeration that is functionally integrated with its neighboring areas (Mattl, 2009; Novy, 2011; ESPON, 2012). The city is growing again since the 1990s and predicted to become a metropolis of 2 million inhabitants around 2030 (cf. Fig. 4). Already, the Eastern Austrian agglomeration is among the biggest in Europe and is still growing in terms of population (Meißl, 2006). Its location close to Bratislava and the regional centers Sopron, Brno, and Györ is potentiating Vienna's claim for positioning as a central European hub, which is recently underpinned by a number of strategic efforts. Thus, there is hardly any doubt that Vienna is about to become a European metropolis again (Mattl, 2000). Yet, for the city's orderly spatial development the current process of constant population growth demands a clear planning agenda concerning inner development and expansion. As not only the city but the whole agglomeration is growing, an integrated metropolitan development vision is needed that tackles the mutual interferences between the city, its outskirts and surrounding urban nodes (ESPON, 2012).

Vienna's Socio-economic Development Path

In the interwar years, Vienna is a city of poverty. Its earlier economic prosperity was fed by its role as the capital of a large Empire. After WWI, though, Vienna is influenced by unemployment, the depression, and a political vacuum. The city is internationally known for its poverty, poor infrastructure and bad housing conditions (Maderthaner, 2006; Pirhofer & Stimmer, 2007).

After 1945, Vienna follows a similar economic development path as other European cities of the 20th century. In the 1950s, the agglomeration profits from structural effects that result in economic growth and increasing wages. Consequently, living conditions of private households change drastically to the better and the economies of scale of Fordist production even increase individual and collective welfare. In Vienna of the 1960s and early 70s, *"[...] sustained growth, full employment, the national welfare state and its local implementation permitted social cohesion to a degree unknown in previous capitalist development."* (Novy, 2011: 244). At that time birth rates stagnate, while local markets demand ever greater numbers of workers to satisfy a booming economy. Thus, migrants are increasingly courted as guest workers to support the productive sector with unqualified workforce (Giffinger & Wimmer, 2002; Meißl, 2006; Kohlbacher & Reeger, 2011).

From the mid-1970s on, Vienna is in economic upheaval due to the breakdown of Fordism. "Austrokeynesianism" is the distinct political strategy applied to reduce unemployment rates by creating jobs in the public sector and investing public money in social welfare mechanisms (Meißl, 2006). The city's traditional inward orientation becomes an increasing problem in a domestic market that stepwise opens and develops an international character (Novy et al., 2001). But it is back then that the traditionally stable Austrian economy can steady itself again. Numbers reveal that the Eastern Austrian region accomplishes the process of economic restructuring very well. The 1990s show a clear shift of employment from the productive to the service sector (Pirhofer & Stimmer, 2007). While the latter has grown in the past decade, production decreased massively. Small-scale enterprises, largely to be accounted to the service sector and valuing the qualities of dense urban environments, take the lead position in inner city areas, while the diminishing productive sector now settles in the outskirts of Vienna and the larger urban region (Bihl, 2006; Meißl, 2006). Relatedly, Vienna is becoming a sought-after business location and a renowned destination for congress and leisure tourism (Mattl, 2000; Meißl, 2006; Musner, 2006). After the geo-political transformation of 1989, Vienna's foreign direct investments to CEE are becoming a backbone to its regional economy, while at the same time new investments from Western Europe rise as well. Specialization, internationalization and highly qualified human capital have in the meantime become the new foundations of the city's economic development. Yet, unemployment rates increase also, showing that the shift to a post-Fordist economy involves new inequalities as well (Meißl, 2006; Novy, 2011).

Fig. 5: Employment development in Vienna, 1964-2001

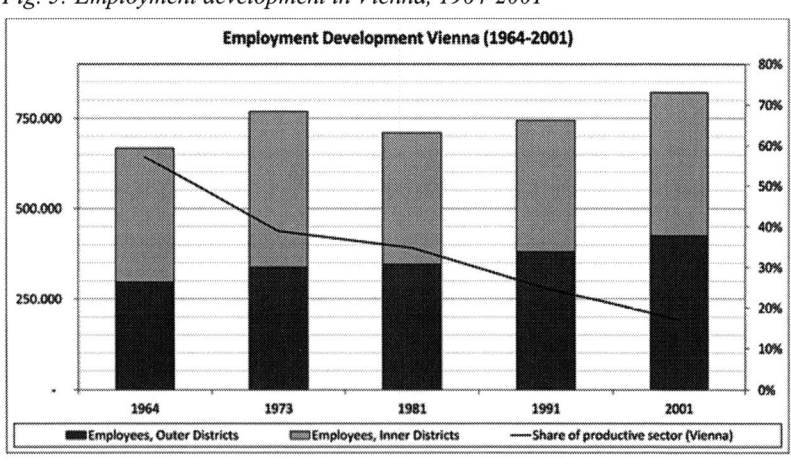

Source: Meißl, 2006: 660f, author's illustration

In the 20th century, Vienna is long determined by a high level of equality, which is to a large degree to be explained through the city's Social Democratic tradition in urban politics. Its socio-economic development is at least until the 1980s largely guided by the ideological principles of Social Democracy. The demands of a working class are at the center of attention, the provision of social welfare mechanisms is meant to avert unemployment and poverty, and planning is guided particularly by equality, which is reflected in equal spatial distribution of social infrastructures and other sports or cultural facilities as central planning goals (Novy et al., 2001; Pirhofer & Stimmer, 2007). At that time, the engagement of labor unions also helps decreasing income inequalities, which forms a more cohesive city in socio-economic terms (Meißl, 2006; Novy, 2011). Only the 80s see a growing socio-economic segregation within the city, i.e. an increasing divide between "poorer" and "wealthier" districts (Meißl, 2006). Today, Vienna's urban quarters are, at least in their appearance and strategic construction, more diverse than ever before (Mattl, 2009), putting Vienna into a dichotomous relation between "unequal diversity" (Novy, 2011) and the still existent political claim for equality (Bihl, 2006; Meißl, 2006). Nevertheless, there is a common sense in planning research until the 2000s that the city is still determined by a comparably low level of segregation (Giffinger & Wimmer, 2002; Kohlbacher & Reeger, 2002). More recent analyses, though, reveal that the persistent segregation of low-income migrant households in certain Viennese neighborhoods might effectuate in an increased socio-spatial polarization (Kohlbacher & Reeger, 2011).

Thus, the greatest challenge to the city's development in this regard is the projected influx of a most diverse group of migrants to the city, of which a large share is low-skilled, vis-à-vis sometimes incomprehensive strategies concerning their inclusion (Statistik Austria, 2010). Although the current scientific discourse labels Vienna as an exceptional example in terms of socio-spatial mixing and cohesion, well-considered measures are needed to mitigate further fragmentation and polarization of the city's population (Kohlbacher & Reeger, 2011; ESPON, 2012). Thus, migration, the inclusion of ethnic minorities, and cohesion in an economically dynamic and growing region will be the number one challenges to Vienna's future development as concerns its socio-economic development.

URBAN POLITICS AND THE CULTURE OF PLANNING

Vienna's urban politics is inseparably linked to the Social Democratic Party (SPÖ). No other big European, democratically organized city has a comparable political tradition of one party determining local governments, related political affairs, holding the majority of seats in the municipal council and providing the mayor since almost 70 years without any interruption (Mattl, 2000; Bihl, 2006). Consequently, Vienna's planning builds upon a long tradition of *"[...] a corporatist form of social democratic urban governance"* (Novy et al., 2001: 131).

At the beginning of the 20th century – and as one of the first cities in Europe – the local government of Vienna begins to nationalize the social and technical infrastructure sector to centrally steer urban growth and spatial expansion without any interference from market forces (Mattl, 2000), as *"[...] the social costs of progress called for more interventionism."* (Novy, 2011: 243) In 1917, the Emperor of the Austro-Hungarian monarchy issues a regulation that protects tenants from housing market speculation, which, in slightly adapted form, is still valid today and forms a central material regulation to the city's comparably stable housing market (Mattl, 2000; Giffinger & Wimmer, 2002; Kohlbacher & Reeger, 2002). Two years later, the Social Democrats win the first free elections with absolute majority. The following years are characterized by social democratic reforms in a city determined by poverty. Political actors begin to develop a local welfare state with a huge social housing program and adjacent other social welfare measures, later to be known as the achievements of "Red Vienna" (Novy et al., 2001; Bihl, 2006; Meißl, 2006; Pirhofer & Stimmer, 2007).

As the first half of the century is determined by political upheaval, Vienna's architectural and planning elites find new confidence only after the post-war reconstruction process of the 1940s and 50s. Following the paradigmatic notion of functional separation as suggested by the Charter of Athens or the sprawling, car-oriented city, planning models and urban development projects largely promote a functionalist but rather sterile and inhuman city. At the turn from the 1950s to the 60s, urban planning is professionalized in Vienna. Famous architect Roland Rainer is selected as the municipality's official urban planner, and the Municipal Department 18 is given new competences as Vienna's planning department. In 1969, a city councilor for planning is installed to finally make Vienna's urban development questions part of the political agenda (Pirhofer & Stimmer, 2007).

It is at that time that the City of Vienna decides to enforce both urban renewal and the conservation of valuable urban structures by issuing laws on urban renovation ("Altstadt-Sanierungsgesetz") and preservation ("Altstadterhaltungsnovelle zur Bauordnung") in 1972. For the first time ever, the physical appearance of parts of the city is thereby put under protection. The whole inner city is labeled a protection zone, with more than 100 similar zones throughout the city following until today. And in the mid-70s, the first neighborhoods within the densely built and partly run-down areas of the city are being regenerated under the roof of Vienna's soft urban renewal policy (Bihl, 2006; Meißl, 2006).

Influenced by its long history as powerful European center, Vienna doesn't see the necessity to interact with its surroundings in terms of planning. Only in the late 1970s and 80s, a strategic re-orientation can be observed in Vienna's planning-political appearance. Its confidence as a city of trans-national importance rises again. Locally, first plans to realize the polycentric agglomeration are envisioned, while cross-regionally, Vienna sees itself competing with other regional centers, such as Munich, Zurich, Budapest, or Bratislava. The city wants to frame its international appearance as place of diplomatic and economic negotiation, political and economic stability, and soft factors, such as cultural facilities and cosmopolitanism. This is particularly supported by the decision of the United Nations in 1979 to choose Vienna as its third seat besides New York and Geneva (Bihl, 2006; Meißl, 2006; Pirhofer & Stimmer, 2007). The city thus begins to orient itself towards other European centers of a similar size to compete economically and culturally after national markets are slowly being liberalized (Pirhofer & Stimmer, 2007; Novy, 2011).

Although this re-orientation is already visible, only in 1976 the political order is given to create a comprehensive plan for Vienna's future urban development within a changed political agenda and planning context (Pirhofer & Stimmer, 2007). The resulting document, the Vienna Urban Development Plan from 1984 ("StEP 84") is the first planning strategy and leitbild for Vienna's spatial development since the 1960s. Despite the new contexts and the political will to re-orient the city, the StEP 84 supports the longstanding political claims for justice and solidarity, participation, and the public provision of infrastructures and amenities to serve a high quality of life for all citizens (Municipal Department 18, 1985).

At that time, new decentralized planning institutions, such as the Vienna Business Agency, are founded to manage cooperation between public and private actors in planning, i.e. to foster governance models of urban development (Novy et al., 2001). The break with traditional urban politics and planning ideologies, though, becomes evident only afterwards. Fuelled by globalization processes and European integration, Vienna's strategies at the end of the century increasingly take a new orientation, focusing on the city's role as an economically vibrant agglomeration. Emphasizing its historically determined relations with Central and Eastern European cities and its outstanding geographic location between East and West, the agendas aim at positioning Vienna as an economic and cultural metropolis of 21st century Europe. The agglomeration's size and its location in an economically integrated Europe give urban politics and planning a new self-esteem for the city becoming a metropolis again (Bihl, 2006; Meißl, 2006). New urban mega projects such as Donau City and the former airfield in

Aspern also become part of the public planning discourse at that time. While huge urban expansion projects have long been banned from political debates due to the failure of similar projects in earlier decades and the parallel success of urban renewal, the contextual changes for Vienna's development make these and other strategically oriented projects central elements of planning-political discussions now (Meißl, 2006; Musner, 2006).

Overall, strategic thinking takes a central position in Vienna's urban development since the late 1990s. The city increasingly becomes aware of its potential for being the political, representational, and economic center of a territory reaching far beyond its administrative boundaries. While its confidence as regional motor of employment, wealth, and innovation is revealed already by the early development plans (Municipal Department 18, 1985, 1994), Europeanization builds the foundation to strategic considerations of cooperating with neighboring agglomerations. Resulting city-regional and trans-national cooperative projects, international networking platforms, and knowledge exchange initiatives evolve at that time, symbolizing a pivotal shift in the envisioning of Vienna's potential urban futures. The city increasingly begins to see itself as an internationally embedded actor, which reflects in the growing importance of competition and cooperation as both planning precondition and objective in planning-political documents of that time. Simultaneously though, visions for Vienna's inner organization are getting ever more blurry, reflecting the uncertainties determining its spatial development since then (Municipal Department 18, 2001, 2004a; 2005).

Notably, economic and technological concerns are the primary themes as the strategy plans issued in 2000 and 2004 reveal very obviously (Municipal Department 18, 2001, 2004a). By suggesting strategic projects that integrate other disciplines and political spheres than the classic fields of planning intervention, planning is increasingly envisioned as a broad and interdisciplinary field (Pirhofer & Stimmer, 2007). The shift towards business-friendly urban politics, though, touches down in Vienna as well, with these development strategies being at the forefront of a new planning ideology. While some describe this new planning approach positively as *"[...] a process of internationally catching-up in terms of locational policies and economic competencies"* (Pirhofer & Stimmer, 2007: 103, author's translation), others reflect upon this shift more critically. As Novy et al. (2001) write, urban development through supply-driven strategic projects solely aims at creating a new urban image of Vienna and activating an urban elite of selected experts and market actors as new partners in planning. Even more: *"Political legitimation via housing has been reduced to a secondary role and instead economic profitability has become the main rationale."* (Novy et al., 2001: 137) Interestingly, in any of these strategies, *"Vienna is growing again"* is a determinant contextual framing of urban planning endeavors and a driver of strategic projects from the early 1990s on (Pirhofer & Stimmer, 2007). There is no doubt about the political will to accelerate Vienna's metropolisation process. The city's embedding in a European urban network is used to position it as competitive partner and hub between East and West (Mattl, 2000). The massive efforts to integrate Vienna in wider economic and political networks in this regard is evident just from the number of networking activities initiated by the local planning administration (Municipal Department 18, 2011). Yet, coping with predicted growth scenarios is recurrently named as a central planning challenge. In this regard, participatory and empowering approaches to urban development will become an even greater challenge. While strategies call for small-scale planning on a neighborhood scale to increase the level of democratic participation in development processes, the growing region and the consequently increasing number of people affected by planning decisions will make this a hard task to realize. And in relation to that, demographic changes, increasing socio-economic diversity and socio-spatial polarization will become threats to the city's praised quality of life if strategies for territorial cohesion and social inclusion are not considered.

THE INSTITUTIONAL SETTING

Following the Austrian Constitution, Vienna is both municipality and federal state – with all legal powers attached hereto. Hence, the mayor simultaneously holds the position of the governor; the municipal council serves as the Vienna regional assembly as well (Bihl, 2006). This legal sovereignty makes the City of Vienna a rather autonomous actor in a variety of planning-political questions. Paired with the continuous control of most of the decisive political posts by the Social Democratic Party, the city is able to form a dense network of state-affiliated bodies, political institutions and planning actors that comprise all relevant governance levels of Vienna's planning, thereby diminishing the influence of oppositional forces and counter-hegemony in urban development (Novy et al., 2001). The local state and corporatist institutions thus play a determining role in the urban social and economic development of Vienna, particularly in the fields of housing, health, social and cultural affairs (Mattl, 2000).

Vienna's political-administrative system of planning is largely determined by the municipal authority ("Magistrat"). It is headed by the mayor and the currently eight city councilors in charge of specific thematic fields and political sectors, e.g. public finances, housing, or culture. The city's administrative body is constituted by the several municipal departments, which are bound by instructions from the city councilors and the directorate of the municipal authority. Among these departments are the ones addressing typical spatial planning questions, such as urban development, architecture and urban design, neighborhood- and land use planning, urban renewal, and housing affairs (Municipal Departments 18, 19, 21, 25, and 50) (Magistratsdirektion, n.d.). Thus, political agenda setting in Vienna's urban planning is evidently influenced by just a small number of political actors, who have a lot of room for maneuver, as they are solely responsible for one policy area.

Affiliated to this political-administrative organizational structure are a number of institutions that are either publicly (co-)financed and thus tied to political agendas or at least co-determined by executive committees or supervisory boards that are staffed with city councilors as decision-making actors. Most prominently, the Vienna Business Agency ("Wirtschaftagentur Wien") is among these institutions. Founded in 1982 by the City of Vienna, the Chamber of Commerce, and two (politically affiliated) banks, the Business Agency aims at promoting the city as business location, managing the establishment of foreign firms and initiating public-private cooperation in this regard. Property management, awarding subsidies for the establishment of innovative businesses, and consulting services are among the activities of the agency today. Its executive board is headed by the city councilor of public finances, Renate Brauner, and the city councilor of housing, Michael Ludwig – both from the Social Democratic Party (SPÖ). Further executive board members are Brigitte Jank, president of the Chamber of Commerce, and Helmut Horvath as representative of a real estate development corporation owned by UniCredit (Vienna Business Agency, n.d.). Subsidiary companies of the Vienna Business Agency are "ZIT – The Technology Agency of the City of Vienna" as a distinct promoter of R&D and media industries, and "departure – The Creative Agency of the City of Vienna", aiming at institutionally supporting the creative industries (ibid.). Evidently, this conglomerate combines political decision-making power and economic capital to determine a great share of Vienna's strategic economic development.

Another state-affiliated agency is the Vienna Tourism Agency ("Wiener Tourismusverband"), which is responsible for Vienna's international appearance, its marketing as destination for both business and leisure tourism, and services for tourists in the city. Being headed by the city councilor of public finances and a mostly politically staffed tourism commission, the Tourism Agency is not at all undetermined by political agendas. And, although it is not member of any decision-making bodies, it acts as the lobbying institution for the tourism-related local economy[1]. While holding an institution for touristic concerns that develops marketing concepts for a destination might not be untypical of any big city today anymore, the Vienna Tourism Agency is solely responsible for actively presenting Vienna internationally. And its legal binding through the Viennese law for tourism development ("Wiener Tourismusförderungsgesetz") in this regard is not very pronounced, leaving plenty of room for maneuver in terms of content, actors to be integrated, target groups, or places of the city to be promoted (wien.at, n.d.b).

On the very local level, Vienna's planning has – earlier than most other European cities – installed another institutionalized planning intervention: the Urban Renewal Offices ("Gebietsbetreuung"). Since the political claim was uttered for regenerating the run-down housing structures in the Gründerzeit-areas of the city in the early 1970s, these offices exist in chosen neighborhoods as both managing actors of the soft urban renewal process and missing link between political-administrative system and local community (Urban Renewal Offices, n.d.). The process of installing Urban Renewal Offices is initiated by the municipal departments 25 (urban renewal) and 50 (housing affairs). Following a public tender, the process is awarded to a private actor (mostly architecture and planning offices) that takes over the agreed-upon tasks. These imply information and inclusion of dwellers and actors of the local economy to participate in urban renewal activities, tenant support, the initiation of economic, artistic or discursive projects with local actors and other community services[2]. In this regard, Urban Renewal Offices serve as two-sided communication channels, offering a more direct transmission of local problems to political decision-makers, while at the same time they are promoters of the political agenda as concerns housing and urban renewal affairs, and neighborhood transformation in general[3].

Also, the district chairpersons play a determinant role in shaping the activities of Vienna's Urban Renewal Offices. District chairpersons are the democratically legitimized representatives from one of the local political parties, elected to assist the mayor in fulfilling the competencies of the municipality in one of Vienna's 23 districts. While their financial margin is rather negligible, they are equipped with a number of competencies to act in order to co-shape the city's local development procedures (wien.at, n.d.a). Holding the decision-making power for permitting the mostly small-scale, ephemeral initiatives conceptual-

---

1   Interview with Norbert Kettner, CEO of the Vienna Tourism Agency.
2   Interview with Kurt Smetana, head of the Urban Renewal Office Ottakring.
3   Interview with Ula Schneider and Beatrix Zobl of Soho In Ottakring.

ized in the course of the guided urban renewal process, the district chairpersons are central players in co-determining the activities set in local planning.

On the city-regional level, two further governance networks influencing Vienna's planning-political setting must be named: the City-regional Management ("Stadt-Umland Management"), and the Planning Association East ("Planungsgemeinschaft Ost"). Both are intended to foster a more integrated city-regional development between the City of Vienna and its surrounding federal state, Lower Austria. The City-regional management focuses Vienna and its neighboring municipalities, aiming largely at technical and formal questions of a more harmonized agglomeration development upon a cooperative program. It is staffed mostly with professional planners from the region – the planning director of Vienna being the representative of the city (City-regional Management, n.d.). The Planning Association East comprehends the whole Eastern Austrian Region and builds on a political commitment from 1978, initiated by the three Federal States to harmonize planning strategies and projects of the respective local authorities. In contrast to the City-regional Management it is a political organization that acts as coordinating and decision-making committee for planning agendas of the future (Planning Association East, n.d.a, n.d.b).

Finally, the Centrope initiative must be mentioned as a planning-relevant project on the cross-regional, respectively the trans-national level of governance. Being set up in 2003 as a multilateral partnership, Centrope currently is the most prominent transnational cooperation in which the City of Vienna participates (Novy, 2011). It builds on the political will to cooperate strategically in the Central-European region in order to clearly promote and position the territory on a growing European market (ARGE CENTROPE Agency, 2013). Centrope is a particularly interesting project as it can be considered characteristic of Vienna's recent planning-ideological transformation. It largely consists of out-sourced or state-affiliated actors and institutions, such as the Vienna Business Agency. The in-depth critical reviews of Centrope's organizational structure, the political agendas and goals of the initiative, and the decision-making processes reveal the determinant position of Vienna in the project, showing how the City of Vienna and its affiliated planning-political network of institutions enforce gaining ascendancy over the Central European region (Giffinger & Hamedinger, 2009; Novy et al., 2013). Hence, while some judge this as a *"[...] shift towards an entrepreneurial type of state"* (Novy et al., 2013: 118), there is at least a common sense that the Centrope initiative is symbolic of an unprecedented pro-active approach to planning in Vienna. All three of these regional bodies reveal the increased governance orientation in Vienna's urban, regional, and its strategic planning ideology in particular, while they also show that strategic urban development questions are still largely expert-led – at least on this spatial scale.

Fig. 6: Vienna's scales of metropolitan governance

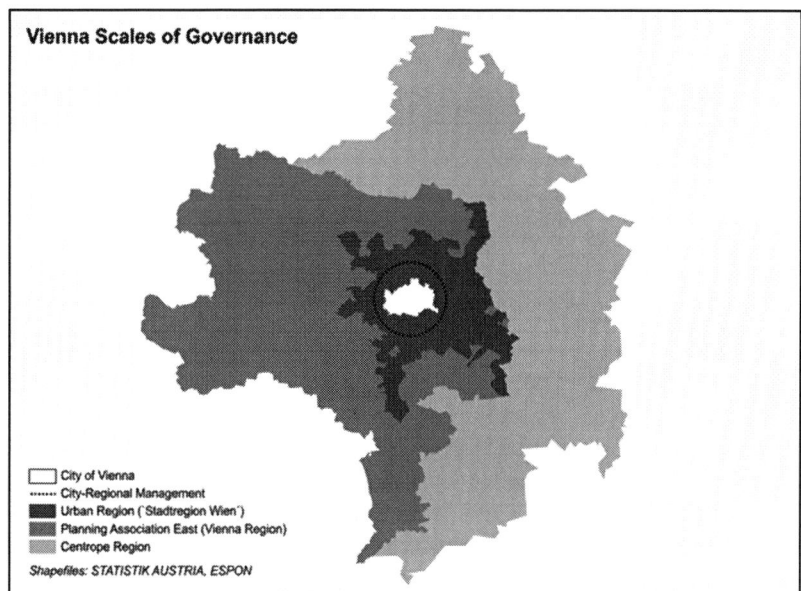

THE STRATEGIC LAYER: VIENNA'S POLITICS OF PLANNING

On the basis of the prior embedding of Vienna's development into its material trajectory, the city's recent strategic orientation needs to be depicted in more detail. Therefore, its recent planning strategies will be analyzed in short in the following section. This will reveal three central points: first, how Vienna's urban development is recently framed and contextualized, second, what planning challenges and potentials are currently emphasized in the strategic documents of the city, and third, which actors, topics and places of the city are named as relevant planning agents in Vienna.

StEP 84 – The comprehensive plan

Vienna's Urban Development Plan of 1984 ("StEP 84") is the first official planning leitbild since the early 1960s. Based upon a number of political principles of how the city's active development should be implemented, the document provides a spatial development concept as its central message. Focal points of planning intervention for the future are presented in relation to the spatial leitbild. None of the city's places, neighborhoods or districts receives particular attention – the whole city is considered as a homogenous territory that deserves a logically structured planning approach (Municipal Department 18, 1985). The aftermath of a very technocratic approach to urban planning is still visible in the StEP 84, although the explicit embedding of the whole concept in political principles of urban development shows a shift in thinking planning. Yet, this needs to be seen in the light of Vienna's strong urban politics. It seems that political actors of that time are not willing to delegate urban development and all related decisions to administrative forces completely:

"In my function as mayor, I want to make unmistakably clear that, despite this plan's flexibility, I will personally verify the compliance of day-to-day politics with the framework of the given plan – not only in terms of its wording, but also as concerns its spirit." (Municipal Department 18, 1985: n.n.)[4]

Contextually, StEP 84 reflects the wide-ranging transformations of the 1970s. It thus accepts the end of the infinite growth paradigm and follows a more humble development vision of preservation, inward orientation, and decentralization as a step towards a more equal spatial distribution of urban functions. All in all, it is a top-down-prescribed strategy that largely reflects long-standing political ideals of development, while neither contextual, nor thematic foci are accentuated (Municipal Department 18, 1985; Pirhofer & Stimmer, 2007).

StEP 94 – Spatial continuity, political-economic transition

Ten years later, StEP 94 is issued as the sequel to the former development plan of the city. While taking up most of the considerations from the early 80s concerning the spatial leitbild for the city, Vienna's urban development as such is completely re-contextualized. The document undertakes a major effort in explaining the potentials of a new geo-political context, the European integration process, and the reversed trend, which is the city's re-urbanization, for its urban development. Strategies for the different parts of the city are still oriented at morphological criteria, such as density and traffic axes, therefore not highlighting particular neighborhoods or places of the city. Yet, topics such as public

---

4 Original quote from Helmut Zilk, former mayor of the City of Vienna, author's translation.

space, urban culture and tourism receive explicit attention for the first time, showing that planning theoretical considerations on these fields of intervention have entered the strategic planning discourse in Vienna as well. Importantly, the whole development process towards the final document is organized differently. Working groups are established to discuss particular topics, and broader citizen participation within these debates is encouraged. In this regard, it is also remarked that StEP 94 is not considered as a product, but as part of a longer process of urban development. Yet, the document is still understood as a reactive political instrument to counter unwished external development trends (Municipal Department 18, 1994). This also underlines the traditionally passive attitude towards planning in Vienna. Due to its decades long peripheral location it was mostly constrained to reacting on external development trends instead of actively enforcing individual development strategies (Pirhofer & Stimmer, 2007). Nevertheless, StEP 94 reveals, what has been mentioned already. Vienna's planning is in the 1990s determined by a re-orientation from public provision and a discourse on social housing to locational policies and the city's economic competencies (Novy et al., 2001; Pirhofer & Stimmer, 2007; Novy, 2011). The new development context has pushed the planning agendas and adjacent political goals into a different direction, which becomes obvious only at the turn of the century and with the publication of the more recent strategic documents of Vienna's planning.

Vienna in a new millennium – strategic, pro-active, European

In the years 2000 and 2004, two Strategy Plans for the City of Vienna are issued. This marks a significant shift in Vienna's politics of planning for several reasons. First, the development process of these strategies comprehends the whole Municipal Authority, thereby making urban development a broader topic that integrates more political spheres than before. Second, it reveals a general reconsideration of urban planning that takes place around this time. While planning strategies had long been considered as reactive instruments in Vienna, the projects and planning approaches suggested here are pro-active attempts to steer urban development into a certain direction. And third, in this regard supply-oriented strategic projects are becoming central to the urban planning agenda, thereby diminishing the prominence of a demand-oriented approach typical of the past decades. The swing to a more entrepreneurial, governance- and outward-oriented planning approach becomes evident not just from the mayor's opening words:

"[The Strategy Plan] encourages Vienna's business community, social groups and organizations, political players and all interested citizens to actively shape Vienna's future in public-private partnership." (Municipal Department 18, 2001)[5]

It is also a novice that with the nomination of strategic projects particular places of the city, specific actors and institutions, and distinct fields of urban development are emphasized and thereby preferred over others. In this regard, also the three case studies to be analyzed are mentioned explicitly as important for the city's future strategic development. Yet, the process of selection of these and other projects is not sufficiently documented each and every time. Anyhow, what is even more notable is the fact that in both documents Vienna's transnational embedding is recurrently used as a framing of the city's development context. While StEP 94 has already at length documented the European integration process and globalization tendencies as a new urban development context for Vienna, both Strategy Plans still seem to be in need of a legitimizing argument for the new approach to planning. It doesn't come as a surprise in this regard that economic policies – and locational policies in particular – are determinant of the two strategies. More interestingly, though, the fields of R&D, science, knowledge production and culture are less considered as attributes of social development of the city, but are primarily put in an economic context and debated as assets for global positioning (Municipal Department 18, 2001, 2004a).

StEP 05 until today – Planning between strategic place-making and neighborhood development

In an adapted manner this approach is carried on to the latest politically legitimized planning strategy so far, the Urban Development Plan 2005 ("StEP 05"). StEP 05 is a progressive planning document building upon a years-long process of development within various thematic groups, consortia, and public events with broad citizen participation. It as well includes the knowledge gained from running urban development processes on the various spatial levels of planning, thereby appreciating the processual dimension of the city. Furthermore, it is the first urban development strategy in Vienna to explicitly point at culturally relevant aspects in planning, such as gender mainstreaming, migration and fragmentation. But what is striking and an innovation to the urban development discourse revolving around earlier development plans is the definition of 13 target areas of planning as a conceptual novelty (Municipal Department 18, 2005). Not only do

---

5 Original quote from Michael Häupl, mayor of the City of Vienna.

these target areas break with the tradition of determining one leitbild for the whole territory of the city, but they reveal, which areas of the city are considered as being threatened by certain challenges or as promising places of development. Most of these target areas are follow-ups to the strategic projects uncovered in the Strategy Plans, meaning they also transport a similar planning ideology. What they show as well is a re-orientation in the city's planning approach concerning its spatial development. While the big wave of urban renewal has already passed, growth scenarios are an argument to take into account new urban expansion projects. For the first time in decades, the debate on brownfield development and urban renewal within existing structures of the city is thus outdone by concepts of urban enlargement. Pushed by the transformations that have put Vienna in a new development context, predicted urban growth, and the path already taken by the Strategy Plans, StEP 05 thus is a self-confident planning document following a strategic planning approach that aims to incorporate both elements of entrepreneurial and justice planning.

The Progress Report to the StEP 05 from 2010 doesn't come up with new planning scenarios. Due to the economic crisis it is again more humble and serves as a marker for the goals reached at half-time. Yet, it again leaves no doubt about the development contexts for the city's future development. The report emphasizes Vienna's position at the heart of the Central European region as a unique development potential. It also points to its on-going growth as a city and region, moving the focus to its related comeback as a European metropolis (Municipal Department 18, 2010). Yet, as concerns the development contexts, Vienna still sees itself in a passive position of accommodation (Smith, 2002), as the following quote clearly shows:

"A city like Vienna is subject to constant political and economic changes. Mostly it cannot influence these transitions at all." (Municipal Department 18, 2010: 15; author's translation)

Currently, the running discussion process concerning Vienna's new Urban Development Plan called "wien2025" is of interest in the context of reviewing the city's planning strategies as well. Although the process is still at a very early stage, a number of contextualizations of Vienna's urban development are already predetermined in the first rounds of discussion held in 2013, thereby intensely framing the future debate. Emphasized contexts are population growth and Vienna's positioning. Interestingly, in a first phase these contexts are discussed merely in terms of feasibility (wien 2025, n.d.). And, as speakers are invited experts only, there is hardly any consideration of the ideas, needs, or attitudes of

Vienna's citizens. So, instead of pro-actively developing a strategy for Vienna's next ten years, a weak political-administrative system is constructed that in its development strategies can only react and adapt to the pre-given external contexts. The consequence is a somewhat deficient debate with a clearly entrepreneurial tone that focuses four topics: "Growth", "Public Space", "Location Vienna 2025", and "Competition" (ibid.). While these might be considerable in a more comprehensive debate on planning Vienna's urban future, they draw a questionable picture of the start to a thematically open strategy building process.

The spectrum of topics analyzed is much broader in the context of the city's Workshop Reports ("Werkstattberichte"). Published by the City of Vienna since the 1990s at erratic intervals, these reports represent those planning-political topics that are considered relevant for the city's urban development by the Municipal Authority. The series comprehends scientific reports from research projects conducted by research institutions, as well as in-house research and politically relevant documents, such as the abovementioned Strategy Reports and Urban Development Plans. Although there is no formal selection process for topics to be published in this series, the almost 150 Workshop Reports published so far draw a distinct picture of topics, contexts and planning approaches considered relevant throughout the years.

Vienna's urban structure is an early determinant topic picked up in the Workshop Reports, accompanied by the traditional fields of urban renewal and housing (cf. for instance Best Practices Hub, 2004; Municipal Department 18, 2004b). Later, city-regional cooperation in planning and the international context to urban development become central to the debate. Besides this up-scaling to a trans-national level, a more differentiated involvement with neighborhood development appears at the same time. Social fragmentation becomes a pivotal element of the discussion in this regard, although some parts of the city traditionally receive greater attention than others. Yet, this thematic development highlights the general notion appearing in Vienna's planning discourse and practice at that time. It constructs two scales of planning intervention independent from one another – the neighborhood level and the European level – which, of course, makes any integrated planning vision for the city and its parts impossible. Looking at the more recent examples, Vienna's role as European city is emphasized even more. Europeanization and globalization are recurring planning contexts that receive particular attention in distinct Workshop Reports (Municipal Department 18, 2012a, 2012b). Interestingly, an evolving awareness of public space as a distinct field of planning intervention is documented in the years 2007-2009 with a distinct report on the topic being issued each year (Municipal Department 18, 2007, 2008, 2009).

Consequently, a clear shift can be perceived in Vienna's ideology of planning since the 1990s. Early Viennese strategies were determined by a claim for justice planning in a far-developed social welfare state. While political goals had been very obvious in this regard, they didn't leave much room for maneuver as concerns planning decisions. Geo-political and economic re-contextualizations thus were an impetus for more self-confident development visions to evolve. The related dual re-scaling of the city as Central European hub and kaleidoscope of distinct local places multiplied the possibilities in planning, leading to manifold approaches of either neighborhood planning or strategic projects, while simultaneously de-politicizing the urban development process.

STRATEGICALLY APPROACHING CULTURE: VIENNA BETWEEN HUB AND HERITAGE

At the very beginning of this chapter, I introduced the Ringstraße as an important symbol of the city in morphological, as well as in political and cultural terms (Schorske, 1981). Still today, it marks one of the culturally decisive parts of the city and is probably deeply rooted in the mental maps of each and every Viennese. But it not only forms one decisive part of Vienna's architectural and institutional cultural heritage. At the same time it is a boundary distinguishing the inner city from the rest in cultural terms (Mattl, 2000). Since the early 20th century Vienna is perceived as a relevant touristic destination and in this regard, it has ever since been promoted with the representational architecture of the Habsburg Empire, cultural events, and contemporary arts (Mattl, 2000). The legacy of the Austro-Hungarian monarchy was thus always considered as *the* valuable touristic resource of Vienna in the 20th century, thereby diminishing the representation of more contemporary modes of cultural expression in the city's international appearance (De Frantz, 2005, 2011; Steinert, 2009). Although an alternative cultural scene began to grow since 1968, the city's international reputation still built upon the subject of the imperial city and high cultural institutions (Mattl, 2000; Musner, 2006; Hatz, 2009). As Hatz (2009) explains, the largely unchanged physical appearance of the two centuries old architecture of the inner city and its surrounding ostentatious Ringstraße even make them the logical image carriers of Vienna. Consequently, even today cultural institutions and cultural tourism are to a large degree concentrated in the inner city.[6]

---

[6] Interview with Norbert Kettner, CEO of the Vienna Tourism Agency.

As Vienna began to strategically orient itself towards other European agglomerations in the late 1970s, the city's cultural facilities – and its architectural heritage in particular – had finally become vehicles for its outward image. At a time when urban tourism became a relevant economic factor as well, Vienna began to invest in cultural infrastructures and new forms of a culture of consumption, events and spectacle in the inner city area to make this form of culture a driver of leisure tourism (Mattl, 2000). In this regard, cultural planning approaches increasingly pushed the spatial concentration of a representative marketable culture in the city center. Former mayor Helmut Zilk and city councilor for culture Ursula Pasterk were the first to reinforce the focus on Vienna's inner city, yet, in reaction to the critique on an overwhelming presence of imperial culture, with an effort to promote Vienna's fin de siècle and contemporary fine arts as a modern counter-narrative of Vienna. With the renovation of the Secession and Gustav Klimt's Beethoven Frieze and the creation of a path of culture through the inner city, a new era of a culture of spectacle started that would promote the conviviality of tradition and modernity as the city's new cultural image (Mattl, 2000; Musner, 2006). The aim was to use the well-received cultural picture of Vienna for making the city the cultural center of Central Europe, regardless of any existing political blocs (Mattl, 2000). Cultural events or exhibitions, such as the famous "Dream and Reality" ("Traum und Wirklichkeit"), held at the WienMuseum Karlsplatz in 1985, supported this effort by promoting just this new duality of tradition and modernity in Vienna's cultural self-esteem (Musner, 2006).

Back then, culture had finally become a truly political and economic instrument in Vienna's urban politics and planning. Former vice mayor Erhard Busek from the Austrian People's Party (ÖVP) began to transform the inner city into a place of cultural spectacle by initiating an annual city festival ("Stadtfest"), while the Social Democrats established a huge music festival at the Danube Island ("Donauinselfest"). In the following years the Wiener Festwochen, the path of New Year's Eve ("Silvesterpfad"), and the Viennese Filmfestival were brought to life to make the inner city a place of spectacle and high cultural events from then on. Furthermore, diplomatic relations with historically related cities, such as Bratislava, Budapest, Prague or Ljubljana were promoted – particularly by former mayor Helmut Zilk – thereby reinforcing the image of the Central European metropolis of culture Vienna had once been (Mattl, 2000; Bihl, 2006; Musner, 2006). Today, this strategy is still pursued by the political and economic successors as the massive promotion of Opera Ball, Life Ball, and Christmas Markets clearly show (Hatz, 2009).

This rather conservative approach to the cultural development of the city, but the conservation of the architectural heritage in particular, ultimately led to the reward of the historic inner city and its surroundings with the UNESCO world heritage title in 2001 (Municipal Department 19, 2006). Consequently, the preservation of the historic substance was given even more significance in Vienna's urban development considerations. And through decentralization of political functions and social infrastructures, the spectacular heritage and event culture received even more space for representation and greater significance as symbol of the city than before (Hatz, 2009).

Due to the new status of Vienna's inner city and the general claim made by Social Democrats for more equal spatial distribution, culture-led planning agendas had to be displaced to the neighboring districts with their efforts to redevelop cultural institutions or even build new ones. And, they were successful. Since the year 2000, a number of cultural institutions were expanded, regenerated or newly built in Vienna – most of them outside the inner city (Hatz, 2009). The realization of a new Central Library and the Museum Quarter ("Museumsquartier") are the most prominent ones in this concern – the latter also being one of Europe's largest cultural institutions (ibid.). The Museum Quarter marks the currently last step in a strategy to make Vienna a culturally competitive city with high quality institutions of contemporary arts and heritage representation (El Khafif, 2008). Peppered with spectacular inner city events around the year, the city offers the kind of event culture that is being promoted since the 1980s, thereby creating a hegemonic cultural representation of Vienna that supersedes any other cultural process in the city.

But the link between cultural politics and planning is not reduced to the city's big outward-oriented institutions only. In the early 2000s, Vienna's planning increasingly began to intervene "culturally" on the city-local level as well. At a time when urban development agendas increasingly consider the cultural economy as a new foundation of economic success, the traditional knowledge base is expanded to the creative industries as a potential field of economic growth in Vienna, too (Municipal Department 7, 2008; Mayerhofer, 2009). In order to support this new form of economically relevant cultural activity and its presumed positive effects on local economies and neighborhood development, "departure – The Creative Agency of the City of Vienna" is founded as a subsidiary of the Vienna Business Agency to promote *"[...] those creative professionals who consider themselves active participants in business life."* (Departure – Die Kreativwirtschaftsagentur der Stadt Wien, n.d.)

At about the same time, the staging of culture spreads from inner city museums to central public spaces as well. In 2004, the city's departments of culture, housing and planning together found the Fund for Art in Public Space ("Kunst im Öffentlichen Raum GmbH"), a publicly financed institution aiming to *"[r]evitalize and enhance urban space [or] positioning Vienna better in an international context"* (KÖR, n.d.a). Thereby, public space is increasingly becoming a representational arena of a certain form of culture and, even more importantly, a decisive planning instrument to regenerate places of the city through culturalization (Hatz, 2009). It is thus not surprising that within the last years both departure and the Fund for Art in Public Space have put a noticeable focus on pioneering artistic and creative projects that deal with urban development and regeneration areas of the city. Obviously, planning-political actors of the local state have become aware of the transformative power of artistic and cultural-economic interventions in city space in the past decade. While big cultural institutions have been part of Vienna's planning-political strategy for its outward reputation and attractiveness since long, only recently the local city government integrated culture and creativity into its repertoire for intervening in local urban development as well (cf. Fig. 7).

Fig. 7: Annual public subsidies for cultural activities (2001-2011)

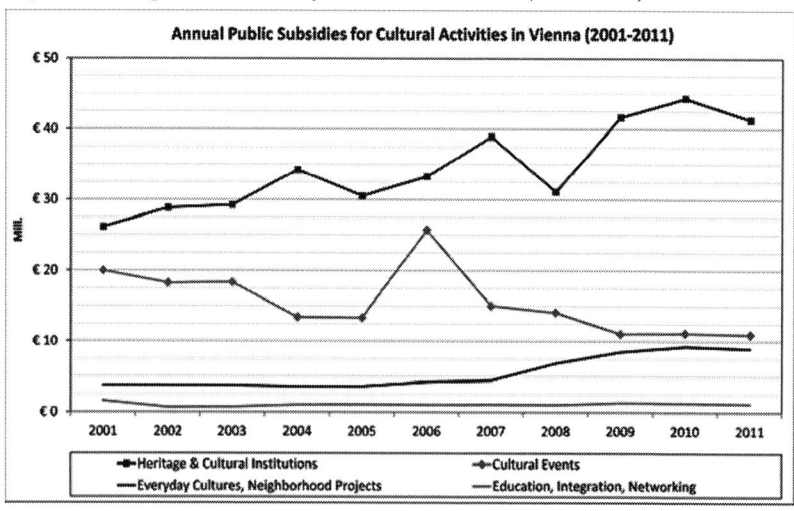

Source: Municipal Authority – Municipal Department 7, author's illustration

On another front, the city is recently confronted with another challenge in cultural terms as well. Vienna's current efforts to strategically position itself as a hub between East and West and the on-going migration to the agglomeration make it a globalizing city where a multitude of cultural identities and value constructs constantly collide, conjoin, and transform (Giffinger & Wimmer, 2002;

Kohlbacher & Reeger, 2002, 2011; Novy, 2011). Thus, in cultural terms the conflict between hub and heritage is more evident than ever. An imbalance in terms of financial and political support between the city's heritage as the Empire's capital and Europe's cultural metropolis on the one hand and an avant-gardist cultural field on the other hand is a long-known conflict in the city (De Frantz, 2005, 2011; Steinert, 2009). But while this struggle must be dealt with in cultural politics, the more relevant question for urban planning points to the other cultures of the city that are neither art-based, nor shaped by a particular marketable historic narrative of the city. Obviously, these are excluded from any of the abovementioned debates. Yet, a growing, globalizing and thus culturally diversifying city like Vienna demands a broader interpretation of "culture" to include these manifold cultures into the planning discourse and let them equally participate in economic processes of culture-led urban development.

Fig. 8: Advertising "Cultural Vienna" as competitive business location

Source: Austrian Chamber of Commerce: "Advantage Austria – Innovation und Fakten Österreich – Infografik" (Video-still, retrieved from www.youtube.com/watch?v=0xyUtM Kyudo, November 12, 2013)

In the city's past cultural planning though, "culture" has largely been reduced to the city's architectural heritage and related prominent institutions – at least in public perception, which accounts for the city's international image in large parts. As the city councilor of culture, Andreas Mailath-Pokorny, states in the Art & Culture Report 2005:

"Art and culture are essential determinants of the life in our city and Vienna's reputation in the world." (Municipal Department 7, 2005: 7; author's translation)

Although this approach to culture was expanded in the 1980s with a new political agenda in cultural politics and planning, the integration of contemporary fine arts from that time on still reduces the city's cultural activities to consumable products. This must be read in the context of the early framing of culture as a potential for tourism and the traditional focus on high-cultural institutions in this regard (Vienna Tourism Agency, 2005). The shift in Vienna's cultural politics about three decades ago initiated the development of even closer links between cultural politics and planning that hadn't existed before. At the time of Vienna's growing awareness of Europeanization and globalization processes, any public discourse on cultural projects implied an intense debate about potential effects on the city's international perception. Thus, culture has become a vehicle of a new outward-oriented planning philosophy in Vienna, which has hardly changed until today (cf. for instance De Frantz, 2005, 2011). This is even further underlined by recurring references to the city's architectural and culturally branded landmarks in advertisements promoting the city as economically vibrant location and tourism destination (cf. Fig. 8).

A culturized understanding of the city though, implying also identities and signifying practices, is still marginal within the discourse on Cultural Vienna and leaves hardly any space for cultural processes, self-determined, bottom-up initiated projects and the evolvement of counter-hegemony to the city's current powerful cultural framing. While topics such as youth, education, learning, or integration are indeed increasingly dealt with in the city's cultural politics (Municipal Department 7, 2012), the city's big institutions are still determinant financially and in terms of representing the hegemonic cultural image of the city (Hatz, 2009). Thus, Vienna is currently determined by two conflictive cultural identities that are equally promoted in the planning-political debate: first, a backward-oriented strategy building upon the city's cultural heritage, which is recurrently held liable for its touristic success and international reputation, and second, its identity as a metropolis in the making, determined by diversity as a driver of development. Yet, as these follow two diametrically opposed paths as concerns the interpretation of culture as either a hegemonic historic narrative for accumulation or culture as lifestyle diversity and a plurality of representations, they don't seem compatible in Vienna's future planning.

So, Vienna is determined by a hegemonic cultural representation that is primarily considered as an instrument in economic, i.e. touristic and creative industry strategies. It is interpreted as a tool to attract attention among an outward target audience of a new middle-class and recently receives even greater attention as an instrument in local urban regeneration as well. All this is reflected in the city's various development agendas, which have been reconstructing a largely identical approach to culture in the city since almost 30 years.

In the StEP 84, Vienna is already described as a cultural metropolis, highlighting the city's popularity as concerns the density of high-quality cultural institutions. The culture emphasized is the traditional architectural and cultural heritage of the late 19th century, while at least "access to culture for all" ("Kultur für alle") is a guiding principle in this regard. Also, cultural policies are meant to foster new forms of culture in order to support social and economic innovation. But despite all openness transported in the text, StEP 84 suggests that Vienna's quality of life and economic success would solely derive from its heritage culture, thereby paving the way for the consolidation of this cultural imaginary in the city's development (Municipal Department 18, 1985).

Ten years later, in the StEP 94, the culture debate is more self-reflective and self-critical, discussing for instance the clinch between heritage and modernity in Vienna's economic development and identity formation. Anyhow, Vienna is still culturally conceptualized between international reputation, image, and tourism upon the hegemonic physical appearance and economically successful arts institutions. And for the first time, cultural institutions are not primarily a function of the social democratic claim of providing culture for all anymore. Instead, they are explicitly considered as instruments of urban transformation and a city's economic success. On the other hand, culture is also defined as everyday practice, everyday life and local cultures for the first time, pointing to its potential in urban regeneration and the construction of urbanity. Autonomous groups, youth cultures, and the socially innovative character of critical civic practices are named in this context and advocated as important cultural fields that deserve support. Yet, it is made clear that the focus has to remain on the city's established high-cultural facilities to secure future economic success.

"Vienna must be positioned as a Central European entertainment center on a domestic market of 300 million potential visitors." (Municipal Department 18, 1994: 299)

The strategy plans following in the first years of the new millennium consequently reinforce this self-esteem: *"Vienna is world (capital) city of culture"*, states former city councilor of planning, Rudolf Schicker in the 2004 document (Municipal Department 18, 2004a: 187). And this culture, of course, is the city's heritage and contemporary high-brow institutions as the report shows. Even more, the two Strategy Plans are absolutely clear about the role of this (narrowly defined) culture as economic and locational factors for the city's strategic positioning and for attracting tourists and investors. Yet, while they are also marked by the evolving commodification-of-culture discourse and adjacent claims to promote the creative industries, they promote the freedom of the arts at the same time. So, while the cultural projects referred to in the reports mostly convey spectacular tourism and an aestheticized nightlife culture of consumption, art and culture are at the very same time considered as resources that need public financing and must be sheltered from commodification (Municipal Department 18, 2001, 2004a). This contradiction can only reasonably be explained as a strategy of political legitimation of this new form of planning the city with culture. The most recent Urban Development Plan for Vienna, the StEP 05, already seriously attempts to consider a culturized planning view in some parts. It is also self-reflective as concerns the imbalance of the very few culturally representative places of the city and the many unrecognized others:

"Due to their historic, cultural, political or social importance, only very few urban quarters determine the image and identity of Vienna in a particular way." (Municipal Department 18, 2005: 192; author's translation)

Hence, culture is also conceived as a central factor for identity formation and societal development, although the fact that respective processes can hardly ever be planned is not mentioned. Yet, public space development moves to the center of attention as a pivotal element of an urban culture, an instrument for constructing urbanity and, relatedly, a city's image and identity. Nevertheless, the culture for competition paradigm upon a politics of visibility is still central in Vienna's culture-led planning in 2005:

"[T]he targeted investment in constructing and expanding the houses of culture (e.g. Museum Quarter, Karlsplatz, Central Library, ...) strengthens the re-positioning of Vienna as international metropolis of culture, and its innovative and dynamic side." (Municipal Department 18, 2005: 84).

This pro-active approach to utilizing culture in Vienna's planning is underlined also by the fact that in 9 of 13 target areas, culture is mentioned explicitly as an element of planning (Municipal Department 18, 2005). Although StEP 05 already was progressive concerning some aspects of a culturized planning approach, its Progress Report in 2010 plays the safest card by returning to the path of a hegemonic heritage culture again. In its description of the inner city, one of the 13 target areas, the report refers to it as the *"historic, cultural and adminis-*

trative center" of Vienna (Municipal Department 18, 2010: 62). This is even more striking as culture is not mentioned anymore in any of the other target areas. Instead, the long known equal spatial distribution of cultural infrastructures and the erection of another new museum in the near future are the only explicit goals in Vienna's cultural planning in 2010 (Municipal Department 18, 2010: 99). Thus it seems as if culture – in whatever form – has again been used just as a legitimizing strategy for promoting an urban development agenda in 2005. The recently started discussion process "wien 2025" for the new Urban Development Plan of Vienna reveals no explicit or implicit references to cultural concerns either. As introduced above already, the documentation of the first public debates of this still young process rather points at a distinct consideration of locational policies, economic growth, and mobility as central fields to be debated (Wien 2025, n.d.).

Reviewing how culture is employed in Vienna's planning strategies also demands an analysis of the city's cultural policies – the distinct culture strategies of Vienna. Yet, there are none. Although culture is a recurring theme in inward- and outward-oriented development strategies of Vienna since long, there are no distinct strategies on cultural planning, cultural politics or whatsoever that would make goals, visions, challenges and future development potentials of the city with culture explicit. Hence, there is also no public participation in broadly discussing citizen's attitudes, needs and visions as concerns the city's cultural image and multiple identities. The only specific documents are Vienna's annual Art & Culture Reports (since 2001). Yet, these are no strategies, but mere reports of subsidies, investments, and projects realized within the city's cultural politics. Hence, the City of Vienna does not issue any explicit culture strategy. Yet, recently Vienna's Tourism Agency published its own Tourism Concept ("Wiener Tourismuskonzept") that in fact is the only detailed strategy on employing culture in (economically) developing the city (Vienna Tourism Agency, 2009).

In this concept, Vienna is contextualized as a city threatened by fierce interplace competition for attention and global tourists, in which the "creativity index" and a city's "cultural quality of life" are important marketing tools. Although the report lengthy debates the new multiplicity of culture(s) and the changed contexts of urban development, Vienna is still framed as the place of a distinct heritage culture, high-brow contemporary arts institutions, and spectacular cultural mass events. These favor the inner city and its attached attractions of consumption – there is no place for any processes of cultural production, though. Single measures in the concept even attempt to determine explicit planning questions by suggesting the preservation of (mostly inner city) traditional coffee houses through forbidding retail speculation in surrounding areas on the one hand, while simultaneously recommending the active regeneration and aestheticization of "run-down" (mostly migrant) neighborhoods in the surroundings through clustering local "ethno-premises" (sic!) (ibid.: 81). Also, public space development is among these suggested measures as a potential asset in destination branding:

"It should be a long-term goal for Vienna to develop a number of distinct basic aesthetic principles of public space design, applicable to different places of the city to make them equally effective assets as the monuments and sights of the city." (ibid.: 105, author's translation).

Hence, the whole concept promotes a strategy of culturalization, where diversity is an exclusive marketing construct, staging "authentic" encounters with a distinct Viennese culture to suit a diversified, yet capital-rich and educated audience of visitors. And, as tourism is framed solely as an economic factor, its potentials for intercultural dialogue, learning, or as a networking platform for future cooperation are ignored.

Yet, no other strategic document in Vienna is so detailed and clear about what culture actually is, and what its use for the city is and might be in the future (although the definition employed is highly questionable). The Tourism Concept for Vienna even has qualities of an urban development plan, as it implicitly intervenes in planning questions by making suggestions for or against local urban transformation, sets guidelines for public space development and cultural planning in general, evaluates the current institutional setting, and names important governance actors that need to be activated in the one or other urban development matter. Its influence on recent Vienna's planning is very obvious in this regard, as links between recently promoted urban development projects and measures suggested by the Vienna Tourism Agency in 2009 can be found, for instance the regeneration of Schwedenplatz and Naschmarkt, among others.

To conclude, links between cultural politics and planning became closer and multi-layered in the past decades. Very early, Vienna began to utilize its potential in high-quality traditional cultural institutions to position itself on an integrating European market. Yet, more recently the local state has become aware of the potential of cultural initiatives for supporting neighborhood development, which is evident just from the creation of departure and the Fund for Art in Public Space as two institutions aiming at better steering the potentials of local creative economies and art-led public space development. Anyhow, the city government doesn't seem to follow the path of a transparent strategy building process in terms of culture-led urban development. While Vienna's Urban Development and Strategy Plans largely reproduce the hegemonic cultural imaginary of a duality of heritage culture and contemporary arts, the only serious culture strategy originates from the state-affiliated tourism agency, which thereby not only demonstrates its power in Vienna's politics of planning with culture, but reinforces a culturalization strategy, i.e. a framing of culture as commodity in competition.

Karlsplatz

A cultural economy for global tourism

DEVELOPMENT BACKGROUND

Karlsplatz is one of Vienna's central public spaces with a history of 800 years. Evolving around Vienna's first suburb, Wieden, it was largely influenced by the Wien River and the adjacent transport route between old Vienna and its Southern surroundings. The already predetermined use of the area influenced the fact that it was excluded from urbanization processes of the 19th century. Quite the opposite is true. It was at about that time, around 1850, that Karlsplatz was for the first time conceptualized as a public square (Geschäftsgruppe Stadtplanung, 1981).

Today, its location close to the inner city has made it both a traffic hub and the somewhat undefined urban space serving as the collective link between some of Vienna's most renowned cultural institutions. Thus, the city's relation to Karlsplatz is ambivalent. Although named a square, its urban design is a patchwork of green space and solitary buildings and rather comes as the result of surrounding developments – Otto Wagner's plans to develop this part of the city could never be finished. At the same time though, it is a symbol of Vienna's achievements in culture and engineering, represented by the surrounding houses of culture, and the underground that began its triumphant advance just here (ibid.).

The 20th century saw a number of physical transformations of both the public space and the surrounding institutions of Karlsplatz – some of them having substantial structural consequences. The functional separation of public transport, pedestrians, and car traffic that was realized around the area in the 1970s is among the most determinant ones still today. The erection of a first temporary, then permanent second building for the Kunsthalle is another influential transformation of the following decades. This dynamic of the cultural institutions, the frequent design regenerations of the public space, and the continuous planning debate about the role of this place for the city somewhat determine Karlsplatz as a place in constant transition.

There is hardly anything else so obvious about Karlsplatz's material preconditions than its surrounding cultural institutions. "karlsplatz.org", the association promoting Karlsplatz's cultural revitalization, names 10 cultural and 3 further large educational institutions located in close vicinity to the place, among them for instance St. Charles Church, the Musikverein, and the Vienna University of Technology (karlsplatz.org, n.d.). Most of them are looking back on a long period of existence – from the erection of St. Charles in 1737 to the Secession (1898), and more recent projects, such as the WienMuseum (1959) (Geschäftsgruppe Stadtplanung, 1981). Hence, it doesn't come as a surprise that these institutions have increasingly become determinants of any planning consideration for Karlsplatz. Its function as a place of the arts was even further emphasized in 1992. Due to the construction works for the Museum Quarter, the Kunsthalle needed a place to reside and thus moved to a temporary container at Karlsplatz. After its relocation to the completed Museum Quarter in 2001, the Kunsthalle replaced the vacant container with a permanent external branch, the Kunsthalle project space, which would from them on promote ephemeral, interventionist artistic practices, art in public space, and events in the new location at Karlsplatz (Kunsthalle Wien, n.d.). It was particularly the Kunsthalle project space, which from then on accentuated the relations between artistic practices and urban space by stimulating public space interventions at Karlsplatz. This suited the anyway long history of Karlsplatz as the place of art in public space in Vienna. Starting with an intervention in 1976 initiated by famous architects Christo and CoopHimmelb(l)au, a number of other temporary and permanent public space projects followed until now. Henry Moore's monument "Hill Arches" (1978), Public Netbase's "nikeground – rethinking space" (2003) or the "100 instructions" by a hundred international artists are among the most famous ones in this regard, which influenced the appearance and symbolic of Karlsplatz in the past (KÖR, n.d.b).

The area's dominant use is determined by its function as nodal point in Vienna's public transport network and the neighboring cultural infrastructures. The people crowding public space are rather passers-by than active users – public transport passengers, students heading to university, and the audiences of exhibitions and performances. Occasionally this picture changes when cultural events use the location of Karlsplatz, and the undefined space "in between" obtains another purpose – the spectrum ranging from Christmas markets to music festivals and public lectures (karlsplatz.org, n.d.).

Until recently, Karlsplatz also housed large parts of Vienna's drug scene, showing a less desirable picture of urban societies. The wide and branched structure of the subterranean pedestrian pathways was a safe refuge for a fringe group of Vienna's society. Addicts and dealers were tolerated by the authorities for being controllable and better supporting drug assistance (Sucht- und Drogenkoordination Wien gemeinnützige GmbH, 2010). This shows what a sensitive subject the transformation of Karlsplatz is, as the most diverse groups of society and interests need to be respected in order to enhance the place without excluding certain groups' demands – from a high-brow cultural economy to educational institutions, from students to passers-by, and from well-off tourists to needy drug addicts.

The institutional setting undoubtedly shapes the development of Karlsplatz as a place of Vienna's cultural economy. In this context, two specific influencing factors must be highlighted, which largely shape this part of the city since the 2000s. The Fund for Art in Public Space: with its foundation in 2004 and its content-related links to Kunsthalle project space, the number of art in public space projects even increased at Karlsplatz (KÖR, n.d.b), thereby attracting attention and, consequently, transforming the public perception of the area. Yet, the development of Karlsplatz as the place of contemporary visual arts is influenced by a material regulation that aims at promoting and protecting another picture of Cultural Vienna: the world heritage title. Awarded to the inner city of Vienna and its neighboring districts by UNESCO in 2001, it aims at the conservation of the city's historical substance, architectural heritage, and ensembles of the past (Municipal Department 19, 2006). In the past years it has gained the status of a determinant factor in inner city regeneration purposes, mostly hindering physical restructurings and thus forming a specific context, also for Karlsplatz transformation.

These two local particularities and a number of other specific strategic considerations concerning Karlsplatz's development point to its top-down imposed planning goals. Karlsplatz is already in 1981 extensively presented as an achievement of Vienna's urban planning. The workshop report issued back then by the Municipal Authority aims at illustrating the past urban design attempts to conceptualize a coherent public space vis-à-vis the just successfully finished construction works for functional separation at Karlsplatz as an achievement of urban engineering. Thereby the report anticipates, what Karlsplatz will be seen as in the coming years: a traffic hub, a (mono)functional building, and a merely technical solution to a comprehensive urban development challenge (Geschäftsgruppe Stadtplanung, 1981).

In the late 1990s Karlsplatz appears on Vienna's planning agenda again. The Strategy Plan 2004 is the first official planning document to take it up as a concrete planning project, naming Karlsplatz a place of the arts ("Kunstplatz Karlsplatz") and pointing at the intent to re-interpret it with culture. Its urban design is still a central goal to the new development endeavor, only this time upon a wide-ranging art-led makeover of both overground and subterranean areas. Also, a networking initiative to jointly promote the cultural institutions surrounding Karlsplatz is foreseen. And, on another front a management concept for dealing with the increasing number of fringe groups and drug addicts in the subterranean pedestrian passage is suggested (Municipal Department 18, 2004a: 90f). One year later, in StEP 05, Karlsplatz has become part of the target area "City". The world heritage status is mentioned as the greatest challenge to its development. A bit puzzling though: at the same time the conservation of valuable historic structures is a central goal. Interestingly, the maintenance of existing and the creation of new non-commercial cultural niches is among the development goals as well, while the enforcement of tourism is as important (Municipal Department 18, 2005: 208). Within this somewhat conflictive agenda, Karlsplatz gets no special mention. Instead, it is referred to in another context of the document as the number one place of cultural transformation (ibid.: 84f).

In the coming years, the strategic discourse reinforces the framing of Karlsplatz as *the* place of fine arts in Vienna:

"The project was completed in 2006 with the Kunsthalle zone; today, 'Kunstplatz Karlsplatz' may be called a cornerstone of Vienna's regional and international positioning as a city of the arts." (Municipal Department 19, 2006: 133).

Others even call it *"[...] an international shop window"* that represents the city's modern arts (Weber, 2006: 269, author's translation). And recently, the strategic planning discourse even refers to Karlsplatz as a good practice (cf. for instance Municipal Department 18, 2009), pointing to the fact that its image has changed from traffic and drugs to arts and aesthetics. It might even have become a role model of state-led public space development in Vienna. Hence, its recent material transformation is solely top-down initiated. Its planning is influenced by a pre-determined government agenda that clearly frames Karlsplatz's cultural development into a certain direction.

The central location of Karlsplatz in the city and its role as a so far undefined large public space make it an exceptional case study concerning Vienna's urban development in general. Being the link between a number of institutions that are at the forefront of Vienna's cultural economy also makes it an interesting transformation process in cultural terms. It is clear that these institutions will play a role in Karlsplatz's makeover, as they have ever since been determinant of discussions about the cultural identity of place. But it is not yet ultimately defined, which role the public space constituting Karlsplatz itself will play in the development process. Hence, the material transformation of these public and semi-public spaces forming Karlsplatz should be of particular interest in its planning. As was already stated above, its transformation demands a sensitive approach that takes into account the different uses of space that do already exist, and the currently unconsidered future uses. The re-interpretation and material regeneration of Karlsplatz thus need to incorporate a broad view of culture being a signifying practice. Planners at stake ought to consider the development of public space as a chance to realize a not fully determined space that is open to the representation of difference. Being the last undetermined public space in the city center, Karlsplatz holds a huge potential for becoming a global representation of contemporary Cultural Vienna. The only question is whether this representation is the continuation of an anyway powerful elitist imaginary of high culture for capitalizing on tourism, or if the potential is used for setting an example of a metropolis in the making, where Karlsplatz serves as a new agora and symbol of Vienna's cultural development.

THE DISCURSIVE CONSTRUCTION OF KARLSPLATZ

Fig. 9: Top-10 terms per year in Karlsplatz mediatic discourse

Fig. 9 gives a first rough overview to the place-specific mediatic discourse. Covering 178 newspaper articles since 2005, the word cloud reveals three important things. First, it points to the fact that the arts are the pre-eminent topic in the transformation of Karlsplatz in the younger past, while other planning-relevant aspects are not covered at all or, at least, only in a negligible intensity. Second, it shows that this debate is focusing the place-specific cultural institutions only, leaving no room for other culturally specific aspects of place in the discourse, thereby unhiding the hegemony of these institutions. And third and most importantly, it already very clearly sketches, who the powerful and discourse-forming actors in Karlsplatz transformation are, indicating an elitist debate determined by the political force of the city councilor of culture, Andreas Mailath-Pokorny (SPÖ), and the actors and institutions mostly subsidized by the department he governs.

As media discourse on Karlsplatz transformation reveals, only a very small group of actors from the political sphere and associated actors from established cultural institutions shape the debate about Karlsplatz's culture-led transformation. In fact, these "cultural experts" frame the discourse from the very beginning, making the place's regeneration, as well as its discursive construction an elitist planning debate. The city councilor of culture, Andreas Mailath-Pokorny (SPÖ) is among the major influencing actors. His occurrences in discourse and the thematic shifts within these are of particular interest, as they are in line with the overall discourse transformation – and this is not only due to his frequent appearance. While his early statements emphasize the cultural institutions at Karlsplatz as a distinct cultural context, he soon goes on to interfere particularly in discursively promoting Karlsplatz as a flagship of Vienna's cultural competitiveness, thereby determining a context of inter-urban competition as concerns the city's cultural development. His statements frame Karlsplatz as a place of cultural consumption and express the need for active public space development to exploit the potentials of this central public space. He is also closely related to the most influential actor in this case study, Wolfgang Kos, director of the WienMuseum, who intervenes in almost completely the same fields and even at about the same time as the city councilor, thereby already indicating a powerful discourse coalition in Karlsplatz transformation.

Fig. 10 illustrates that only a few actors play a central part in determining the place-related debate, showing their power over discourse as opinion leaders. This thematic coalition consists of a cultural-political elite of established holders of a political office and state-affiliated cultural managers with high reputation: mayor Michael Häupl (SPÖ), the traditionally powerful city councilors of culture (Andreas Mailath-Pokorny, SPÖ), planning (Rudolf Schicker, SPÖ, and, since 2010, Maria Vassilakou, Green Party), and public finances (Renate Brauner, SPÖ), Norbert Kettner (Vienna Tourism Agency, CEO), and a number of institutionalized cultural actors with an at least financial affiliation to the local state, most notably Wolfgang Kos (WienMuseum, director), Christoph Möderndorfer (karlsplatz.org), and alternating representatives from KÖR. Being equipped with both discursive and material planning power, it is largely this cultural-political elite coalition that constructs the picture of Karlsplatz as an inner city representative place of the arts. And, it is them who enforce Vienna's cultural image as a duality of tradition and modernity in this part of the city.

Fig. 10: Theme-based mapping of actors in Karlsplatz discourse

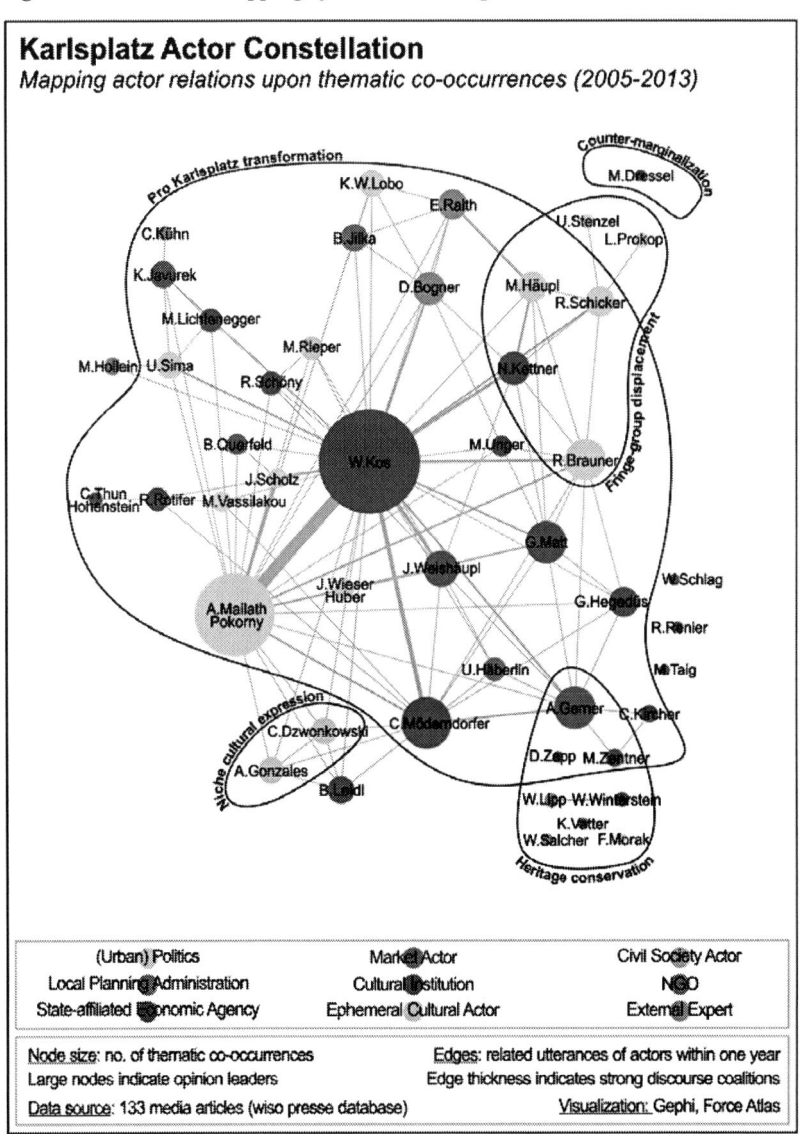

If existent, the mapping would as well allow for depicting counter-hegemony in discourse. Yet, apparently in Karlsplatz discourse such a counter-hegemonic coalition does not exist. Heritage conservation, for instance, is in parts even incorporated in the pro-transformation debate, although – as explained above – normally being a powerful argument against inner city planning considerations. Also, modes of niche cultural expression stay marginal, as well as arguments against fringe group displacement.

As was indicated already by the initial content analysis, two topics are determinant in Karlsplatz discourse: the cultural context, and the identity and image of the place. No other thematic fields are discussed with a similar intensity and, simultaneously, with an equal variety and number of actors. At the same time, the cultural context, referring to the institutions and place-specific development path of the place for this case study, is the only strand that is continuously emphasized in the debate on Karlsplatz transformation without any interruption. Concerning the other thematic fields, the related cultural economy, the contextual framing of inter-urban competition, and public space development at Karlsplatz are of comparable significance. On the other hand, civil society concerns, such as integration, education, learning, or community do not play any role in the place-specific media coverage. This can only partially be explained by the fact that Karlsplatz is not a residential area. Rather, it points at a narrow understanding of civil society and the exclusion of social aspects of culture in the context of Karlsplatz's transformation, which is revealed by a closer investigation of actors' statements in discourse as well. Notably, societal transformation and fragmentation are determined by a very much state-centered discourse on displacing fringe groups, while after 2007 these and related topics are completely excluded. Interestingly, even infrastructural concerns, which refer largely to the old urban design question of Karlsplatz, play only a secondary part.

As concerns the composition of actor groups in Karlsplatz discourse, actors from the political sphere play a remarkable role.[1] They are the only actor group to intervene in all thematic fields within the analyzed time frame that get a mention at all. Even more, urban politics constitutes the major discursive actor as concerns place image and identity.

---

1   Visualizations of the chronology of discourse illustrate the place-specific debate and its development from 2005 to 2013. Actor statements were grouped in 9 thematic fields in a bottom-up approach, thereby pointing to prevalent topics and shifts in the thematic focus of the project-related debate. Colors do again indicate actors' affiliations.

Fig. 11: Visualizing the chronology of Karlsplatz discourse

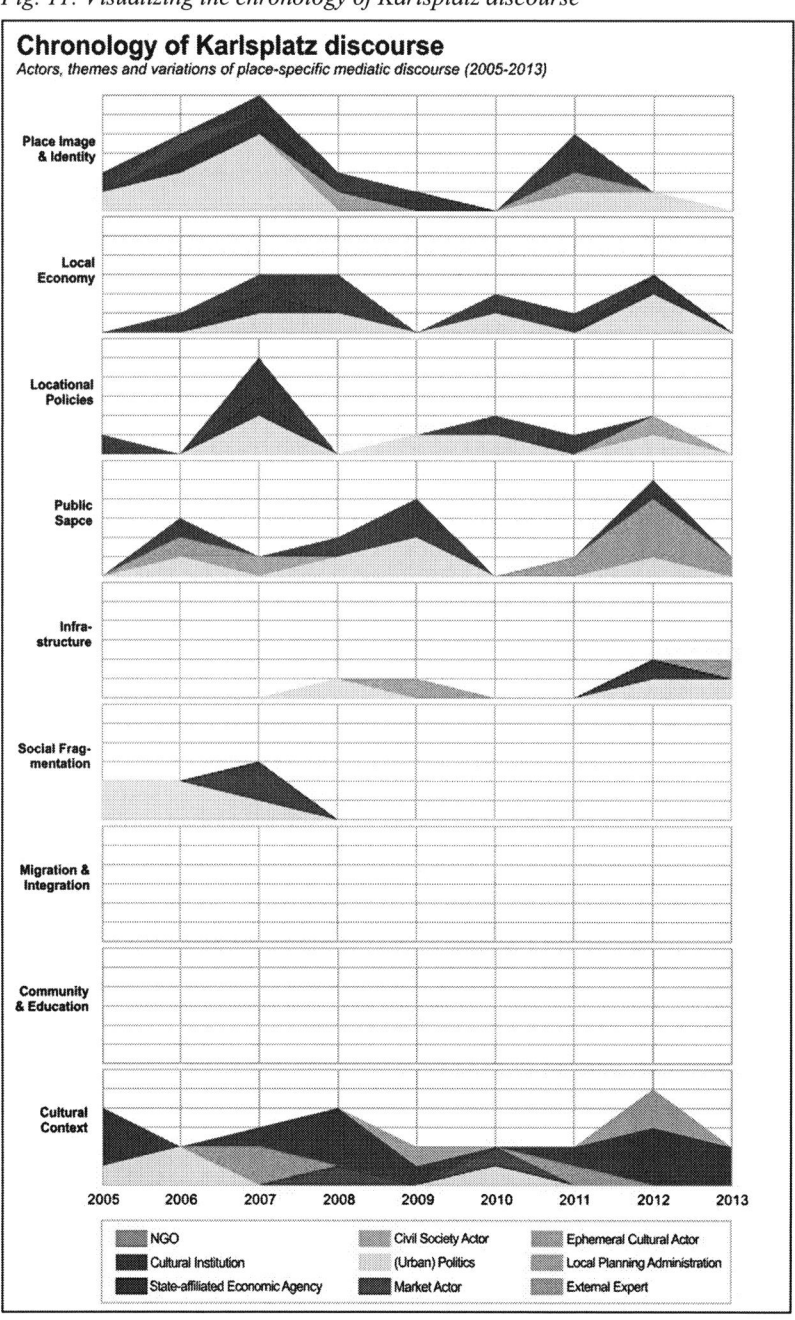

From that time on, art and culture are only discussed as economic questions anymore, shifting the culture discourse into the direction of a cultural economy debate. Consequently, there is no concern about any societal goals to be reached with cultural processes at Karlsplatz. The prevalence of culturalization goals in the transformation of Karlsplatz also removes the largely state-led debate about the drug addicts there from discourse. Interestingly in this regard, it is the same cultural-political elite discursively legitimizing the displacement of this fringe group. Norbert Kettner (Vienna Tourism Agency, CEO) emphasizes in this context that an aesthetic and clean city is necessary for attracting tourists[2], thereby of course legitimizing the displacement of this group from Karlsplatz. *"We do not want to ban the drug addicts, but they shall not dominate"*, says former city councilor of planning, Rudolf Schicker.[3] These and other statements leave no doubt that the art-led regeneration of Karlsplatz is meant to attract a very particular audience, while forcing out another.

Hence, tourism becomes an increasingly important factor in the debate since 2007, largely supported by the elite cultural coalition. Culture as such is only discussed in the context of art institutions, and in this regard the contextualizations of Vienna play an ever increasing role as legitimizing arguments for an art-led place transformation. Vienna is framed as a city in fierce global competition, while at the same time its competitiveness and world city status in terms of art institutions are repeatedly emphasized. These early framings and the continuous discursive dominance of the cultural-political elite throughout the years help promoting a hegemonic culture at Karlsplatz that is synonymous with the city's art-led touristic image. The dominance of these elite actors in discourse even increases in the coming years. From 2008 to 2010 it is almost exclusively this established political and cultural elite framing Karlsplatz discourse. And increasingly, planning questions at Karlsplatz are determined by the discursive duo Mailath-Pokorny and Kos. With the appearance of karlsplatz.org, another group of cultural managers are equipped with the power to plan under the courtesy of powerful political actors. This further consolidates the art-led image of Karlsplatz in discourse as a hegemonic construction. *"[W]e want to present the real Vienna and Karlsplatz."*[4], highlights Christoph Möderndorfer, head of the association karlsplatz.org, pointing of course at the artistic diversity of the city.

---

2 "Unsere Liga ist sicher Berlin" (Die Presse, April 09, 2007).
3 "Lavendel statt Drogen am Karlsplatz" (Der Standard, May 19, 2006; author's translation).
4 "Kultur statt Kicken am Karlsplatz" (Kurier, June 06, 2008; author's translation).

Following, the discourse narrows down to two central planning projects. From 2009 on, the new WienMuseum is one central discursive element. It is framed as the savior in a discussion peppered with increasing claims for enforcing entrepreneurial planning. Vienna's outward-orientation, tourism, consumption, and image construction are pivotal arguments in an expert debate framed by politics and closely related cultural experts. *"Vienna needs an architectural signal – a landmark."*[5], is one representative statement among many in this concern. Importantly, Karlsplatz regeneration – and the new WienMuseum in particular – are recurrently implicitly referred to as important symbols of the separation of Vienna from Federal cultural politics. Thereby, the regeneration and expansion of WienMuseum is also largely legitimized, as it has a totally different and more contemporary focus than the heritage-based Federal museums.[6] The regeneration of the pedestrian passage is the second central topic. It is meant to complete the re-interpretation of Karlsplatz into an art space. The weak argumentation for its reconstruction unhides that its renewal has never been a question of substantially re-building a somewhat unskillfully planned subterranean traffic hub, but of transplanting the art-led regeneration strategy also into the pedestrian pathway, in order to communicate the contemporary arts image of Vienna to an even greater group of people.

Hence, Karlsplatz discourse constitutes a great example of the construction of a hegemonic cultural imaginary. While the multi-level transformation of this inner city public space touches upon a diverse range of planning-relevant questions, its regeneration is discursively determined by just a few non-planning actors. Instead, its strategic importance as a representative place of Vienna is recognized particularly by a cultural-political elite that claims the prerogative of (re)interpretation of this part of the city upon the existence of art institutions in vicinity to Karlsplatz. This is the beginning of an intense discursive reinterpretation of the place from an undefined area into *the* art place of the city. Notably, there has never existed any doubt about the fact that culture at Karlsplatz *must* be interpreted as contemporary arts. In this regard, Karlsplatz transformation very skillfully combines two political goals in Vienna's planning situated on different scales of intervention: the promotion of a more modern cultural image of the city in global tourism, and the re-interpretation of an undefined and problematized inner city public space. These goals are interchangeably utilized in discourse as arguments to enforce the realization of the respective other. Vienna's image as a

---

5 "Das Stadtmuseum bleibt in der Stadt" (Die Presse, March 03, 2010; original quote from Andreas Mailath-Pokorny, author's translation).
6 "Das Potenzial ist sichtbar" (Falter, March 26, 2008).

world city of contemporary arts legitimizes the enforcement of art-led transformations at Karlsplatz, while Karlsplatz's art-led regeneration itself serves as a powerful representation of Vienna's contemporary art-based image.

The culture defined in Karlsplatz discourse is by and large an economic resource of consumption and a representation instrument serving the consolidation of a hegemonic cultural image, i.e. a culturalization strategy. The produced imaginary reinforces Vienna's image as world city of culture, yet in a very narrow sense of contemporary (visual) arts. The cultural-political elite that mostly determines place-specific discourse promotes a high-brow, contemporary-arts culture that represents a very exclusive part of Vienna's cultural spectrum. It is narrowed down to a commodity in tourism development and global competition, while excluding other cultures from the generated economic process.

MATERIALIZATIONS OF THE CULTURAL IMAGINARY

As was shown for the case of Karlsplatz, the construction of a dominant cultural imaginary could be revealed. Yet, the question whether these discursive strategies were actually able to influence the material development of the place is another aspect. Therefore, it is necessary to collect the important moments of material transformation since 2005. These can be divided into different strategic phases: first, the regeneration of the public park in 2005 and the progressive displacement of fringe groups from Karlsplatz in the coming years as an aestheticization approach; second, the funding of an association to culturally curate Karlsplatz revitalization upon networking the surrounding cultural institutions as an identity construction process; third, the intensification of art-led projects with an increasing amount of spectacular mass events as an attention strategy; and fourth, the regeneration of the subterranean pedestrian walkway as representation of "Kunstplatz Karlsplatz". These strategic moments of material intervention – aesthetic, identity, attention, representation – can all be traced back to earlier processes of meaning-making in the analyzed local planning and media discourse and shall thus be discussed now in more detail.

- **Interventions in urban design**: A central point in the manifold planning efforts at Karlsplatz within the past decade is the re-design of public space. In 2005, the "Resselpark", one of the central green spaces forming Karlsplatz, is regenerated. Yet, it is not aiming at improving the long criticized design situation by implementing a comprehensive public space concept, but at restoring the view axes between the cultural institutions to make them more visible in the urban fabric. This material intervention's orientation towards the large institutions at Karlsplatz is largely determined by the preceding framings made by the cultural-political elite coalition. Their discursive strategy shapes the picture of Karlsplatz as the unmistakable place of these institutions, thereby pre-determining that any material planning intervention would need to take them into account. Even more, this strategy is legitimized upon references made to the original park design concept from the 1970s: *"The whole arrangement will again look like 30 years ago, when it was planned."*[7] Actually, though, the original park concept was not at all focusing the surrounding institutions, nor the view axes between them (Geschäftsgruppe Stadtplanung, 1981). Hence, the first urban design intervention in 2005 is clearly a strategic approach to materially aestheticize the place and stage the surrounding institutions. Yet, this material intervention is obviously shaped and legitimized through a discursive construction placed in media debates by the powerful cultural-political elite coalition.

- **karlsplatz.org**: On August 01, 2006 the association "karlsplatz.org" starts its work at Karlsplatz. Led by the cultural managers Christoph Möderndorfer, Gabriela Hegedüs, and Peter Melichar, it is the association's goal to link the cultural institutions surrounding the area and *"[...] initiate and moderate a process of identity formation for an authentic 'Artspace Karlsplatz'."* (karlsplatz.org, n.d.) The project is assigned to the curating team by the Vienna Municipal Department for Cultural Affairs (MA7), which is affiliated to the city councilor of culture, Andreas Mailath-Pokorny (SPÖ). The fact that the project is initiated by the city councilor himself, and the goal orientation of karlsplatz.org both indicate that the initiation of the project is the materialization of the political strategy to further promote the anyway hegemonic institutions around. Although the association is open to non-institutionalized cultural projects[8], its specified task from the very beginning is focused on promoting the established cultural players. Hence, karlsplatz.org is a continuation of the discursively shaped idea of how to combine culture and planning in the transformation of Karlsplatz. Even more, as was already analyzed above, the delegation of constructing an art-led place identity to karlsplatz.org, and the simultaneous disappearance of political actors from discourse as regards identity-

---

7 "Grauer Schicker, schicke City" (Die Presse, August 25, 2005; original quote from Rudolf Schicker, author's translation).
8 Interview with Christian Dzwonkowski and Richard Natiesta from Buskes Festival Vienna.

and image-related questions must be considered as the targeted depoliticization of the culture-led transformation discourse, while the strategic goals of Karlsplatz's cultural re-interpretation are carried on. This is underlined by the fact that the selection of the curating team and its program was anything but a transparent process. It was actively enforced by the city councilor of culture, although open questions about the development of Karlsplatz were not resolved at that time. And, with the "popfest", a popular music event held each summer by karlsplatz.org, also the attention strategy for Karlsplatz is enforced. The event was initiated by the city councilor of culture as well. And notably, it co-occurs with the councilor's increasing number of statements concerning Vienna's positioning as world city of music. Hence, it is not only another materialization of the imaginary produced for cultural Karlsplatz, but it consolidates Karlsplatz's role as one of Vienna's most important places in terms of its contemporary cultural image.

- **Kulturpassage Karlsplatz**: The last step in a strategy of transforming Karlsplatz into a representative place of the arts is the renewal of its subterranean pedestrian passage, which connects Karlsplatz with the Ringstraße. In 2008, gerner°gerner architects win the urban design competition held by Vienna's public transport association (as the owner of the passage) to renew Karlsplatz Passage. The goals are manifold: besides optimizing pedestrian's mobility, orientation and security, or suggesting high quality design while conserving the architecture under heritage protection, a central aim is to design the passage as a lively path of art and culture to promote the cultural institutions surrounding Karlsplatz (gerner°gerner plus, n.d.; Wiener Linien, 2013). Interestingly, the biggest planning project at Karlsplatz since the design intervention in 2005 is largely unquestioned, which is due to two important discursive strategies. First, the complexity of the transformation process is increasingly emphasized by the involved actors, thereby making the debate about the pedestrian passage an elite discourse. Technical matters are often highlighted, which excludes non-experts from participating in the debate. Heritage protection, for instance, is an interesting contextual factor in this regard. By signaling the consideration for the existing architectural heritage, critical voices are largely muted. And second, although the name would suggest something bigger, the "culture passage" is a mere marketing instrument for the cultural institutions, implemented into the urban fabric of Karlsplatz. It is the ultimate consolidation of the discursively constructed imaginary that culture at Karlsplatz is synonymous with the large art institutions. Hence, it is the result of a previous discursive construction and, thus, a perfect example of Cultural Imagineering. Even more, the "logical" integration of art works by Peter Kogler and Ernst Caramelle, two of Austria's internationally most renowned visual artists of the past decades, makes the hegemonic culture that has consolidated at Karlsplatz even more obvious.

- **Wien Museum**: An open question in analyzing the materializations of a cultural imaginary at Karlsplatz is the new WienMuseum. Although the construction of its new building is fixed in the political agenda of the local government, the debate, which has intensified since 2010, did not bring any satisfying result so far. Anyhow, the particularly intense WienMuseum discourse reveals the influence of a number of factors as concerns planning the city with culture in Vienna. First, it unhides the dependency on ideological paths of past cultural planning politics. The Social Democratic claim for a more equal spatial distribution of cultural facilities within the city became as well a central claim in the discursive strategy of the Social Democratic city councilor of culture. It also points at the (anyway questionable) primate position of institutions in relation to cultural processes in Vienna's culture-led development. Second, it reveals the peripheral role of world heritage-related restrictions as an extra-discursive influence by contrast with tourism- and image-related contextualizations. The latter two were also decisive arguments in diminishing the number of potential new locations for WienMuseum to inner city places only. While Karlsplatz was originally considered as just one among a number of potential locations, the discursive strategy of the city councilor of culture, Andreas Mailath-Pokorny (SPÖ), and the director of the WienMuseum, Wolfgang Kos, has in my eyes already decided the fate of WienMuseum. Their simultaneous shift in discursively transforming Karlsplatz from an improper place and no-go-area of the city into the *"optimal museum location"*[9] already set the ground for re-constructing a new WienMuseum at its current location. Broadly speaking, the new WienMuseum at Karlsplatz is already built – the only question left is, when it will materialize. This also indicates the dominance of the imaginary enforced also at Karlsplatz that culture is meant as an

---

9 The changed attitude of Mailath-Pokorny and Kos towards Karlsplatz as museum location becomes obvious by comparing their discursive interventions between 2009 and 2012 (cf. for instance "Wien-Museum: Neubau am Hauptbahnhof?" (Wiener Zeitung, November 27, 2009) and „Ein architektonisches Signal für Wien" (Kurier, July 25, 2012)).

instrument to promote tourism and the city's cultural image and that in this regard Vienna's old city center is the logical place.[10]

TRANSFORMATION AS HEGEMONIC MATERIAL PRACTICE?

Karlsplatz is a great example of powerful actors intervening in discourse to legitimize the culture-led transformation of the city. The narrowing down of culture to art, established art institutions, and the carrier of a global city image was adopted wholesale in the material transformation of the place. Most materializations analyzed were set already years ago in a strategy aiming at the aesthetic and symbolic upgrading of Karlsplatz. Hence, their implementation as such was hardly influenced by the more recent place-related discourse. Anyhow, in some cases the legitimation and framing of planning interventions upon the discursively constructed imaginary could be detected. Even more, the analysis of culture-led material processes at Karlsplatz allowed for demonstrating that their unquestioned shaping as art-led projects for representation in a *"global capitalist cultural economy"* (Scott, 1997: 324) is the evident result of a discursive construction of a cultural imaginary.

Overall, Karlsplatz transformation must be read as follows. The process started around 2005 as a pure planning initiative upon the political will to regenerate a problematized urban public space. In order to enhance acceptance and aestheticize the place, it was soon peppered with artistic interventions. Hence, the notion of Karlsplatz as *the* place of the arts in Vienna soon became dominant in discourse. Consequently, coming transformative efforts were increasingly legitimized upon their art-led orientation. These prepared the ground for ever bigger planning interventions at Karlsplatz, ultimately leading to the attitude that this place would need a new spectacular landmark museum. Interestingly though, the hegemony of the arts as determinant of Karlsplatz has become so strong in the meantime, that it is unquestioned that the debate about this huge planning project is governed exclusively by a cultural-political elite.

This is also reflected by the fact that there is no such thing as counter-hegemony in Karlsplatz transformation. Interestingly, although Karlsplatz is a huge central public space with a large number and great variety of users day by day, there are no signs of representations of a different culture of the city. Instead, a small number of political and cultural actors with high reputation was

---

10 On November 12, 2013 and after the empirical analysis of this research had already been finalized, the decision for Wien Museum to stay at Karlsplatz was made public.

able to stabilize their cultural economy of touristic consumption and an exclusive high culture in the transformed materialities of place. The growing number of public space events and the art-led aestheticization of large urban infrastructures point to a strategy of spectacular urban regeneration for the sake of promoting this anyway established cultural economy. The sporadic popular cultural processes that evolved since 2005 must also be read in the context of this strategy, supporting either the project of representing a hegemonic cultural image (e.g. the popfest), or a culture of touristic consumption (e.g. the Christmas market). The removal of stores from the subterranean passage in the course of its regeneration also points to the supremacy of a cultural economy as the objective of place transformation. The imaginary of art for global reputation and touristic consumption legitimizes their non-inclusion, as aesthetic factors for success in a tourism economy outdo other local economic considerations. Thus, the transformed cultural materiality of Karlsplatz is nothing but the consolidation of the hegemonic high-cultural, institution-oriented cultural politics of Vienna.

Hence, the wrap-up of Karlsplatz transformation ends with a critical tone. The regeneration process did not improve the pedestrian pathway or green spaces in their functionality for its everyday users. As a planning project it was hence not oriented towards improving the usability or variability of urban space for the diverse user groups of a multifunctional inner city public space. Instead, it was an exercise in aestheticizing the last undefined central public space of Vienna in order to promote the practices of the established cultural and tourism economy of Vienna. A handful of powerful cultural-political actors were able to influence local place transformation upon a distinct cognitive construct of culture's role in Vienna's development, which will reasonably be very influential of future Cultural Vienna. And this powerful elite constellation is not at all untypical of Vienna's cultural planning processes, as I am still going to point out in the comparison of case studies. Hence, Karlsplatz's new materiality now joins the other central public spaces of the city in their function as representative places of a hegemonic art-led capitalization strategy – only this time not upon heritage, but upon contemporary arts to complete the materialization of the long promoted image of tradition and modernity. By materially implementing a marketing campaign for the surrounding cultural flagships, these institutions and the companies of an also well-established inner city tourism-dependent service economy are the winners of Karlsplatz's remaking.

Seestadt Aspern

Cultural symbolism for entrepreneurial urbanism

DEVELOPMENT BACKGROUND

Seestadt Aspern (or "Aspern Urban Lakeside") is among the largest urban expansion projects in Europe and constitutes Vienna's biggest urban development process ever since. As part of Donaustadt, Vienna's 22nd district in the Northeast of the city, it is located on the left side of the Danube River – a part of the city that has long been neglected by the urban development process. The area of 240 hectares is the leftover of a former airfield, which is closed in 1977 due to the development of Schwechat south of Vienna as the city's primary airport. In 1980, the disused airport facilities are demolished, and only two years later, General Motors opens a branch next to this wasteland. While these transformations as such do not influence the city's spatial development agenda immediately, the fall of the Iron Curtain in 1989 and Austria's potential accession to the EU in the early 1990s do. In 1992, former mayor Hans Mayr pushes through his will to let the City of Vienna acquire the properties of the former airfield in order to be prepared for the forecasted influx of people in the near future.[1]

Development visions for this part of the city are way older than the now realized master plan. In Vienna, urban visions about the city's spatial development and structural organization have always considered a second city center beyond the Danube River since the 19th century (Mattl, 2000). Today, this planning vision still exists. Backed by constant urban growth and the attempt to come up to the city's former image as the Danube metropolis, concepts to develop the city beyond the Danube are recurrently reinforced. With StEP 84, the longstanding idea of developing polycentric Vienna is revived for the first time since decades, only that time with very little success. Only in StEP 94, the vision of creating a second city center beyond the Danube is taken up again after the Danube City

---

1   Cf. "Seestadt Aspern: Utopia reloaded" (Die Presse, June 22, 2012).

has become an economic success story and symbol of Vienna's start into a new era as European metropolis (Pirhofer & Stimmer, 2007). In fact, StEP94 is the first planning strategy taking up the idea to develop the former airfield as a new urban quarter outside "old" Vienna and beyond the Danube, herewith grounding existing visions for the trans-Danubian parts of the city in concrete concepts for the first time (Municipal Department 18, 1994).

In 1992, as the City of Vienna buys the land of the former airfield, a first plan to develop the location is created on behalf of a competition held by the City of Vienna, which Roland Rainer, Vienna's former municipal urban planner of the 1960s, wins. Rainer's concept foresees the development of an urban quarter of 10.000 inhabitants and 6.000 workplaces in the northern part of today's Seestadt Aspern area (Wien 3420 Aspern Development AG, n.d.c). Although both a master plan and the general development intention exist, the project is not realized due to a number of limitations. Although forecasts predict urban growth for a near future, the longstanding paradigmatic preference given to renewal instead of expansion in Vienna's planning forms an insurmountable planning-political barrier. And, big infrastructural projects linked to the Aspern development, such as the underground expansion from the old city center to the new urban satellite, are postponed again and again due to financial constraints. Yet, although Rainer's plan is never realized, it sets the preconditions for any future concept to be envisioned for this part of the city (Tovatt Architects & Planners & Projektteam Flugfeld Aspern, 2007).

The fact that "Vienna is growing again" is repeatedly referred to in the strategic considerations for the city's future orientation – also in the debate on realizing a new urban center in Aspern (Municipal Department, 1994, 2005). Yet, in-migration to the city was and still is determined by a low-skilled, low-income population (Statistik Austria, 2010). Hence, the socio-economic development context of the city makes the expansion project of Aspern a difficult task. It implies that the new urban quarter would also need to serve the diverse economically and culturally determined lifestyles of migrants besides serving the demands of a local population.

Seestadt Aspern's development itself is also shaped by a number of other material cultural influences. For instance, the former airfield has a very ambivalent heritage. It had once been the location of pioneering aviators and technological innovation in aeronautics, while at the same time it is remembered as the place where Heinrich Himmler landed in 1938 to announce Austria's annexation to the German Reich. Hence, in 1987 the City of Vienna erects a forest ("Gedächtniswald") on the edge of the property to serve as a symbol for the collective memory of the victims of the National Socialist regime (wien.at, n.d.b).

Yet, Aspern is hardly existent on Vienna's mental maps[2] – a fate it shares with most trans-Danubian parts of the city since long. The development of a densely built new urban center is most likely going to change this fact. Yet, it is problematic concerning its embedding in the surrounding fabric, which is determined by rural structures, single family houses, and a notable skepticism of neighboring residents towards the urbanization of this part of the city.[3]

This is also one of the reasons for cultural processes to materialize on the construction site. Although it took a while for cultural aspects to become a visible part of the planning project, they have recently become the most apparent processes in Seestadt Aspern's development. In 2011, the development agency launches Seestadt Publik, a program subsuming performing arts and community projects of all kinds that are meant to communicate an image of openness and evolving urbanity (wien 3420 Aspern Development AG, n.d.d, n.d.e).[4] So, they begin to actively implement cultural events as communicative tools to create acceptance for a large-scale urbanization process. All these projects point at a distinct audience and group of users: the wished-for future dwellers of a new, well-off creative middle class.[5] On the other hand, processes that do not fit the brand image are excluded, most prominently the "Wagenburg Gänseblümchen", a nomadic artist group, that is only reluctantly given the temporary permission to stay at Seestadt Aspern (Gänseblümchen, 2013; wien 3420 Aspern Development AG, n.d.f). This already points at a very exclusive interpretation of culture in the development of Seestadt Aspern.

Importantly for this case study, urban expansion as such is not a favored planning vision in Vienna due to the miscarried attempts of the past. Hence, although the area is on Vienna's planning agenda since the early 1990s due to the favorable property relations, only in 2005 the project is finally kicked-off. Today the development area is largely publicly owned, although ownership is distributed among three public or at least state-affiliated bodies: the Federal Real Property Management Corporation ("Bundesimmobiliengesellschaft" – BIG), the Vienna Business Agency, and the Fund for Housing and Urban Renewal

---

2   Interview with Josef Lueger, former planner at wien 3420 Aspern Development AG.
3   Interview with Bernd Rießland, former CEO of the Vienna Business Agency; interview with Daniel Aschwanden, performing artist from the artist collective content.associates.
4   Interview with Josef Lueger, former planner at wien 3420 Aspern Development AG.
5   Interview with Daniel Aschwanden, performing artist from the artist collective content.associates; interview with Josef Lueger, former planner at wien 3420 Aspern Development AG.

("wohnfonds_wien") (Tovatt Architects & Planners & Projektteam Flugfeld Aspern, 2007). Together with the Vienna Insurance Group and the Bausparkasse bank as two major investors, these actors contribute to a specifically established development agency – the "wien 3420 Aspern Development AG" – which is in charge of developing the project successfully from an economic viewpoint[6] (wien 3420 Aspern Development AG, n.d.b).

StEP 05 is a new impetus for the development considerations of the former airfield. In 2003 and as part of the development of the new plan, the Strategic Environmental Assessment "SUPerNOW" of the whole trans-Danubian part of the city is commissioned by the City of Vienna. The project concludes that a huge urban development potential would exist, while insisting that it could only be exploited in combination with an expansion of the city's public transport network – a longstanding political claim in Vienna's planning. The assessment, which covers also the Aspern area, is the kick-off for seriously developing the former airfield. Relatedly, the Urban Development Plan 2005 suggests the combined development of the underground line U2 and the development of a new urban center at just this location as one of its 13 target areas – "Zielgebiet U2 Donaustadt – Flugfeld Aspern" – leaving no doubt about the will to realize what has long been an urban development vision. Tovatt architects win the following urban development competition for the airfield in Aspern in 2005 and, after a broad discussion process, present the master plan in 2007 (Municipal Department 18, 2005; Tovatt Architects & Planners & Projektteam Flugfeld Aspern, 2007; Wien 3420 Aspern Development AG, 2011).

While development goals for the new urban center in Aspern are only superficially discussed in StEP 05, the 2007 master plan contrastingly reveals a very complete planning vision, including an architectural design concept and planning process guidelines. The plan foresees the development of an independent urban quarter of 20.000 dwellers and 26.000 work places that serves as the center for both a growing Viennese district and cross-border metropolitan region. The programmatic goals are to incorporate high quality public and green spaces from the very beginning of the urban development process, develop a city "open to all" in terms of different (also temporary) uses, realize mixed uses and high densities to construct urbanity, and enforce the establishment of companies from the productive and service sector. Furthermore, the developers undertake to harmonize real estate and infrastructural development. And, a Local Area Management ("Gebietsmanagement") is to manage tasks of the public hand in the future. Despite

---

6   Interview with Bernd Rießland, former CEO of the Vienna Business Agency; interview with Josef Lueger, former planner at wien 3420 Aspern Development AG.

the clear objectives, openness in planning is central for being able to better react to future contextual transformations and changing demands (Tovatt Architects & Planners & Projektteam Flugfeld Aspern, 2007: 14f).

Interestingly, these goals and guidelines are not at all dissimilar to the ones already promoted in 1992 in Rainer's concept. As Pirhofer and Stimmer (2007) describe, a guiding principle defined back then is to accept the plurality of demands towards a new urban quarter and the unforeseeable as part of the urban process. Further central goals are to save wasteland for future utilizations through dwellers, an economic concept for ground floors including temporary use, consolidated car parks ("Quartiersgaragen"), multifunctional facilities and multiple uses of public space, and flexibility concerning final planning decisions. All of these are still crucial to the current planning concept[7], revealing how little the development vision for the area has actually changed within 15 years.

Yet, the most apparent difference in Aspern's new development vision lies in the fact that for the first time in history a huge urban development project is privately managed. This allows for a planning approach that largely differs from prior Viennese planning, as it aims at economic viability and largely builds its development process upon a branding campaign. Until today, no other urban planning project in Vienna has seen such a comprehensive attention strategy, even more, one led by a profit-oriented development agency. And this, of course, is critical vis-à-vis a much broader public interest. So, while Aspern's development was publicly induced, property ownership and decision-making power lie in the hands of semi-public and private, economically oriented actors.

What the review of all strategic planning documents referring to the development of the former airfield Aspern shows, is that its realization must be read in the ambivalent context of Vienna's more recent planning culture, which is torn between reacting on forecasted city-regional growth as an external development determinant and the long wished-for impetus for active urbanization as a metropolis in the making. The following quotes indicate the recurring attempts to conjoin these somewhat opposing planning attitudes in the Seestadt Aspern development:

"The outstanding strategic location on the Vienna-Bratislava axis [...] creates the opportunity to develop the Airfield Aspern as an international center of attraction and a hub for economy, science, and research in the border-crossing Centrope region." (Tovatt Architects & Planners & Projektteam Flugfeld Aspern, 2007: 4; original quote from Rudolf Schicker, former city councilor of planning, author's translation)

---

7   Ibid..

"aspern is the city for 21st century lifestyles that harmonizes private needs and professional requirements, business success and social responsibility" (Wien 3420 Aspern Development AG, 2010: 9)

Within this cleavage of pro-active and reactive planning in Aspern's development, it will be interesting to see, which role culture is meant to play. If Seestadt Aspern marks a new era in Vienna's self-esteem of urban development, where inner transformation is joined by urban expansion as a symbol of the declared belief in growth and metropolisation, what does this new era entail for Vienna's cultural development? After all, the construction of a new urban quarter from scratch constitutes a huge potential for a culturized planning approach, where experimental methods, self-determined urban interventions, and the expression of cultural difference should be determinant considerations. Hence, in this specific case of place transformation we need to ask, whether the apparent utilization of certain cultures for a profit-oriented urbanization project can reasonably be combined with the expectations of the many cultures to be accommodated there towards this area's development.

THE DISCURSIVE CONSTRUCTION OF SEESTADT ASPERN

Fig. 12: Top-10 terms per year in Seestadt Aspern mediatic discourse

As can be seen from Fig. 12 and in contrast to the word cloud shown for Karlsplatz, culture is not at all an obvious part of the place-specific discourse. Instead, classic planning-related topics – most evidently housing and economic concerns – play the central part in the Seestadt Aspern development discourse in recent years. Nevertheless, this first approach to analyzing the discursive foci reveals more than one might think at the first glance. It uncovers a number of planning-cultural specificities that must be read in the context of Vienna's development trajectory. First, housing is central to urban development also in the context of Aspern, which is due to the material context of stable in-migration to Vienna since 2005 and the effects of the global financial crisis on Vienna's housing market (Tockner, 2012). Second, Vienna's historic inner city is an important point of reference in the discursive formation of Seestadt Aspern development, as it is recurrently referred to as an architectural role model for the project. And, the public transport connection linking the traditional center with the new one is a conciliating argument *for* the urban expansion project. Also, the conglomerate of architecture and urbanity as an inseparable duo to consider in developing the project is a central planning-cultural influencing factor. In this context, public space development evolves as a new pivotal element of the discussion in more recent years.

What can be said in general about the actors intervening discursively in the construction of Seestadt Aspern is that the determinant group reflects the recently prevailing notion of Vienna's governance structures in planning. Actors from the political-administrative system representing the sovereign planning agent are joined by state-affiliated economic institutions as partners in promoting a development strategy aiming largely at growth and efficiency objectives. These longstanding networks in Vienna's urban development affairs, which become obvious in Seestadt Aspern's development, constitute a corporatist governance regime (Pierre, 1999). Similar governing coalitions are often referred to as typical of Vienna's more recent politics of planning (Novy et al., 2001; Pirhofer & Stimmer, 2007; Novy, 2011). And they are also discursively framed as the only feasible governance approach to developing Seestadt Aspern, as this exemplary quote from Rudolf Schicker (SPÖ), former city councilor of planning, reveals: *"This area particularly shows, how close urban planning, investors and subsidized housing must cooperate."*[8]

Interestingly, it is not primarily the city councilors or the mayor, who significantly shape the development path of the project, but a small group of representatives from powerful state-associated economic players in Vienna's planning landscape. As can be seen (cf. Fig. 13), two poles of dense actor relations exist within the dominant pro-urbanization debate that advocate entrepreneurial planning and place branding as adequate approaches to the project's realization.

---

8 „Zurück in die Zukunft der Ostregion" (Der Standard, May 21, 2005; author's translation).

Fig. 13: Theme-based mapping of actors in Seestadt Aspern discourse

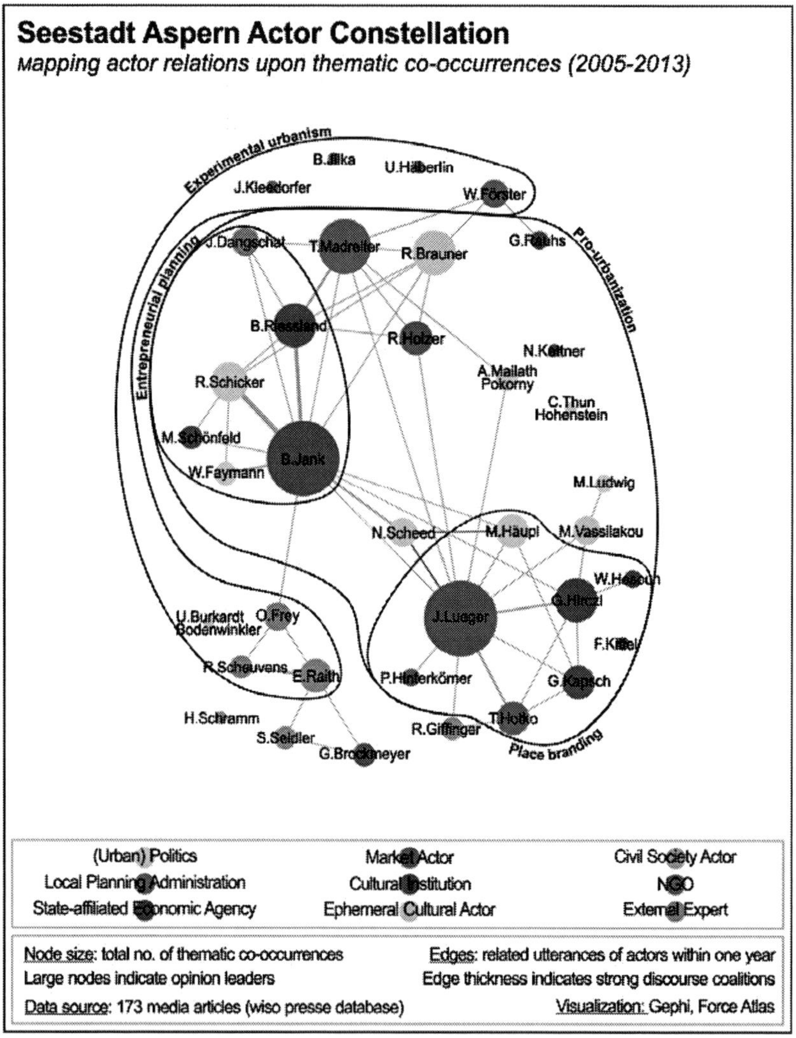

Seestadt Aspern Actor Constellation
Mapping actor relations upon thematic co-occurrences (2005-2013)

[Network diagram showing actor nodes including: B.Jilka, J.Kleedorfer, U.Häberlin, W.Förster, J.Dangschat, T.Madreiter, R.Brauner, G.Fruhs, B.Rießland, R.Holzer, N.Kettner, R.Schicker, A.Mailath Pokorny, C.Thun Hohenstein, M.Schönfeld, B.Jank, W.Faymann, M.Ludwig, N.Scheed, M.Häupl, M.Vassilakou, U.Burkardt, O.Frey, Bodenwinkler, J.Lueger, W.Hatzl, G.Hirczi, F.Kittel, R.Scheuvens, E.Raith, P.Hinterkörner, G.Kapsch, H.Schramm, S.Seidler, G.Brockmeyer, R.Giffinger, T.Hobek, Place branding]

Categories:
- (Urban) Politics / Local Planning Administration / State-affiliated Economic Agency
- Market Actor / Cultural Institution / Ephemeral Cultural Actor
- Civil Society Actor / NGO / External Expert

Node size: total no. of thematic co-occurrences. Large nodes indicate opinion leaders
Data source: 173 media articles (wiso presse database)
Edges: related utterances of actors within one year. Edge thickness indicates strong discourse coalitions
Visualization: Gephi, Force Atlas

The first includes Brigitte Jank, president of the Vienna Chamber of Commerce, and Bernd Rießland, former CEO of the Vienna Business Agency. Although particularly the actions of the latter are to a large degree dependent from decisions made by the city's political bodies[9], it is these two who exercise an exceptional influence on the discursive determination of the future thematic orientations and

---

9   Interview with Bernd Rießland, former CEO of the Vienna Business Agency.

utilizations of Seestadt Aspern by determining a number of planning-relevant questions: *"We are in constant discussion, also about transport issues and the overall cubature."*[10] This unhides how central the state-affiliated economic agencies are in shaping Aspern's planning discourse, and how powerful they are in determining this area's material development. On the other hand, planners and planning experts are only peripheral actors when it comes to placing topics in discourse to influence the debate and the future materialities of place. As will be shown in the next section, they advocate a different imaginary of open planning processes, while the above illustration already indicates that these actors are only marginal in place-specific discourse.

The thematically subdivided discourse development over time since 2005 (cf. Fig. 14) draws a precise picture of prevalent topics and actor groups in the discursive construction of Seestadt Aspern.[11] Dominant topics are the construction of place image and identity in Seestadt Aspern, the implementation of locational policies as a consequence of the contextualization of urban development in inter-urban competition, the targeted development of public spaces and, relatedly, experimental forms of urbanization. Yet, no other thematic field than public space development shows a comparable density and variety of actor groups. And, only place image and identity, and public space are referred to without any interruption throughout the years analyzed, unhiding the pivotal position of the two in the strategy to developing this urban quarter from scratch.

As concerns the variety of actor groups represented in discourse, the diversity is greater than in the case of Karlsplatz discourse. Yet similarly, non-institutionalized actors do hardly ever appear in discourse at all, indicating also an expert-led mediatic framing of the project-specific development. Actors to be associated with state-affiliated institutions, local politicians, representatives from Vienna's planning administration, and the development agency as a powerful market-oriented actor are determinant of the Seestadt Aspern discourse.

Interestingly though, comments focus a conglomerate of economic processes, place identity and, relatedly, the role of public space. In this context, the named actor groups appear regularly, sometimes even together to form a thematic discourse coalition. Contrastingly, socio-political topics are clearly underrepresented, being hardly ever mentioned at all.

---

10 "Aspern wird neuer Stadtteil mit Ost-Orientierung" (WirtschaftsBlatt, May 03, 2006; original quote from Bernd Rießland, former CEO of the Vienna Business Agency, author's translation).

11 The critical discourse analysis referred to in this context is based on 173 case study specific articles covering the period from January 01, 2005 to May 13, 2013.

Fig. 14: Visualizing the chronology of Seestadt Aspern discourse

Chronology of Seestadt Aspern discourse
Actors, themes and variations of place-specific mediatic discourse (2005-2013)

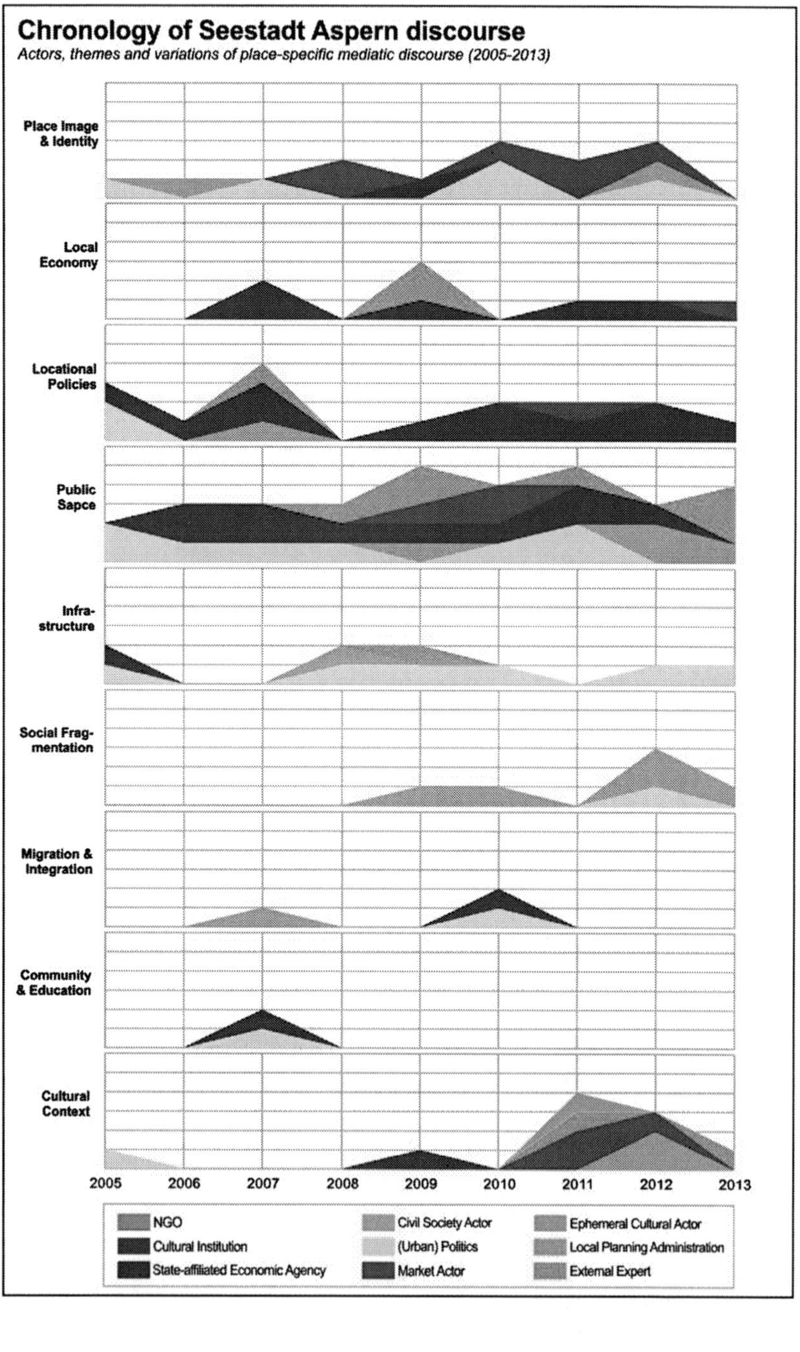

The fact that culturally relevant questions regarding community, migration, or societal formation are only peripherally considered by just a few actors, points to the prevalence of a planning ideology that has not yet integrated a culturized understanding of urban development.

In the first years, discourse is largely dominated by urban politics and institutions affiliated to the local state, or, to be more precise, by three individual actors: the former city councilor of planning, Rudolf Schicker (SPÖ), the former CEO of the Vienna Business Agency, Bernd Rießland, and the president of the Vienna Chamber of Commerce, Brigitte Jank. Only since 2007/08, after the master plan for Aspern is adopted by the municipal council and the branding concept is published, the variety of actors intervening discursively increases. Thomas Madreiter, head of Vienna's Municipal Department for Urban Development (MA18), appears more often, and so does Josef Lueger from the development agency "wien 3420 Aspern Development AG", as well as a number of external planning experts. From then on, it is particularly Madreiter, who broadens the debate about the soon-to-be city, while all carry on the formerly intense political framing of Seestadt Aspern as image carrier of the business location Vienna and promoter of a knowledge-based economy.

Overall, thematic fields hinting at a more entrepreneurial planning ideology are evidently overemphasized in relation to socio-cultural aspects of place transformation and planning. These economy-, competition-, and image-oriented framings become even more dominant after 2009. Considerations about public space development and the cultural identity of place are increasingly emphasized from that time on as well. This points to an important discursive moment that deserves further attention. The analysis shows that both public space development and (cultural) identity projects are referred to by some actors as tools in an entrepreneurial development strategy. This discursive pre-determination of such fundamental urban cultural questions by just a few (mostly market-oriented) actors is important to the construction of a cultural imaginary in the context of Seestadt Aspern development, as will be shown later in this section. And, in these fields of debate the discourse has also not consolidated yet. For the most part, the number and institutional variety of actors still fluctuates in the place-related discourse – individual topics are still discussed by diverse actor groups. This is largely due to the fact that the development project is still in the making and that individual interests of most actors are still not materially represented, which is particularly true for image- and identity-related questions, and the adjacent public space and cultural place identity discourse.

In general, it is easily depicted how strong the influence of a coalition of a small number of political actors and state-affiliated economic agencies in the discursive path-shaping of Seestadt Aspern is. Particularly in the first years, Aspern development is an expert discourse, determined by politicians and related actors in executive positions of semi-public institutions. They appear as early framers of the area's future development, leaving no doubt about Aspern's necessary realization as a business-friendly nieghborhood and symbol in competition for investments. Introduced arguments do not just promote the development of the peripherally located area. They aim at legitimizing a new planning ideology based on a strategic supply-oriented approach in order to reach for new European markets and position Vienna as a Central European hub: *"We have the unique chance to realize here what hadn't been possible in other urban quarters."*, states Rudolf Schicker, former city councilor of planning.[12]

Throughout the years, Seestadt Aspern is utilized by several actors as an object for Vienna's positioning, either as a city of KBE and R&D potentials, or as a business-friendly metropolis with claims for a minimal state, entrepreneurial planning and the construction of a metropolitan image. This is particularly done by the anyway powerful discursive actors Bernd Rießland (Vienna Business Agency), who solely determines central planning questions[13], and Brigitte Jank (Vienna Chamber of Commerce), who not only does the lobbying for business interests in Seestadt Aspern development, but intensely intervenes in shaping the general debate on physical planning in Vienna on the shoulders of place-related discourse.[14] These path-shaping strategies are yet constantly counteracted by discursive demonstrations of power of local politicians, who claim the continuation of Vienna's longstanding planning-ideological traditions in realizing Seestadt Aspern:

"There will be no urban expansion without subsidized housing."[15]

Its intangibility as a not yet realized project hence makes Seestadt Aspern a door-opener to place almost any planning-political agenda in discourse. This is

---

12 "Vom Stadtrand zur Stadt" (Der Standard, October 06, 2005; author's translation).
13 Cf."Urbanisierung im Marchfeld" (Der Standard, August 18, 2007); „Stadt für 18.500 Bewohner nimmt langsam Gestalt an" (WirtschaftsBlatt, April 30, 2008).
14 Cf."Wiens Zukunft heißt Wissen und Forschen: Brigitte Jank sieht Wien als Stadt der Forschung" (WirtschaftsBlatt, May 15, 2007); „Wien plant einen Start-up-Bezirk" (Die Presse, March 17 2013).
15 "Wir geben mit der Bildungsmilliarde Gas" (WirtschaftsBlatt, January 21, 2008; original quote from Renate Brauner, city councilor of public finances, author's translation).

visible also from the increasing appearance of topics such as sustainability, smart cities, and energy-related aspects of architecture and urban design. These sometimes detailed reports of distinct projects not only exclude non-experts from the discourse, but legitimize the discourse-forming actors as experts. This is also the moment, around 2008, that the central discourse coalition begins to change, increasingly representing actors from the development agency, external architecture and planning experts from the Vienna University of Technology, and varying representatives of the Vienna Business Agency. Politicians, though, appear only selectively anymore, emphasizing the one or other existent claim made by others, respectively referring to Seestadt Aspern in day-to-day politics.[16] Otherwise, the discourse is shaped by the triad of Vienna Business Agency, Chamber of Commerce, and development agency, with rare appearances of urban researchers and planning administration representatives. This also draws a very distinct picture of Vienna's recent planning culture, at least as concerns discursive power and the path-shaping of future planning ideological developments.

An important discursive strategy points to the constant emphasis of urbanity as a leitmotif of the development of the former airfield from the very beginning of its envisioning. Urbanity is discursively referred to as density and mixed use (which is a very static and rather anachronistic view that ignores diversity, social and economic innovation, or democracy as other important urban qualities). The production of this kind of urbanity is inseparably linked with the realization of large-scale infrastructures to accommodate the large numbers of people to put this idea into practice. Hence, Seestadt Aspern is doomed to fail if these infrastructures are not realized, thereby largely legitimizing particularly the underground expansion fixed in 2007.[17] The underground and the leitmotif of urbanity are thus mutually dependent legitimizing arguments for Seestadt Aspern. While this urbanity by definition needs a high-level public transport connection, the underground expansion, on the other hand, determines Seestadt Aspern's fate as a dense urban center to adequately use the infrastructural capacities.[18] This is also interesting in terms of the materializations in Seestadt Aspern as I am going to explain in the following section.

In 2007/08, first references to culture are made – implicitly, by the former head of the Vienna Urban Development Department (MA18), Thomas Madreiter, who points out that current migration tendencies call for a more cul-

---

16 Cf."Startschuss für Seestadt Aspern" (Österreich, October 24, 2012).
17 Interview with Bernd Rießland, former CEO of the Vienna Business Agency.
18 Cf. „Violette U-Bahn fährt ins Grüne" (Kurier, October 03, 2010).

turally sensitive planning,[19] and more explicitly, by the development agency, which at about the same time begins to exclusively determine the approach to developing Seestadt Aspern with a distinct place branding concept. This approach is legitimized as an efficiency measure, in order to attract only those, who really want to live in the evolving urban center.[20] However, it is the continuation of an exclusive development strategy determined by entrepreneurial principles. And, it gets obvious how hegemonic this planning approach has become in the meantime, as it is not just largely unquestioned, but even supported by contextualizations of other actors, who suggest that place branding and entrepreneurial urban development approaches can be the only logical reaction to these environing transformations.[21]

Also, place branding is legitimized as a planning approach upon the argument that everyone would know that branding a city is more complex than branding a product. Although this notion can only be supported, it serves just as a legitimation of an urban development practice that includes entrepreneurial methods to sell an urbanization process to a market of future investors and dwellers with no consideration of other (culturally important) factors, such as lifestyle diversity or socio-economic differences within an urban population. This also uncovers how exclusive the process of constructing a brand for Seestadt Aspern is. A development agency guided by economic principles determines who they want or don't want in the new urban center. This is very questionable and reveals to what degree Seestadt Aspern's urbanity and diversity are mere discursive constructs following the rules of a developer's branding strategy to attract particular audiences for the sake of economic viability. Culture, in this regard, is nothing but a brand constructed for enforcing a certain wished for place image and identity:

"Based on the characteristics of the new urban quarter determined in the brand, it can be decided for each building if it generally fits the concept or if it needs to be rejected."[22]

Hence, the branding concept serves as a door policy for Seestadt Aspern's future inhabitants. Also, the complexity argument appears in the Seestadt Aspern de-

---

19 Cf. "Prognose: 28 Prozent Ausländer in Wien" (Die Presse, April 02, 2007).
20 Cf. "Mit der Macht der Marke" (Die Presse, May 31, 2008).
21 Cf. for instance "Verbindlichkeit statt Lippenbekenntnisse" (Kurier, September 15, 2010).
22 "Nike, Red Bull, Amsterdam" (Die Presse, October, 07, 2009; original quote from Rainer Holzer, CEO of the wien 3420 Aspern Development AG, author's translation).

bate. It suggests that the development of an urban quarter is such a complex matter that it needs a branding campaign to be tangible, thereby excluding non-experts from the discourse and the material development process. As will be discussed later, the non-inclusion of alternative lifestyle groups and niche cultures in decision-making is a recurring problem in the culture-led place transformation processes of Vienna.

Overall, the discursive framing of culture in the context of the place transformation is largely done by the development agency and certain planning experts, and hardly ever by those actors "doing" culture. Even the processes initiated in the course of the development-agency-induced culture- and communication project "Seestadt Publik" (wien 3420 Aspern Development AG, n.d.d) receive only very little mediatic response. On another front though, a thematic counter-coalition of urbanists attempts to broaden the project-related culture discourse since 2009. By increasingly emphasizing public space, ground floor development and architectural form as identity-forming forces, they broaden the urban culture debate in the Seestadt Aspern planning process, and thereby implicitly diversify, yet substantiate a more general debate about the distinct urban identity of a 21st century European city. This coalition includes Thomas Madreiter, former head of Vienna's Urban Development Department and current planning director of Vienna (City of Vienna), and Rudolf Scheuvens and Erich Raith, professors of architecture and planning (Vienna University of Technology). Herewith, two oppositional actor groups independent from each other attempt to place their urban cultural vision in discourse to frame a certain urban cultural development vision of Seestadt Aspern transformation. While Rudolf Schicker (former city councilor of culture, SPÖ), Brigitte Jank (Vienna Chamber of Commerce), Bernd Rießland and Gerhard Hirczi (Vienna Business Agency) largely see Aspern as the image carrier of a competitive business location,[23] the counter-coalition promotes a different economic model and more culturized picture of urbanity with no consideration of spectacular urbanism or competition, but founded on open, self-determined processes of urbanization. While we will only in the future see which of these urban cultural visions and strategic orientations of Seestadt Aspern – and Vienna in general – will prevail, certain recent materializations indicate the dominance of the first.

The only discursive appearance of a cultural actor is in 2011, as Ute Burkardt-Bodenwinkler from the artist collective "content.associates" attempts to describe the links between processes of cultural expression, the production of space and planning. Herewith, she places a flashlight of an innovative, performa-

---

23 Cf. "Leuchtturmprojekte für die Seestadt Wiens" (Kurier, April 20, 2011).

tive planning practice in an otherwise largely technical discourse aiming solely at economic development objectives. The promoted openness in planning, the interpretation of culture as a form of experimental urbanism, and the links drawn between cultural actors and planners as urbanists are all important interpretations of culture in urban development and reflect, how some of the projects realized in the context of "Seestadt Publik" are interpreting culture-led development. Nevertheless, this understanding does not become dominant, as it is not taken up by any other actor in discourse. Anyhow, it adds to a generally broadening debate about culture in the Seestadt Aspern transformation from a non-place to an urban center in recent years.[24] Yet, the consideration of cultural processes as temporary rentiers, or the utilization of their symbolic power in communicating an aesthetic, cosmopolitan and intellectual image and constructing place identity[25] all point to a culturalization strategy, which reduces cultural processes to attention- and image generators. Although the variety of culture-led processes actually *is* broad, thereby indicating also a broad understanding of culture, its role in urban development is determined by an imbalance between a patronizing developer knowing about the image value of these processes[26], and tolerated cultural actors considered as luxury goods in an affluent society.[27]

Also, the general trend in the discursive production of planning in Vienna must be mentioned in the context of Seestadt Aspern. In the past years, a number of actors besides those from the economic agencies have been promoting urban development approaches, which emphasize market conformity and private investments as preconditions to any planning effort.[28] The planning administrations follow in 2012 by framing the city as located in a competition for attention and a new middle-class of high-skilled, creative workforce[29]. Such proclamations become dominant, as they fit also the entrepreneurial attitude of the deter-

---

24 Cf. "Aspern: Wo (Lebens)Künstler auf der Baustelle wohnen" (Die Presse, August 12, 2011).
25 Cf. "Zwischennutzung soll in Wien größeren Stellenwert bekommen." (Wiener Zeitung, July 28, 2012).
26 Interview with Josef Lueger, former planner at wien 3420 Aspern Development AG
27 Interview with Daniel Aschwanden, performing artist from the artist collective content.associates.
28 Cf. "Wiener Mix" (Die Presse, September 24, 2011).
29 Cf. "Zwischennutzung soll in Wien größeren Stellenwert bekommen." (Wiener Zeitung, July 28, 2012); "Die Stadt muss in den Randgebieten kompakter warden" (Wiener Zeitung, September 09, 2012).

minant discourse-forming coalition of market-oriented institutions, while culturized considerations from other actors get lost in the shuffle[30].

Hence the cultural imaginary of Seestadt Aspern must be viewed in strong opposition to the one discussed before for Karlsplatz. The Aspern discourse is, of course, shaped by classic questions of physical planning that are concerned with supply and demand, system efficiency, and general urban functions. Culture, in this regard, has only an implicit role to play and is thus not that easy to reveal in discourse analysis. Its discursively determined role in urban planning, though, can be read from diverse statements. All references made to cultural processes in the Seestadt Aspern development consider culture as a tool to construct identity and image, to attract attention and communicate a distinct branding concept. Which culture that is, who is supposed to become active, and how decisions are made about these and other relevant questions, stays largely unclear even after a detailed analysis.[31] Yet, this only implicit framing of culture allows for a broader debate to evolve in more recent years that – also implicitly – turns to culture as concerns the construction of urbanity. This debate implies public space and ground floor development, and the continuation of Vienna's architectural perimeter block structures from the Gründerzeit as distinct urban cultural qualities of Vienna, thereby attempting to reconstruct the city's structural qualities as part of its identity in Seestadt Aspern. Yet, this only concerns the physical appearance of the city and not the equally important identity forming forces of socio-cultural processes. Even more, it shows that the discourse is also in this regard constructing a culturalization strategy towards developing Seestadt Aspern, where cultural processes are meant just as aestheticizing add-ons, yet not path-shaping ingredients to an urban development project. Hence, while the discourse on the definition of culture is rather broad, it is hegemonic as concerns culture's role in urban development as a tool for safeguarding an accumulation strategy. Broadly speaking, the cultural imaginary for Seestadt Aspern promotes an idea of urbanity as a particular physical appearance of the city, in which cultural processes are just the icing on the cake.

On a meta-level, the discourse also tells a lot about Vienna's local planning culture. It unhides the governance structures in recent planning as concerns actor constellations and the determinant actors discursively influencing planning outcomes, showing the predominance of few state-affiliated institutions guided by economic principles in steering planning processes into certain directions. Furthermore, it reveals the prevalent attitude towards active urban development and

---

30   Cf. "Wien 2030: eine Stadt für zwei Millionen" (Falter, January 16, 2013).
31   Interview with Josef Lueger, former planner at wien 3420 Aspern Development AG.

how it is contextualized and, thus, legitimized, revealing two largely oppositional clans of business-friendly, entrepreneurial planning, and open processes of self-determined identity-formation. And, it points to the distinct approaches discussed in actively shaping the city and steering its development strategically, highlighting again the abovementioned dichotomy between the self-confident, growing metropolis and the reactive city adapting to unchangeable external influences.

MATERIALIZATIONS OF THE CULTURAL IMAGINARY

Depicting the cultural imaginary for the case of Seestadt Aspern development demanded an in-depth analysis to reveal the often only implicit references made to culture in discourse. Nevertheless, discourse analysis was able to unhide the dominant construction of culture and its role in planning. References to culture in Seestadt Aspern discourse are largely based on local urban development traditions and dominant interpretations of urbanity and Vienna's distinct urban identity. Hence, they rather revolve around attempts to determine a distinct *urban* culture of Vienna.

In this regard it can be uncovered, who the central actors are in the project-specific imaginary construction and contest over determining the place culturally. Two oppositional thematic coalitions place their urban cultural vision in discourse to frame the material development of Seestadt Aspern into their favored direction. One consists of market-oriented representatives of Vienna's state-affiliated economic development agencies, who promote a business-friendly model of planning and the notion of attracting enterprises as development motors. The other is a group of urbanists and representatives of the city's planning administration, who consider targeted public space development and ephemeral and open planning processes as the more adequate approach. Interestingly, both construct a somewhat similar imaginary of culture and its particular role in determining urbanity in discourse, which considers cultural events as useful tools in top-down-constructing an aesthetic place identity and spectacular, positive image.[32] And for both, these cultural processes seem to be just add-ons to market an anyway pre-determined development strategy. The following section points out three distinct materializations of these imaginaries of the culture of place to highlight, in which concerns discourse has reasonably affected Seestadt Aspern's material transformation.

---

32 Interview with Josef Lueger, former planner at wien 3420 Aspern Development AG.

- **Constructing urbanity I: from unwanted urban expansion to appealing "Urban Lakeside"**: The transformation of the former airfield Aspern into a new urban center was long influenced by the ambivalent urban development history of Vienna concerning urban expansion projects as such. The obvious dominance of the historic city center paired with the negative images associated with some of Vienna's early mono-functional expansion projects largely determined the characteristic of the Seestadt Aspern development approach. As explained above, the peripheral location of Aspern raised critical voices concerning its meaningfulness in the first years. Yet, two external influences allowed for the further elaboration of concepts and development visions for this part of the city: first, constant population growth as a material influencing factor since the 1990s, and second, the framings made by the strategic planning discourse of the early 2000s with its recurring references to Europeanization and globalization processes as contextual transformations demanding a more active urban development attitude. As can be seen from discourse analysis, references to Centrope, European positioning and inter-urban competition in the context of Aspern's development are particularly dominant in the first years after the publication of StEP 05. Yet, only two further discursive strategies achieve the wide-ranging commitment to the expansion project it enjoys today. The planned connection of Aspern with Vienna's inner city through the expansion of underground line U2 is constantly used by the politically responsible city councilor of planning, Rudolf Schicker (SPÖ), and the property owners as an argument to diminish concerns about the development project. Although the City of Vienna and the Federal Government agree on a financing model for the underground construction only in 2007, the promise alone safeguards the continuation of the planning process in the years before. Furthermore, the whole project can only develop in its current form as it is legitimized upon a skillful branding concept. In June 2008, the branding agency "brainds" and the Aspern development agency present a branding concept to the public (brainds, n.d.) that is so intensely communicated that it ultimately displaces Aspern's designation as an urban expansion project from the minds of all critical forces and from discourse by re-framing it as the "Urban Lakeside". Hence, the future materializations to come in Seestadt Aspern's development would not be possible without the successful re-interpretation of the place from periphery to urbanity.

- **Constructing urbanity II: cultural events and public space development for identity and image**: Initiated by the development agency, the artist collective content.associates develops a concept for an art-, culture-, and communication project called "Seestadt Publik" in 2011, which aims at creating public attention, reputation, and identity for the development area. In the following two years, diverse cultural projects are held in Seestadt Aspern under the roof of Seestadt Publik – from urban gardening projects and a bicycle recycling workshop to open air theaters and cinemas, from participatory arts performances and artists in residence, to an architecture festival and modern circus performances (wien 3420 Aspern Development AG, n.d.e). This was made possible not only by the branding concept, which determined the Seestadt Aspern development approach as one building upon an entrepreneurial communication and attention strategy. It is as well evident from discourse analysis that the increasing commitment to the project and the consequently broadening debate about its urban cultural development since 2009 are a decisive impetus to the realization of this variety of cultural processes. The discursively formed hegemonic notion that art and culture would serve as valuable instruments in identity formation and image construction processes ultimately allowed for the unquestioned realization and private financing by the development agency, while the curatorial work for Seestadt Publik was even handed over to external cultural actors.[33] Although powerful actors in Vienna's politics of planning with culture had an obvious interest in realizing a flagship cultural institution in Seestadt Aspern[34], the construction of a different picture of urbanity and a "calmer" cultural imaginary did not allow for this development vision to materialize. Instead, the recent materializations of culture had to happen on another layer. With the naming of parks and streets after famous Austrian women, Vienna's cultural politics and the actors engaged in the development agency of Aspern constructed not a symbol of gender equality in Vienna, but a symbol of the cultural openness of Seestadt Aspern, while simultaneously constituting a less spectacular intervention in developing public space (wien 3420 Aspern Development AG, n.d.a). At the same time though, these and other cultural materializations point to the still dominant claim in Seestadt Aspern's development strategy to attract exclusive outward audiences upon a culture-led place image. "Sprungbrett Aspern", for instance, is a temporary project testing Do-It-Yourself-Urbanism. The "Microhaus" realized in the course of the EU-funded PROGREENcity project documents challenges and potentials of sustainable architecture. And the "Flederhaus", a 16 meters tall wooden building has moved from Vienna's famous "Museumsquartier" to Aspern in 2012 as

---

33 Interview with Josef Lueger, former planner at wien 3420 Aspern Development AG.
34 Cf. "Die Sandkastenspiele der Museumsdirektoren" (Der Standard, July 11, 2009); interview with Norbert Kettner, CEO of the Vienna Tourism Agency.

another symbol of sustainability and a cultural place (Schulz, 2012; wien 3420 Aspern Development AG, n.d.d). Valuable as they might be, all of these projects are aimed at a well-off, well-educated and self-confident new middle-class of potential dwellers, thereby constructing a very exclusive place identity and image. On the other hand, the potential of broad integration upon open cultural processes is not fully exploited due to the dominance of a different discursively formed rationale of planning with culture in Seestadt Aspern.

- **aspern IQ**: As described above already, a duality of two largely oppositional forces in discursively framing the prevalent future development path of Seestadt Aspern can be seen. One is based upon Vienna's planning-political tradition of adapting to contextual transformations and resulting local demands with classic government approaches of public provision, paired with the still dominant Social Democratic claim for equal distribution and access. The other is largely entrepreneurial and supply-oriented, aiming at a pro-active, business-friendly development that is meant to tackle inter-urban competition for attention and capital. It is not yet decided in the development process of Aspern, if one will prevail in the long term. Yet, the inauguration of the office building "aspern IQ" as the first permanent building of the new urban center in 2012 indicates a dominance of the latter planning model, which is backed also by a look at the actor constellation in the development agency and their dominant statements in discourse. Interestingly though, this dominance has not yet turned the development path completely into their favored direction. Instead, the discursive framings, although very dominantly placed in the project-related mediatic debate, are constantly contradicted by statements from other powerful actors in Vienna's politics of planning, who recall the city's urban planning traditions, urging their continuation also in Seestadt Aspern development.[35] This is also recently materially represented by the vast number of housing projects constructed right now. These developments unhide the materialization of a planning-political contest fought out in discourse over determining Aspern as either a business location with adjacent housing, or a residential urban neighborhood in conjunction with work places. This primarily reveals to what degree the context framings placed in discourse are determinant of the materializations in Vienna's planning. While Europeanization and Vienna's potential hub function in Central Europe shape the Aspern debate of the first years since 2005, constant population growth and the following housing shortage are re-

---

35 Cf. "Wir geben mit der Bildungsmilliarde Gas" (WirtschaftsBlatt, January 21, 2008); "Wien 2030: eine Stadt für zwei Millionen" (Falter, January 16, 2013).

cent powerful framings shifting its development into another direction since 2008. The latter is of course also determined by Vienna's long planning-political history, which is a powerful contextual influencing factor in the current materializations of Seestadt Aspern.

TRANSFORMATION AS HEGEMONIC MATERIAL PRACTICE?

Apparently, the transformed materiality of place in the Seestadt Aspern area is influenced by two determinant interpretations of culture. One refers to Vienna's previous development path as social, participatory and shaped by distinct architectural patterns, which forms a unique urban identity to be applied also to Aspern as a culture of place. The other refers to cultural events as part of an attention strategy and foundation for creating a distinct image of place. Together, these two form a reductionist interpretation of culture as a top-down assignable or pre-determinable quality of place. This allows for keeping the prerogative of interpretation of Seestadt Aspern in the hands of the developing actors from the political-administrative system and the adjacent semi-public agencies. Consequently, it assists the maintenance of economic and political hegemony of the corporatist governance network in Vienna's planning upon the realization of this urbanization project.

From the culturized planning view, which I employ to review culture-led transformation processes in Vienna, the resulting material practices in Seestadt Aspern's development are critical for Vienna's cultural development for a number of reasons. For one thing, the consolidated planning model determining the past and coming material transformation of place is highly critical. It could not be revealed by the author even in the course of the conducted narrative interviews, how the private actors in charge of decision-making processes might be able of safeguarding a broad public interest, while at the same time representing economic efficiency and viability as primary development goals.[36] This becomes particularly obvious from the early utilization of on-site art-led interventions. While these employed an experimental and participatory approach to space production in order to carve out the qualities of place as contributions to a potential urban identity, the development agency saw the primary benefit in the creation

---

36 Interviews with Bernd Rießland, former CEO of the Vienna Business Agency; interview with Josef Lueger, former planner at wien 3420 Aspern Development AG.

of an added value for the brand "Seestadt Aspern" and the image of place.[37] Hence, these first materializations on a largely undefined construction site clearly served a capitalist interest of creating surplus value upon exploiting the image value of art-led processes. This is confirmed by the fact that now that the phase of creating attention and image is replaced by the construction of the first permanent buildings, the initial cultural processes are not extended.[38]

Of course, being an area without any dwellers, Seestadt Aspern couldn't bring about any local, self-determined cultural signifying practices so far. Anyhow, the accompaniment of this urbanization process by cultural and artistic practices could have enabled perspectives that go beyond the marketing of cultural uniqueness, while having the same positive economic effects in the long run. Hence, now that the area is slowly being populated, the new residents should be empowered to initiate self-determined signifying practices for the creation of identities of place. Yet, this demands undetermined spaces, as well as the authorization to appropriate these spaces for the expression of cultural difference. The question is, whether this is still possible in the already much determined development process. In any case, Roland Rainer's early vision of creating an open urbanity with undefined spaces that can constantly be re-interpreted will not be realized – particularly due to the converse claims made by the investors.[39] Nevertheless, some of the cultural events at least opened up the chance to establish an idea of cultural processes as expressions of a new urbanity and difference.[40] Yet, this doesn't owe much to a successful planning approach, but to the engagement, openness and instinct of individual actors with decision-making power in Aspern's development.

Consequently, the culture-led processes realized as part of the branding strategy seem to tackle mostly a global capitalist class of business investors and a new creative, cosmopolitan middle-class of wealthy, well-educated and high-skilled dwellers. But at the same time, numbers show that in-migration to Vienna, which has become the main legitimizing argument for realizing Seestadt Aspern development in recent years, is not determined by this group of people (Statistik Austria, 2010; Kohlbacher & Reeger, 2011). While culture-led imaging

---

37 Interview with Josef Lueger, former planner at wien 3420 Aspern Development AG; interview with Daniel Aschwanden, performing artist from the artist collective content.associates.
38 Interview with Daniel Aschwanden, performing artist from the artist collective content.associates.
39 Interview with Josef Lueger, former planner at wien 3420 Aspern Development AG.
40 Ibid.

was on top of the development agenda until 2013, the project so far largely passes over urgent questions in Vienna's cultural development, particularly those of an aging society, increasing value diversity due to constant in-migration, and a growing underprivileged class that demands affordable infrastructures and inclusive measures. Hence, the current materializations of urban cultural visions are part of a culturalization strategy for safeguarding the economic benefits of property owners and investors.

After its discursive and material analysis, the project cannot convince that it will take the increasing societal diversity of globalizing Vienna serious enough. Instead, culture is utilized merely as a communicative tool for creating acceptance and attention by promoting a diversity that had never been the primary development goal of Aspern. Instead, the goal is to use the potential of predicted urban growth for capitalizing on an urbanization process by employing so far marginal economic objectives in Vienna's urban development policies. The number of material planning interventions that preceded the current construction of buildings (e.g. the underground expansion, the creation of public spaces, and the launch of aspern IQ) must hence be read as instruments to safeguard investments from both future dwellers and market actors. The material cultural processes, in this regard, are only meant to facilitate an urban expansion project that has become too big to fail for the city.

Thus, the new materiality of place in Seestadt Aspern needs to be understood as a process of culturalization for capitalization. While the discursive path-shaping of the area supported the de-stigmatization of urban expansion projects in Vienna, it simultaneously constructed a simplistic picture of culture's role in planning, which has reduced the distinct qualities of place to unique selling propositions for a hegemonic economic project. While the demands for basic amenities of a growing population are an important argument for the project's realization, the first practical considerations circled around the construction of a brand that would safeguard surplus value for those who invested in the large-scale urbanization project. Hence, Seestadt Aspern might become a good practice of urban expansion in the contemporary European city as concerns the important planning objectives of efficiency, consensus, civic participation, and even social orientation in some regard. But it cannot make a good example of planning for cultural development, as it never allowed for more than one commodity culture to evolve.

Brunnenviertel

Capitalizing on cultural diversity

DEVELOPMENT BACKGROUND

Brunnenviertel is an urban neighborhood in Vienna's 16th district, Ottakring. It is located in the Northwest of the city, close to the Gürtel, the city's outer ring and most important transport route. Brunnenviertel's core are the pedestrian area around Yppenplatz, a pivotal public space and meeting place in this part of the city, and the neighboring Brunnenmarkt, one of Europe's biggest street markets and the neighborhood's lively commercial center (Rode et al., 2010).

Most areas surrounding the Gürtel are shaped by a distinct building pattern, the perimeter blocks, which were constructed during the Gründerzeit, as Vienna was determined by industrialization and a fast growing population. These Gründerzeit structures allowed for population densities that are still today co-determinant of the urban character of these parts of the city. Yet, their age and poor facilitation – a large share of the housing stock is more than 100 years old – effectuated in a down-cycle of the neighborhoods close to the Gürtel and their stigmatization as poor, run-down no-go areas of Vienna (ibid.). The City of Vienna became aware of these unsatisfying developments in the early 1970s, and thus created the legal basis for large-scale urban renewal projects.

In 1974, one of the first Viennese Urban Renewal Offices ("Gebietsbetreuung") is launched in the Wichtelgasse in Ottakring in order to realize the city's just issued soft urban renewal strategy to increase the quality of the district's housing substance.[1] Yet, these housing structural interventions are the only attempt to regenerate an area that has long been forgotten by a planning agenda oriented largely at the city center.

Only in the 1990s, the need to develop a comprehensive strategy for the future of Brunnenviertel and other neighborhoods close to the Gürtel is voiced

---

1   Interview with Kurt Smetana, head of the Urban Renewal Office Ottakring.

again. It is due to Austria's EU accession at hand that the city of Vienna is awarded with the funding of a project that aims at regenerating the Gürtel and its surroundings – "URBAN. Wien – Gürtel plus". Hence, from 1995 to 2001, the western parts of the Gürtel are regenerated on multiple levels. The Otto Wagner designed monumental urban railway construction running through the middle of the boulevard is revived as a hotspot of Vienna's young urban nightlife, squares and other infrastructures around the Gürtel zone are renewed, and working groups discuss the development challenges and potentials of the urban quarters surrounding the Gürtel. In the course of the project, Yppenplatz, a pivotal public square within Brunnenviertel, is regenerated as well (Municipal Department 18, 2012c), making Brunnenviertel a reviving urban quarter only due to the notable physical makeover of public infrastructures.

The material cultural preconditions to Brunnenviertel's more recent transformation can be considered decisive in both the material transformation and discursive re-interpretation of the neighborhood (Rode et al., 2010; Suitner, 2010). Compared to Vienna's average, Brunnenviertel is since long determined by a specific population and employment structure. In the 1990s, comparably low rents attract particularly a low income population with an above average share of (mostly Turkish) migrants and typical urban pioneers, i.e. students and artists. The otherwise run-down commercial structures and weak local economy are slowly revived upon the engagement of these new groups of dwellers. The quarter is henceforth characterized by an unusual socio-cultural diversity for Viennese conditions, which first reflects in a diversified ownership and product range of stores and market stands at Brunnenmarkt with an obvious influence of the Turkish minority (Rode et al., 2010). This causes crass periphrases of the neighborhood as *"Little Istanbul"*[2], which fuel the stigmatization of Brunnenviertel in its outward appearance until the late 2000s.

On the other hand, the evident density of artist dwellings and studios in the area prompt local cultural actors to engage in networking activities to use this newfound potential. The most famous one is Ula Schneider's attempt to start a local art festival – "Soho In Ottakring" – which is first held in spring 1999. Its success as attractor of audiences from all over Vienna leads to its annual continuation as a 14-days art festival each spring until 2012. The event causes huge mediatic attention and makes "Soho" the buzz word referred to in an arising discourse of Brunnenviertel's regeneration and re-interpretation from a no-go area to Vienna's up-and-coming neighborhood (Suitner, 2010).

---

2 Cf. "Schlafen oder auf Istanbul schauen" (Der Standard, July 5, 2005; author's translation).

Hence, Brunnenviertel is widely perceived as an area shaped by a number of cultural processes – from the unique street market that enlivens the neighborhood day by day, or the socio-economic and socio-cultural diversity of a local population that becomes visible in public space, to the art-led events that not only add to a functioning local economy, but communicate a distinct image of place to an outward audience.

In the year 2000 and after the finalization of the EU project around Gürtel, Kaitna/Smetana architects take over the Urban Renewal Office in Ottakring to continue a slightly adapted urban renewal initiative in and around Brunnenviertel. Besides further renewal of the local housing stock, the Urban Renewal Offices have particularly become service centers for a local population, information and networking platforms, and initiators of diverse community activities.[3] Yet, the focus of financial contributions is still on carrying on with the city's successful soft urban renewal model. From 2001 until today, 18 residential houses were renewed and modernized in Brunnenviertel with the City of Vienna subsidizing the projects with € 12,7 million (Municipal Department 25, n.d.a). Nevertheless, the City of Vienna enforces its planning efforts in this part of the city with the initiation of another EU-funded project – a huge local citizen participation process that should last five years from October 2002, and which should bring about a number of further, mostly infrastructural measures within the area[4] (Municipal Department 21A, 2009; Municipal Department 18, 2012c). Also in 2002, the target area Gürtel is initiated by the City of Vienna as a sequel to "URBAN. Wien – Gürtel plus". It is a continuation of the new comprehensive planning approach for a distinct urban quarter delimited upon similar structures and development challenges. And, target area Gürtel is also the prototype of the 13 target areas defined in the 2005 issued Urban Development Plan of Vienna (Municipal Department 18, 2005; Rode et al., 2010). Hence, throughout the years, the western Gürtel – and Brunnenviertel in particular – have become important grounds for Vienna's planning as forerunners of a new urban development approach. And, they moved to the center of attention in public planning discourses due to the recurrent initiatives revolving around this part of the city and the resulting material and symbolic transformations.

The City of Vienna's efforts to accompany the transformation process at Brunnenviertel are laid down in the distinct report on the target area Gürtel (Municipal Department 18, 2012c). It documents the whole spectrum of projects realized in and around the Gürtel area within the past almost 20 years, from the

---

3   Ibid.
4   Interview with Hans Staud, owner of Brunnenviertel-based company Staud's.

EU-funded re-vitalization project to one of Vienna's biggest citizen participation processes ever. The report unhides the strong political commitment to a participatory approach in regenerating this part of the city. In this regard, it largely refers to Vienna's past planning-cultural achievements ("Wiener Modell") and the resulting responsibilities for today's planning (ibid.: 118). This leaves no doubt about the continuation of a planning model shaped by traditional government objectives, which for the case of Vienna are largely determined by the values of a Social Democratic planning ideology and a strong local state (Novy et al., 2001; Pirhofer & Stimmer, 2007; Posova & Sykora, 2011). At the same time, the grassroots art-led event of Soho In Ottakring and related local initiatives empowered by the Urban Renewal Office point to a different interpretation of planning as bottom-up processes of neighborhood transformation. This duality is characteristic of recent neighborhood transformation in Vienna and so conspicuously materializes in Brunnenviertel that it forms a great example of analyzing the contest over space in culture-led place transformation.

Brunnenviertel is the culturally most diverse of all three case studies, which is of course due to its dense urban structure and the related social mixing. This makes it a challenging planning object, as the most diverse interests from all spheres of society – state, market, and civil society – constantly collide in attempts to transform it. At the same time, these flexible structures, the cultural diversity and an apparently active and empowered civil society are what makes Brunnenviertel a transformation process full of potentials for a culturized approach to planning. Regarding the material preconditions, the neighborhood might even become a role model of how difference can contribute to social innovation, how cultural expression and art-led projects can foster inclusion, and how planning can add to a city's cultural development at least on the small scale. On the other hand, its re-interpretation and remaking *"from Ghetto to Grätzel"*[5] prompts desires of utilizing the positive drive of regeneration for individual economic or political benefits.

Hence, one of the important questions for the current development of Brunnenviertel is, whether it can be considered a self-determined process of transition in a mixed neighborhood – with all positive and negative implications from destigmatization to gentrification – or, whether it must be viewed as an example of the active culturalization of urban life in metropolitan Vienna. Broadly speaking, I ask if the transformed materialities of Brunnenviertel can be considered as the continuation of a well-functioning bottom-up neighborhood development process for a diverse population, or if individual interests succeed upon the material-

---

5   Cf. interview with Hans Staud, owner of Brunnenviertel-based company Staud's.

ization of different cultural imaginaries? The analysis of potential processes of Cultural Imagineering in the following sections is supposed to shed light on this question.

THE DISCURSIVE CONSTRUCTION OF BRUNNENVIERTEL

Fig. 15: Top-10 terms per year in Brunnenviertel mediatic discourse

The analysis of frequently appearing terms in the place-specific discourse already shows the prevalent thematic orientation of the Brunnenviertel discourse within the past years (cf. Fig. 15).[6] It unhides the great influence of two distinct cultural projects on the place-related debate – the art-led neighborhood festival Soho In Ottakring, and the more recently launched "Brunnenpassage", a community arts project initiated by Caritas, a traditional Austrian NGO affiliated to the Catholic Church. These two are central to the discourse on the quarter, while other, more typical topics in the context of neighborhood transformation, such as local economy, real-estate development, or integration, are rather subordinate. Interestingly, these two art-led projects and the place transformation are discussed in close relation to particular spatial scales of the city – the Grätzel (i.e. neighborhood), the urban quarter, and the district Ottakring. This already implies two important points: first, it shows that in the case of Brunnenviertel these projects are very much influential of the mediatic perception of a neighborhood in transition, and second, it already points to a distinct cultural imaginary, in which local art-led processes are considered as constitutive of the meaning of place. At

---

6   The results presented in this section are based on 133 place-specific media texts covering the period from January 01, 2005 to May 13, 2013.

the same time, other topics that shape the neighborhood's development, such as migration and integration, housing, and gentrification are less often referred to in discourse.

What is important to be highlighted concerning Brunnenviertel's re-interpretation is that the discourse forming actors are to a large degree local actors who work and live in this part of the city. Herewith, image and identity constructions are largely based upon local attitudes and value constructs, and not – as in the other two case studies – based on external attributions. Furthermore, the overall number of actors and diversity of actor groups appearing in discourse is much higher than in the other two case studies, pointing at a more diverse and more balanced representation of individual values and urban cultural development visions. As Fig. 16 shows, also NGO-representatives and civil society actors emerge occasionally in discourse. And, many of the decisive discourse forming actors are also part of a local population and thereby implicitly represent also civil society interests. Hence, it can be stated that the debate is largely local, characterized by actor diversity and no dominant relations between individual actors. Instead, those shaping the place-specific discourse basically constitute a representative group of the actors actually involved in material place transformation. Overall, Brunnenviertel mediatic discourse is less of an elite debate than Karlsplatz and Seestadt Aspern transformation, which is particularly reflected by the non-institutionalization of a large number of actors appearing in the mediatic debate. State-affiliated institutions and planning administration representatives hardly ever appear. Instead, more market actors and external experts shape the place-specific debate, forming a different picture of the politics of planning with culture than the other two case studies did. Opinion leaders and central discourse forming actors have varying institutional affiliations and stand in for diverse development issues, which is another decisive difference in comparison with the prior cases analyzed. The number of central actors is also more diverse. Yet, sort of a local urban development coalition can be highlighted that consists of actors equipped with both discursive and material power over space. This group includes a number of political representatives, most notably the district chairperson Franz Prokop (SPÖ), Ula Schneider from Soho In Ottakring, Hans Staud, owner of a long-established, locally based company ("Staud's"), and representatives of Brunnenpassage. This group of actors represents different spheres of urban life, creating a balanced discursive construction of cultural Brunnenviertel. Even more importantly, the majority is local actors with an internal view on place-specific processes.

Fig. 16: Theme-based mapping of actors in Brunnenviertel discourse

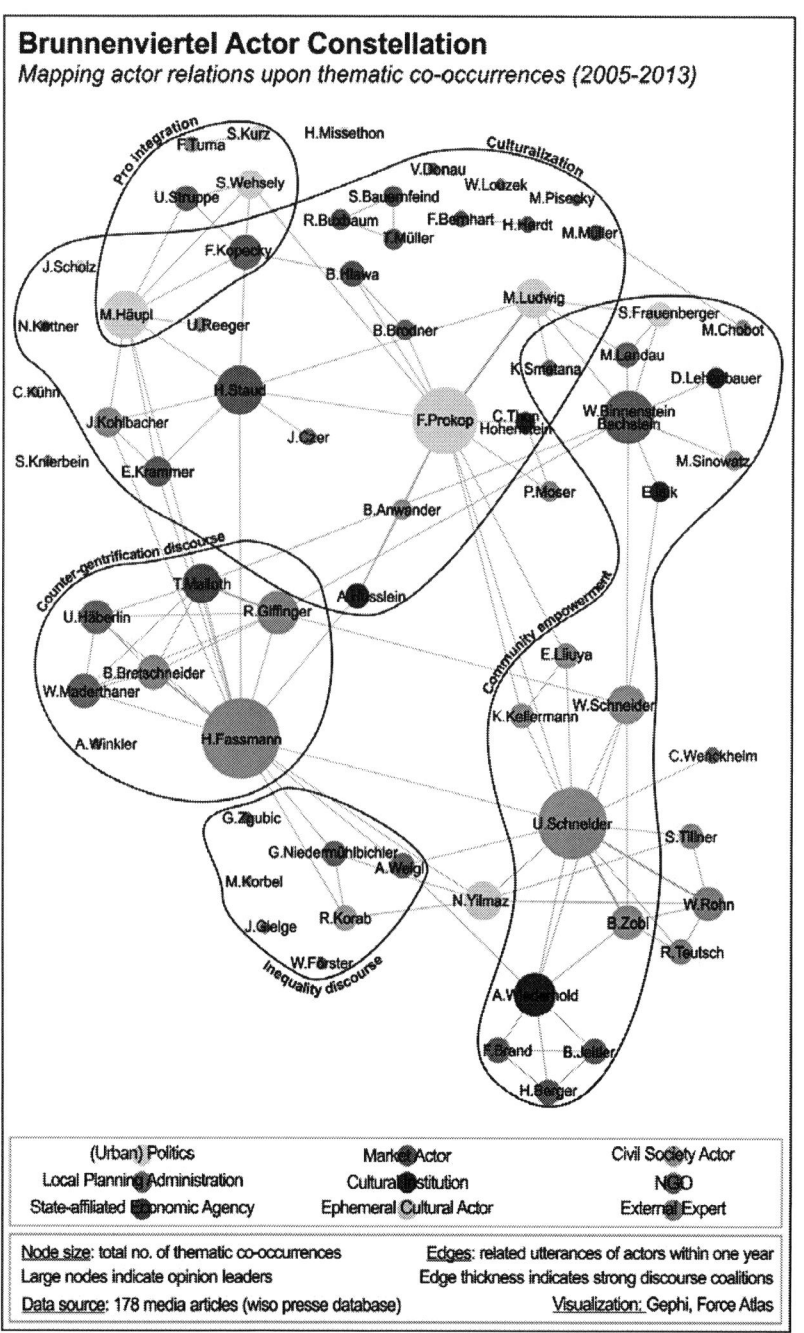

The only exception is Heinz Fassmann, professor of geography and designated expert on migration and ethnic segregation from the University of Vienna. His frequent appearances in discourse on questions of migration, integration and segregation in the context of Brunnenviertel transformation assign him with a pivotal position in the discursive actor network, raising the general awareness for migration and integration as important topics in the whole place transformation debate.

Compared with the above case studies, the thematic actor distribution in Brunnenviertel discourse looks way different (cf. Fig. 17). The thematic focus is largely on four topics: a fluctuating physical planning debate on infrastructures, i.e. housing, mobility and urban design, a very much expert-led discussion on the neighborhood's socio-economic development, an obviously contested migration/integration discourse, and a very determinant debate on the place-specific cultural context shaped by a variety of cultural actors. Other thematic fields are touched upon only sporadically and rather in relation to one of the discourse-determinant fields, for instance references to public space, a distinct local economy, or a discourse on community development. Interestingly, place image and identity appear in discourse in 2009 as a new determinant topic. This field is largely discussed by cultural and market actors with two clearly oppositional claims. While market actors emphasize the image value of Brunnenviertel, cultural actors point at the identity forming forces of distinct local cultural processes – a contest reflecting also in the dominant cultural imaginary of Brunnenviertel, as I am still going to show.

Actors from the political sphere often co-occur in discourse with planning administration representatives and external urban development experts, meaning they refer to similar topics at the same time. Taking into account the supposed objectivity assigned to the latter two, this co-occurrence might be an indication of a strategy of conflict avoidance, which is typical of Vienna's politics of planning (Novy et al., 2001). Hence, conflictive topics such as segregation, displacement, or inequality and exclusion are discussed rather unemotional, yet still not always fact-based. Anyhow, Brunnenviertel discourse is a good example of how actor groups largely stay within the frame of their actual qualified expertise. Planning experts from research and practice largely appear in the context of planning-related topics, market actors determine market-related thematic fields, while non-institutionalized cultural and civil society actors make most of their statements on local community-related concerns. Only urban politics and external experts vary largely across the thematic spectrum of place transformation, while only few of them are central to the overall place-specific discourse.

Fig. 17: Visualizing the chronology of Brunnenviertel discourse

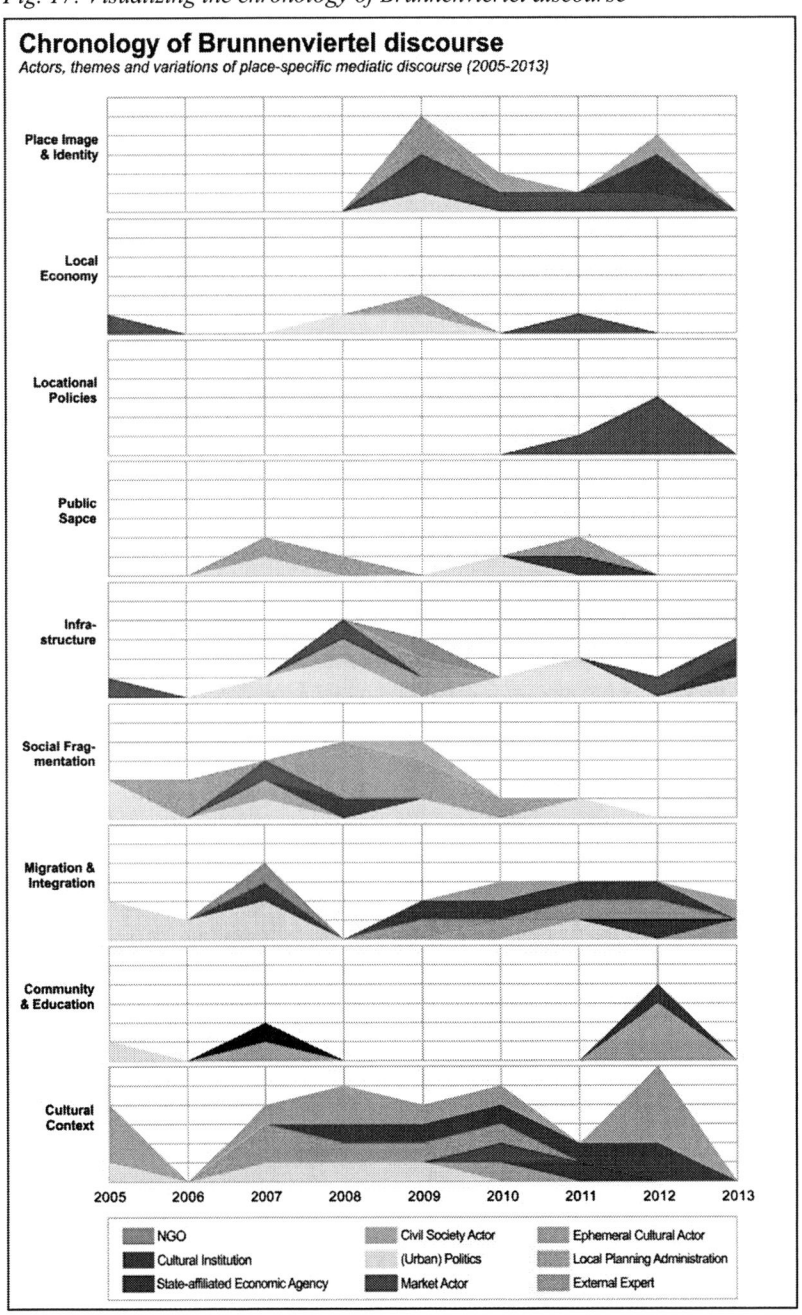

Overall, Brunnenviertel discourse is largely consolidated. Actors from the same actor group revolve around very clearly bounded thematic fields. Although this indicates the stabilization of an otherwise very dynamic urban transformation process, the debate between profit-oriented real-estate development and housing as a public infrastructure will still be an important line of conflict in the future development of this urban quarter. And in this context, the recently emphasized triad of place-specific culture, image, and real-estate development as a distinct cultural imaginary in the making will play a decisive role.

As is obvious, the quarter's material development challenges – a large share of migrants among the total population and a low quality housing stock – are determinant of the discourse from the very beginning. Representatives from the political administrative system thus frame Brunnenviertel's wished-for socio-economic development path very early, discursively determining its future material planning as a mixed urban neighborhood. Herewith, they carry on the longstanding ideological goal of social mixing and public infrastructure provision in Vienna's politics of planning (Pirhofer & Stimmer, 2007). Yet, statements also unhide the unreflected attempt of hindering residential segregation, which is also largely legitimized upon Vienna's previous urban planning strategy.[7] This already indicates the influence of a hegemonic traditional Social Democratic planning-political ideology, which is discursively endowed with additional power in Brunnenviertel transformation. CDA also reveals the importance of a successful regeneration of Brunnenviertel for Vienna's Social Democratic Party. As part of Ottakring, the homestead of Vienna's Social Democratic movement, Brunnenviertel's re-interpretation and physical renewal are increasingly understood as symbols of a not yet anachronistic planning ideology that dominates Vienna's urban development.[8]

Brunnenviertel discourse integrates not only Vienna's planning elites, but a local population of dwellers and entrepreneurs, political and cultural actors as well. In this regard, the discourse allows for a very open and positively connoted debate on otherwise very emotionally discussed topics such as migration, integration and ethnic economies. This bottom-up framing of Brunnenviertel is determinant of the whole future discourse, which considers cultural diversity not as a challenge, but as a local development potential. This attitude is repeatedly supported by a few very powerful actors in Vienna's politics of planning, such as the city's mayor, Michael Häupl (SPÖ):

---

7   Cf. "Alles neu in 'Klein Istanbul'" (Neue Kronen-Zeitung, April 22, 2005).
8   Cf. "Neuer Frühling für den Brunnenmarkt" (Kurier, March 23, 2005); interview with Ula Schneider and Beatrix Zobl from the association Soho In Ottakring.

"Areas like Brunnenmarkt with a higher concentration of foreigners have not become parallel societies but multi-cultural centers that are an enrichment to the city."[9]

Interestingly, urban transformation in Brunnenviertel is often legitimized upon the large share of migrants in the neighborhood. As explained above, ethnic segregation is per se considered as a negative condition. Hence, the target audience of planning interventions in Brunnenviertel is thus solely an Austrian population:

"Young families shall be attracted to the neighborhood so that the mix of nationalities is not too one-sided."[10]

Such statements enforce also the stereotypical differentiation between poor migrants and a wealthy local population – a distinction utilized in more recent culturalization strategies, too.[11]

From 2006 on, the obvious material transformations of the quarter cause an increased mediatic debate on negative implications of the neighborhood regeneration, first and foremost linked to the gentrification matter. In this regard, *"Vienna is different"* becomes the common phrase referred to and the legitimizing strategy to mute any oppositional voices in the place transformation process. Collectively, local planners, politicians, and external experts alike largely neglect the suspicion of displacement of prior (migrant) dwellers due to Vienna's particular legal housing regulations and urban development traditions.[12] Yet, these references to Vienna's planning as an unswayable, socially responsible system legitimize almost any planning approach. These attributions also allow for a different discourse to rise in 2009/10, which is led by a variety of representatives from the real estate sector. They designate Brunnenviertel as an up-

---

9 "Unsere Stadt hat kein Problem mit Integration" (Die Presse, May 17, 2005; original quote from mayor Michael Häupl, author's translation).
10 "Alles neu in 'Klein Istanbul'" (Neue Kronen-Zeitung, April 22, 2005; original quote from Sonja Wehsely, city councilor of integration (SPÖ), author's translation).
11 Cf. "Wenn Sie als Museumsdirektorin vom Belvedere über Wien blicken, ..." (Kleine Zeitung, August 30, 2009).
12 Cf. "Bobo-Grätzel under Construction" (Der Standard, April 22, 2006); "Niederer Stadtadel" (Falter, August 13, 2008), "Inselbewohner mit Stadtadresse" (Die Presse, October 07, 2009); interview with Kurt Smetana, head of the Urban Renewal Office Ottakring.

and-coming neighborhood, enforcing a culturalization strategy upon the neighborhood's diverse cultural representations without any discursive opposition.[13]

Within all that, the discourse on culture and its role in Brunnenviertel's transformation stays broad. This is largely due to the cultural actors' frequent discursive appearance, who are thus as central to the discourse as holders of a powerful political office. They highlight the relevance of a culturized view on urban development by emphasizing culture's role in integration efforts, local networking activities, community building, and empowerment. Thereby, the dominant interpretation of culture draws clear links to planning by highlighting urban development as transcultural processes and a question of multi-ethnicity, integration and inclusion.[14] The self-reflection and local embeddedness of these cultural actors are decisive for the constant place-based re-formulation of culture-led processes in this regard. It allows them to take up the ever changing contextual challenges of an urban neighborhood in transition. In this regard, the efforts of Soho In Ottakring are supported and their claims even broadened by the appearance of the Brunnenpassage as a second cultural project to combine arts and integration at Brunnenviertel. Together with diverse sporadically appearing actors from the political-administrative system and a number of urbanists, they further promote a positively connoted discourse of cultural diversity as an urban quality.[15] Interestingly, this largely rests upon two encouraging arguments: first, Vienna's wished-for role as a Central European metropolis, which understandably demands in-migration and, hence, cultural diversity, and second, references to the city's past as melting pot in the Austro-Hungarian Empire. Hence, migration is also largely discussed with a positive tone, although being biased by stereotypes, which rather indicate the discursive construction of a culturalized society at Brunnenviertel.[16] The latter is particularly evident since 2009/10, as the distinct culture of place is increasingly re-interpreted into a USP, with ethnic diversity being reduced to food cultures, a culture of consumption, and an image for diverse capitalist accumulation strategies.

The increasing understanding of cities as constant processes of change appears more than once in Brunnenviertel discourse since 2010, constituting an

---

13 Cf. "Investieren im richtigen Grätzel" (Der Standard, November 03, 2012).
14 Cf. "Multikulti ist Vergangenheit" (Der Standard, November 22, 2005); "Brunnenmarktviertel wird zu einer riesigen Bühne" (WirtschaftsBlatt, May 24, 2005).
15 Cf. "Inselbewohner mit Stadtadresse" (Die Presse, October 07, 2009).
16 Cf. "Die neue Republik Bionade" (Die ZEIT, October 22, 2009); "Die Vielfalt als Lebensgefühl ..." (Kronen Zeitung, February 21, 2013); interview with Hans Staud, owner of Brunnenviertel-based company Staud's.

implicit legitimation of its top-down regeneration. Together with repeated claims that Vienna is different in all respects, particularly as concerns its socially oriented planning culture, this again allows for an undisputed continuation of the running transformation process. Although affordability problems and socio-economic inequalities also increasingly appear in Vienna's planning discourse after 2008 and with distinct references to Brunnenviertel as a case study, local elites and urbanists dispel any doubts about Brunnenviertel's recent development path and confirm the undisputed strength of a socially oriented local state in Vienna's planning.[17] Yet, since 2011, representatives of the real estate sector begin to metaphorically flood the place-specific discourse, promoting a more differentiated economic assessment of Vienna's urban neighborhoods – Brunnenviertel being an often cited example in this regard. The so-called micro-location ("Mikrolage") is introduced to the planning discourse as a discursive strategy to stimulate a greater differentiation of prices on the Viennese housing market.[18] This is particularly interesting, as it seems to suit the dominant notion of place-based planning very well. Neighborhood branding strategies building upon ethnic diversity, art-led aestheticization, and other cultural transformation processes are becoming pivotal in this context. But this rising debate is not just an indication of an increasing focus on small-scale neighborhoods in the material development of the city. It is another argument for the continuation of emerging accumulation strategies in Brunnenviertel in the coming years, and a sign of the enforcement of a strategy towards unequal diversity in Vienna's development (Novy, 2011).

As concerns the construction of a cultural imaginary for Brunnenviertel, critical discourse analysis revealed a distinct group of actors as determinant of the formation of "Cultural Brunnenviertel". This group is characterized by just a few locally based actors who shape the development context, image, and distinct culture of place. Their varying individual backgrounds and particular interests in place transformation effectuate in the construction of a broad cultural imaginary. And, this imaginary is supported by a number of adjacent, yet only sporadically appearing powerful actors from the political sphere, who recurrently explain Brunnenviertel's positive re-interpretation with the continuing prosecution of Vienna's traditional planning-ideological objectives. Culture, in this regard, is thus largely referred to as the material local art-led processes that employ an art-as-public-space approach, hence functioning as identity-forming forces, community platforms, and socio-political instruments of critique. Building upon a place-

---

17 Cf. "Wiener Blut mischt sich stets neu" (Wiener Zeitung, September 17, 2010); "Im Brunnenviertel bleiben Mieten leistbar" (Kurier, February 18, 2013).
18 Cf. "Anvisiert: Bezirke mit Potenzial" (Die Presse, November 10, 2011).

based approach, these processes also serve as representation instruments of the "other cultures" of Brunnenviertel, thereby expanding the culture discourse to place-specific aspects of migration and social fragmentation. Hence, a very distinct socio-political culture-led approach to community building influences the place-related discourse from the very beginning. As a consequence, only actors engaged in these or similarly oriented material transformative processes were able to enter Brunnenviertel discourse, for example Ula Schneider (Soho In Ottakring), Hans Staud (Staud's), or Anne Wiederhold (Brunnenpassage).

This distinct cultural imaginary affects also the coming materializations, as the next section is going to show. Its place-based character was even able to push the re-interpretation of the neighborhood as a whole into a more positive direction. Consequently, this also increased the pressure on Brunnenviertel transformation, which let a cultural counter-imaginary appear in discourse in 2009/10. This imaginary clearly builds upon a diametrically opposed interpretation of culture's role in urban development as an agent of change in a capitalist re-urbanization strategy. Inequality, poverty and exclusion are increasingly replaced from that discourse, whereas lifestyle diversity, ethnic local economies and the variety of food cultures appear instead as characteristics of "Cultural Brunnenviertel". These almost stereotypical place images serve the newly emerging accumulation strategies upon the culturalization of Brunnenviertel's distinct cultural qualities. Hence, its imaginary and the current and future materializations are determined by a contest between culturized approaches to self-determined and empowering place transformation upon local identities and cultural difference, and capitalist regeneration claims upon the shoulders of a culturalized place image.

MATERIALIZATIONS OF THE CULTURAL IMAGINARY

- **From "Soho" to "Brunnenpassage": the institutionalization of community and diversity**: The art-led event Soho In Ottakring is inseparably linked to Brunnenviertel discourse right from the start. Although it had originally been conceptualized just as a networking initiative for local artists, its place-based artistic approach employed a broad cultural view, which had an undeniable influence on the positive perception and transformed outward image of place (Suitner, 2010). In the coming years, these positive connotations resonated in discourse. The discursive framing sketched Brunnenviertel as an exceptional neighborhood, pointing at a unique mixture of ethnic diversity, art-led events and urban renewal as this area's distinct cultural quality. This discursive construction of place increased the pressure on developing Brunnenviertel as a typical culture-led urban regeneration project. Yet, as it was the essence of Soho In Ottakring's approach to integrate recent socio-political and place-specific transformations in its annual program, the development pressure and its implications were always materially countered by a high-publicity critical involvement with these matters. Hence, the increasingly contested urban development discourse very much influenced the artistic work of Soho In Ottakring as a characteristic material process at Brunnenviertel. And, the project itself was a key influencing factor in the non-materialization of certain wished-for accumulation strategies.[19] Thus, the place-related cultural discourse largely continued framing a culturized vision of place. And with the launch of Brunnenpassage in a vacant market building at Yppenplatz in June 2007, this dominant interpretation of culture materialized in a second art-led project – only this time as a permanent process with a constant thematic focus on community arts and the facilitation of accessibility of art for migrants (KunstSozialRaum Brunnenpassage, n.d.). The vacant market building it uses today was even under consideration for housing a mall.[20] But the dominant cultural imaginary of place allowed for the materialization of a non-profit, community-oriented integration project at the heart of the urban neighborhood instead. Hence, the initiation of Brunnenpassage at just this place of the city is not a coincidence.[21] Quite the opposite. It can be considered as the targeted institutionalization of a civil society attempt of community building in Brunnenviertel. Initiated by Caritas, a renowned Austrian NGO affiliated to the Catholic Church, Brunnenpassage is the ultimate establishment of an imaginary promoting identity and difference as mutually dependent qualities of community. Its thematic orientation perfectly fits this dominant place-specific imaginary. One might reasonably ask why integration and the facilitation of access to art for migrants is a specific challenge for this part of the city – it sure has the same relevance in other Viennese neighborhoods with similar shares of a migrant population. But it was the hegemonic influence of Brunnenviertel's cultural imaginary, which let the realization of this project at just this place seem only logical.

---

19 Interview with Ula Schneider and Beatrix Zobl from the association Soho In Ottakring.
20 Interview with Hans Staud, owner of Brunnenviertel-based company Staud's; interview with Kurt Smetana, head of the Urban Renewal Office Ottakring.
21 Interview with Ula Schneider and Beatrix Zobl from the association Soho In Ottakring; interview with Hans Staud, owner of Brunnenviertel-based company Staud's; interview with Kurt Smetana, head of the Urban Renewal Office Ottakring.

- **Urban regeneration upon hegemonic planning-political ideology and the representation of difference**: Brunnenviertel is a remarkable case study of urban renewal in Vienna. Within little more than one decade, the neighborhood around Brunnenmarkt and Yppenplatz went through multiple phases of physical regeneration. As explained above already, the manifold planning initiatives must be viewed in the context of a committed local political effort to establish a symbol of effective Social Democratic urban politics and functioning integration with Brunnenviertel. This effort is repeatedly placed in discourse by the respective political actors, such as mayor Michael Häupl (SPÖ), who clarifies, *"Our city has no integration problem."*[22], or the city councilor of housing, Michael Ludwig (SPÖ), who recently states, *"Rents will remain to be affordable in Brunnenviertel."*[23] These statements all frame Brunnenviertel as a functioning transformation process and link the supposed success to the distinct Social Democratic urban development interventions. Skillfully, they also incorporate the civic art-led initiatives evolving at about the same time into the discursive construction of this planning model and their cultural vision of place.[24] While the bottom-up cultural processes function as counter-hegemonic cultural expressions of difference, they are (to some degree surprisingly) supported by the political sphere. At the same time though, politicians promote a different, top-down oriented approach to planning. Yet, the distinct combination of a strong and caring local state with the allowance of representations of difference constructs a cultural imaginary of place that is able of legitimizing the neighborhood's intense physical transformations thereafter. Consequently, the variety of planning interventions, ranging from traffic calming and market revitalization to public space development and renewal of the local housing stock (Grüne Ottakring, 2007; Municipal Department 25, n.d.b), are all based on a hegemonic planning cultural construction of a strong, welfare-oriented state, blended with a place-specific cultural imaginary of self-determined development and difference.

---

22 "Unsere Stadt hat kein Integrationsproblem" (Die Presse, May 17, 2006; author's translation).

23 "Im Brunnenviertel bleiben Mieten leistbar" (Kurier, February 18, 2013; author's translation).

24 Cf. "'Gut leben ohne nix' auf dem Soho-Festival" (Wiener Zeitung, May 14, 2009).

- **From "No-Go-Area"[25] to "Little Istanbul"[26] – the commodification of diversity**: The above discussion of the cultural imaginary of Brunnenviertel revealed an increasing contest between two opposing interpretations and utilizations of cultural diversity in recent years. While the variety of local actors appearing in discourse framed a very broad picture of the culture of place as *cultures*, certain market actors increasingly enforce a counter-imaginary by promoting a culturalization strategy of Brunnenviertel. It is particularly real estate developers, who attempt to re-interpret the place-specific imaginary of ethnic and lifestyle diversity into a marketable image for a well-off middle-class that is supposedly attracted by such factors. Advertisements for *"Vienna's new melting pot of the Nations"* (JP Immobilien, 2012: 18) or *"Living in Soho"* ("Wohnen in Soho"; cf. Suitner, 2010) are the obvious instruments in an accumulation strategy that builds upon a different imaginary, where culture is a commodity and agent of change for constructing exclusive cultural grounds. It can't be verified that this evolving imaginary's materialization expresses in a transformed local population, as relevant socio-economic data couldn't be acquired. Yet, the recent beautification of public spaces and the increasing allocation of restaurants representing food cultures that are not as largely, if at all, represented by the ethnicity of a local population indicate also the political will to actively construct a diversity that serves as a selling point in the capitalist regeneration of Brunnenviertel. This increasing commodification of diversity is also recognized and harshly criticized by those cultural actors who initiated a broad culture discourse upon the bottom-up art-led process of Soho In Ottakring. Development pressure and unsatisfying institutional support for civic practices effectuate in the emigration of the festival.[27] Hence, it can be concluded that Brunnenviertel discourse enforced a turn from ephemeral cultural activities as broad, yet versatile socio-political instruments to institutionalized projects tackling single policy areas. This turn goes hand in hand with a shift from self-determined bottom-up neighborhood transformation to a top-down imposed political strategy in planning. Consequently, particular economic interests were increasingly able to enter the discourse and formulate a cultural construction that alienates diversity, utilizing it in capitalist urban development approaches.

---

25 Cf. "Zehnmal Soho in Ottakring" (Wiener Zeitung, May 09, 2008; original quote from Beatrix Zobl from the association Soho In Ottakring).
26 Cf. "Alles neu in 'Klein Istanbul'" (Neue Kronen Zeitung, April 22, 2005).
27 Interview with Ula Schneider and Beatrix Zobl from the association Soho In Ottakring.

TRANSFORMATION AS HEGEMONIC MATERIAL PRACTICE?

The transformed materiality of cultural Brunnenviertel is a special case in Vienna's Cultural Imagineering. At the time being, the strategies of three different actor groups collide in place transformation, all employing a slightly different approach to culture and its role for development. First, a civil-society-determined, empowered approach to culture as art-led socio-political critique, tool for society building, and signifying practice shaped the transforming neighborhood. While this largely influenced the cognitive re-interpretation of Brunnenviertel in the first run, i.e. changing its outward perception, it also paved the way for what I referred to above as the institutionalization of community and diversity. The materializations to follow, from Brunnenpassage to Kulturkuppelfest, can be considered as the direct consequence of a strategy aiming at the representation of a local cultural economy and inclusive neighborhood development.[28]

This, of course, is closely related to the obvious and overly ambitious state-led planning interventions to be observed in the past two decades of this area's transformation. The local state's responsibility towards diverse neighborhoods like Brunnenviertel is repeatedly linked to its past socially oriented planning and history as European melting pot. Yet, these arguments of course legitimize top-down planning interventions, as they emphasize the need for a strong state in Vienna's neighborhood transformation processes. This allows for getting the intense physical neighborhood regenerations described above under way and transforming Brunnenviertel into a symbol of functioning Social Democratic politics of planning in Vienna. The expended intense political effort on regenerating Brunnenviertel gets evident not just from the multiple aestheticizations of public space, or the renewal of street market infrastructures. The exceptional financial contributions to the renewal of the local housing stock (Grüne Ottakring, 2007) and the public subsidies allocated to Soho In Ottakring and Brunnenpassage (Municipal Department 7, 2008 and other Art & Culture Reports) uncover the undoubted will to transform the neighborhood into a socially and economically functioning urban quarter.[29] And, the hegemony of this ideological project gets evident from the collective and undoubted support it receives not only from local Social Democratic politicians, but from other actors alike. Hence, the diverse

---

28 Cf. interview with Hans Staud, owner of Brunnenviertel-based company Staud's; interview with Kurt Smetana, head of the Urban Renewal Office Ottakring; interview with Ula Schneider and Beatrix Zobl from the association Soho In Ottakring.

29 Interview with Ula Schneider and Beatrix Zobl from the association Soho In Ottakring.

top-down regenerations of infrastructures that changed the materiality of place must be interpreted as a political attempt to consolidate the notion of a strong and caring local state. And in this regard, Brunnenviertel's cultural diversity and self-determined civil society engagement are successfully utilized for supporting the material implementation of this hegemonic ideological project.

And third, market actors from outside the quarter increasingly build upon a culturalized re-formulation of local identity and difference as an image carrier and USP in distinct accumulation strategies. Herein, the diversity of Brunnenviertel's local population and the picture of an empowered civil society are utilized by real estate developers as a selling point in neighborhood branding strategies (JP Immobilien, 2012). The unique materialities of place, i.e. the expressions of cultural difference, are re-interpreted discursively into a marketable image in order to create surplus value upon material urban transformation. And, this strategy touches down materially in the form of an exceptional number of housing renewal projects within the past years. Although being state-subsidized to keep rents lower than in the privately financed segment, the market-led construction of a distinct culture of place by which these projects are advertised clearly aims at a financially strong clientele. Hence, the transformed materiality of place in this regard points to culturalization for capitalization in a (re)urbanization process.

Consequently, Brunnenviertel's materialities currently combine hegemonic economic and ideological projects, which both build upon a distinct interpretation of cultural diversity and employing this diversity in planning for maintaining hegemony and power over space. The bottom-up neighborhood development though, which once characterized Brunnenviertel and transformed its image to the better, is now largely supplanted by a top-down, institutionalized approach to culture and economic interests that endanger a functioning community and local economy. Hence, while the neighborhood could long be considered as a good practice of handling diversity in a globalizing city, it is increasingly threatened to lose this image for the sake of individual economic interests and the top-down determination of ideological principles.

To conclude, Brunnenviertel is currently in transition as concerns actors profiting from culture-led place transformation. Of course, the diverse local population benefits from the meanwhile institutionalized community empowerment efforts and the tradition of Brunnenviertel as a sincere seedbed of socio-political critique. Yet, it is exactly this quality of place, which local politics has incorporated through the initiation and financing of manifold planning interventions in the area to further consolidate its powerful role in urban development. And while having positive effects for a local population as well, the politically emphasized re-interpretation of Brunnenviertel into a romanticized multicultural urban sphere largely serves an external group of profit-oriented developers, who have already taken the chance to sell the cleaned-up image of a diverse neighborhood to well-off audiences of potential future investors.

Cultural Vienna revisited

Rationales, imaginaries, and hegemonic practice

UNDERLYING RATIONALES OF PLANNING THE CITY WITH CULTURE

Contextualizations and scaling

Contextual social, economic, and political transformations play a decisive role in any urban development consideration. They form the contexts that shape both the preconditions to and potential outcomes of planning interventions and thus largely determine the chosen approach to active place transformation. The importance attributed to these development contexts is reflected by most planning documents as well, where they constitute the first chapter almost without exception, thereby framing plans and policies. Such context framings also frequently appear in media discourse as constructs that attempt to influence planning decisions. In this research, case study analysis revealed similar contextualizations for Cultural Vienna as legitimizing or stabilizing arguments for or against certain forms of planning and planning with culture.

The embedding of Vienna's development in a greater context is determined by a somewhat conflictive duality, which is interestingly shaped by just one group of actors: the local state and its affiliated economic and cultural institutions. Context framings emphasize Europeanization, globalization, and urban growth as the three important development challenges. Interestingly, they result in two differently oriented strategic motifs that influence the imaginaries, materializations, and non-materializations in urban development: first, an accommodation motif that considers planning contexts as widely external and thus unchangeable influences, and second, a pro-active planning motif, building on the potentials of diminished boundaries (cf. also Giffinger & Hamedinger, 2009 on similar findings). Notably, in discourse, the first is inextricably linked with claims for demand-driven, socially oriented planning: *"Constant migration to Vienna causes an increased housing demand."*[1] The second promotes largely supply-driven, entrepreneurial approaches: *"We are in competition [...] Our level surely is Berlin."*[2]

Either way, in all three case studies Vienna's urban development contexts are one decisive factor influencing material place transformation besides planning cultural traditions. At inner city Karlsplatz, the framing of inevitable competition for attention on global tourism markets enables the utilization of contemporary arts for the city's strategic positioning. This is as uncontested as the focus on established forms of cultural expression in this regard, while the displacement of fringe groups is even considered an undoubted necessity for an aesthetic representation.[3] In Seestadt Aspern, the materialization of aspern IQ as the first permanent building is the consequence of the contextualization of urban development in inter-urban competition for business investments. The recent crisis though brings the opposing contextualization to the fore, which legitimizes Seestadt Aspern's realization upon the accommodation of growth and migration, thereby carrying on the city's socially oriented housing policies: *"More than 2,800 affordable and high-quality dwellings will be realized in the first construction phase until 2016."*[4] And, Brunnenviertel's culturized transformation is long safeguarded upon Vienna's past as European melting pot and the argument that the pro-active development towards a metropolis would demand accepting migration and cultural diversity[5]

The city's migration-conditioned growth and consequent diversification is a central planning-political argument *for* place transformation, particularly in Seestadt Aspern and Brunnenviertel discourse. It largely results in three distinct discourses that influence the place-specific material development. First, it causes an increased debate about public space development upon the acknowledgement of

---

1 "Wien wächst, aber es ist nicht aufblasbar" (WirtschaftsBlatt, May 08, 2013; original quote from Renate Brauner, city councilor of public finances (SPÖ), author's translation).

2 "Unsere Liga ist sicher Berlin" (Die Presse, September 09, 2007; original quote from Norbert Kettner, CEO of the Vienna Tourism Agency, author's translation).

3 Ibid.

4 "Startschuss für Seestadt Aspern" (Österreich, October 24, 2012; original quote from Michael Ludwig, city councilor of housing (SPÖ), author's translation).

5 "Kapsch und Häupl: Immigration bringt uns Standortvorteil" (Heute, January 26, 2010).

its role in identity formation, representation, and the construction of urbanity.[6] In Brunnenviertel it materialized in the physical regeneration of Yppenplatz and revitalization of the street market, while in Seestadt Aspern it effectuated the early construction of public green spaces before any housing construction had started. Second, constant urban growth legitimizes Seestadt Aspern's realization even after outward-oriented locational policies experienced a setback due to economic crisis. In both Aspern and Brunnenviertel, population inflow is the foundation to discursively legitimize and re-emphasize a strong state in Vienna's planning – largely upon its efforts in subsidizing affordable housing for accommodating an increasing number of residents.[7] This successfully sustains the imaginary of Vienna's socially oriented planning, while practically case study analysis reveals that the promoted diversity is either unwished or commodified. And third, growing diversity is increasingly used as a legitimizing argument for place branding strategies in order to attract only "the right" audiences.[8] This, of course, is a very questionable approach to planning and place transformation, as it cannot safeguard democratic, culturized decisions, but is only likely to the construction of materially and discursively exclusive urban environments – particularly, if urban development agendas are handed over to profit-oriented actors.

Hence, in discourse also two distinct, somewhat oppositional scales are constructed for urban planning to intervene. On the one hand, we have Vienna as a global city of the arts – a self-confident metropolis in the making, clearly defined by one cultural identity and image, competing for leisure and business tourists as one of the best in the world. Fig. 18 depicts the cities that are repeatedly referred to in Vienna's mediatic planning discourse, thereby illustrating how this scale is discursively formed. Cities considered equivalent in terms of culture are Berlin, Hamburg, Paris, London, or New York. On the other hand, the constructed picture is that of a kaleidoscope of distinct urban quarters, where the cultural diversity of a growing metropolitan population is to be accommodated. Interestingly, in this discourse the regional or national scale are not of interest. And, only in the context of Aspern, the vicinity to Bratislava was an early framing, while it also disappeared from discourse in the meantime. European integration is also not an important context for Cultural Vienna, it seems; and neither is inter-urban cooperation in urban cultural development. Rather, Cultural Vienna is envisioned as a self-confident competitor on a global scale, which, of course, is

---

6   "Stadterweiterung im Landeanflug" (Wiener Zeitung, November 19, 2011).
7   "Wir geben mit der Bildungsmilliarde Gas" (WirtschaftsBlatt, January 21, 2008).
8   "Nike, Red Bull, Amsterdam" (Die Presse, October, 07, 2009; original quote from Rainer Holzer, CEO of the wien 3420 Aspern Development AG, author's translation).

closely related to the construction of a distinct cultural imaginary, where culture is art and art is a unique selling proposition in inter-place competition.

Fig. 18: Top-10 reference cities in Vienna's cultural planning discourse

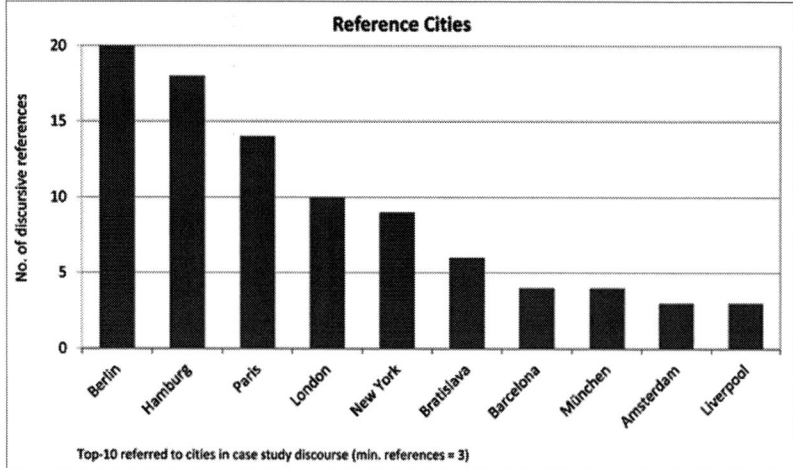

Hence, the resulting scales and the planning strategies of approaching the respective scalar contexts, on which the politics of planning with culture reside in Vienna, point to a cleavage between handling local cultural diversity as an accommodation to external social and geopolitical influences, and constructing one globally accessible art-led identity of the city to dominate global tourism markets.

The dominant application of culture

While the analyzed processes of Cultural Imagineering revealed distinct imaginaries each, they still show a number of commonalities, which can be distilled to one dominant imaginary of Cultural Vienna. Contextualizations and scalar embedding of the city, for instance, are a determining factor of all three place-specific cultural imaginaries, hence forming one part of the hegemonic conception of Cultural Vienna. Yet, there are a number of other characteristic factors of the hegemonic conceptualization of culture in Vienna's development.

Within the transformation of Karlsplatz, a cultural-political elite shapes culture as a representation instrument of a hegemonic arts image to be employed in the politics of global visibility. In Seestadt Aspern, the imaginary frames culture as a tool for communicating a pre-determined place brand as part of an entrepreneurial development strategy. And in Brunnenviertel the transforming cultural symbolic of a diverse urban neighborhood is increasingly re-formulated by market actors and local urban politics alike as an image carrier of the respective strategic endeavor. While art is only at Karlsplatz promoted so heavily as the only imaginable interpretation of culture in urban development, all cases of culture-led development more or less obviously point to the dominance of an imaginary that considers cultural specificity as a mere marketing instrument for attracting attention – either on a local market of potential future dwellers and creative workforce, or on a global market of tourists and investors. Hence, the dominant cultural imaginary of Vienna considers culture as a planning instrument in top-down constructing a distinct place image and identity.[9]

The city is in all case study discourses embedded in a context of fierce global inter-place competition. The power of this contextualization is so strong that the city's successfully marketed heritage is considered an insufficient resource for attracting visitors and investors. Consequently, the strategy is expanded to include modern fine arts in the repertoire of Vienna's image, while there is no doubt that it has to be a resource in tourism, largely neglecting its non-economic functions for development. The hegemony of this culturalization strategy increasingly enters all three place-related cultural imaginaries. It conceptualizes cultural planning as the transformation of the symbolic of public spaces for representing a marketable image of contemporary urbanity.[10] Yet, this top-down construction rejects any self-determined cultural processes aiming at the representation of difference that don't suit the dominant accumulation interests, thereby also excluding niche cultural processes of the city from the economic circuit.

Another dominant influence is Vienna's cultural planning tradition. It is historically determined by large institutions, as chapter 0 already pointed out. Notably, the institutionalization of cultural processes increases, the closer the case study is located to the city center. This is reflected also by the varying importance of a distinct history of place, or the city's cultural heritage in discourse. While history and heritage seem to dominate Karlsplatz transformation, in Seestadt Aspern discourse, the area's burdened past is not at all part of the place-specific cultural imaginary. In Brunnenviertel though, references to the city's glorious history as European melting pot and traditional diversity are a determinant factor in its transformation. This unhides the still existent hegemonic power of a distinct historic narrative of Cultural Vienna, which particularly influences

---

9 Cf. "Ein architektonisches Signal für Wien" (Kurier, July 25, 2012).
10 Cf. "Untergrund wird bunt" (Kurier, June 05, 2012).

the city's central places, while the not yet urbanized parts of the city are not influenced by either the local cultural planning history or this historic narrative.

An equally important point in depicting the cultural imaginary of Vienna is the definition of cultural actors, i.e. those reasonably "doing" culture, and the target audiences of culture-led urban transformation. This shows who is empowered by the discourse forming actors to intervene in the city's cultural formation and who is not, and further consolidates the role assigned to culture in planning. Referring to results from discourse analysis, target audiences of cultural processes in Vienna's planning can be reduced to two large actor groups: global tourists and a well-off middle-class of potential new residents. All cases analyzed explicitly point to either the one or other target group. Yet, while obviously tourists are to be attracted to the central places, future dwellers are the distinct audience of the peripheral areas of the city. This, of course, contributes to the further consolidation of the imbalanced spatial organization of tourism in Vienna and the anyway hegemonic tourism-centered cultural strategy.

As concerns those "doing" culture the case studies do not reveal such a clear picture. While visual and performing artists are central characters in all three discourses, the actors revolving around them largely differ – from cultural managers and curators at Karlsplatz, to civil society and market actors in Brunnenviertel, and urbanophile visitors in Seestadt Aspern. Yet, planners, urbanists, or activists are hardly ever considered a relevant group of cultural actors in discourse. Only the openness of individual actors in Seestadt Aspern development towards activist urban interventions allowed for the consideration of single activist processes such as guerilla gardening. The same is true for the approach of bottom-up cultural processes in Brunnenviertel. The dominant conceptualization, though, defined artists and a cultural-political elite as the decisive cultural actors, while self-determined civic practices are largely neglected and excluded from discourse and the resulting imaginaries.

Altogether, the dominant interpretations of culture in Vienna's planning do hardly allow for self-determined, critical cultural expression as part of the urban development process. The big planning projects are way too much determined by a top-down culture discourse, which promotes the anyway hegemonic interpretation of culture as the arts for attention in competition. Cultural actors attempting to employ an open and, hence, also probably critical process as part of the place transformation are thus often confronted with predetermined moral concepts and envisioned value constructs, which restrict the potentials of material cultural processes in urban development.[11] Even in the case of Brunnenviertel, civic engagement in the culture-led regeneration of a problematized urban neighborhood is from the very beginning confronted with attempts of its utilization in economic capitalization processes and its incorporation in political representation. A culturized approach to planning, though, would demand openness also towards critical civic engagement and its active empowerment as part of a democratic, inclusive process of urban cultural development.

Influential actors: Imagineers of Cultural Vienna

Case study analysis has pointed to a number of discursively and materially important actors, who have power over discourse and power over material planning. The following is meant to collectively discuss the empirical findings on these actor groups. This demands an immediate distinction between those, who appear in more than one culture-led development discourse, thereby potentially influencing the strategic orientation, cultural self-esteem, and material culture-led development of the whole city, and those who are determinant of the transformation of one specific part of the city only. The first group constitutes a clearly delimitable coalition of powerful actors in Vienna's development. It consists of the Social Democratic city councilors of planning, housing, public finances, and culture, the city's mayor, and the CEO of Vienna's Tourism Agency. This elitist group appears in all discourses on Vienna's culture-led development in similar form, shaping the transformed materialities of place upon similar powerful imaginaries. The second group is easily described, as it merely exists in Brunnenviertel. The urban neighborhood in transition is the only case study where place transformation and the related utilizations of culture for a distinct economic or representational purpose are contested. The early art-led process Soho In Ottakring established a counter-hegemonic culture of place both materially and discursively, allowing for the continued materialization of inclusive, critical, and society-building cultural processes, while at the same time opposing to an instrumentalization of place identity for external economic and political interests until recently.

Interestingly, whenever cultural planning decisions are to be taken, they are shaped by political or cultural elites, but never by planners or even civil society

---

11 Interview with Christian Dzwonkowski and Richard Natiesta from Buskes Festival Vienna; interview with Daniel Aschwanden, performing artist from the artist collective content.associates; interview with Ula Schneider and Beatrix Zobl from the association Soho In Ottakring.

actors. This, of course, is shaped by the political tradition of cultural politics in Vienna. But it also indicates the exclusiveness of Vienna's politics of planning, particularly when it comes to representative culture-led development processes. For the case studies analyzed though, the powerful urban politics representatives are not central to the discourse, but appear only as secondary discourse forming actors. Instead, the cultural and economic managers of state-affiliated institutions are those framing Vienna's urban (culture-led) planning. In Seestadt Aspern, the state-affiliated economic agencies promote the politically emphasized development context and planning vision. In Brunnenviertel, the Urban Renewal Office, local politicians, an NGO and external experts strengthen the planning-political imaginary of a strong and caring local state. And even in Karlsplatz transformation, where the city councilor of culture is a central figure, the director of WienMuseum and karlsplatz.org are decisive coalescing partners to push through the hegemonic art-for-tourism agenda.

Also, informal links building upon the close private relationship between decision-makers and local actors in place transformation play a pivotal role in decisions for or against material place transformation. Revealing these links demanded an in-depth empirical investigation of informal planning decisions that might have influenced material practice but cannot be revealed through discourse analysis. All three cases indicated such relations that enabled certain material planning interventions. In Brunnenviertel it is the realization of the pedestrian zone upon the links between local entrepreneurs and the district chairperson.[12] At Karlsplatz the materialization of the festival of street artists builds upon the link between festival curators and a municipal council representative.[13] And the consolidation of distinct patterns of urban development for Seestadt Aspern is based on the link between property owners and municipal planning department.[14] This, of course, points to anything but a transparent decision-making process in the material place transformation of all three case studies and unhides the importance of informal links between actors as powerful determinants of Vienna's planning landscape and decision-making processes. In this regard, the district chairpersons are one largely hidden group that emerged as powerful actors in planning as well. Interestingly, they do not appear often in discourse, because they seem to have enough power over material urban transformations to steer these processes without actively intervening informally, and because they

---

12 Interview with Hans Staud, owner of Brunnenviertel-based company Staud's.
13 Interview with Christian Dzwonkowski and Richard Natiesta from Buskes Festival Vienna.
14 Interview with Bernd Rießland, former CEO of the Vienna Business Agency.

are part of a greater planning-political coalition with the same development goals – at least in the cases analyzed. Apparently, district chairpersons are very influential of the material transformations observed in case study analysis, particularly when it comes to approving self-determined local initiatives. Thereby, they also serve as gatekeepers of the municipal strategies for the development of local places of the city,[15] potentially preventing the establishment of evolving counter-hegemonic processes as well.

An equally important point is, whether the congregation of actors in media discourse constitutes an arbitrary collection, or if actors intervening materially are also adequately represented in discourse. This is further meant to depict, whether distinct actor groups intervene in the process of meaning-making without having a stake in local culture-led place transformation. Generally, in Seestadt Aspern and Karlsplatz transformation, state-affiliated actors have not only taken over former public planning tasks in material terms, but they also largely determine the construction of the cultural and planning imaginaries of Vienna. Hence, in these two cases an extended local state materially and discursively determines the Cultural Imagineering process. At Brunnenviertel, though, broad participation in material and discursive place transformation mutually influence each other to create an open process of urban change, although local politics and certain market actors put increasing pressure on its development. While infrastructure regeneration was largely state-led, the discursive construction of a cultural imaginary and its materialization are contested.

As concerns those actors influencing the politics of planning without having a stake in the formal modes of place transformation, the case studies also point to a number of powerful actor groups. In Seestadt Aspern these are mainly representatives from the political-administrative system, who for the most part do not hold an official position in the planning process but attempt to actively steer the project into their desired direction. In Karlsplatz, the most prominent group intervening from outside the place transformation process is constituted by a diverse range of external experts. They do not add decisively to the museum location debate, but rather support the notion that Karlsplatz is an expert-led planning project, thereby excluding a diverse and integrative public debate. In Brunnenviertel though, a variety of market actors from the real-estate sector appears in discourse, thereby recently biasing the cultural development path of the neighborhood. Overall, the characteristics in governing Vienna's culture-led planning in both material and discursive terms point to an extended local state. Either decision-making power is still held by the local state itself, or, if trans-

---

15 Interview with Kurt Smetana, head of the Urban Renewal Office Ottakring.

ferred to an external partner, the powerful planning-political elite binds planning decisions and materializations to their hegemonic planning ideology by promoting a distinct cultural and planning imaginary via discourse (cf. particularly Seestadt Aspern in this regard and, to a minor degree, Brunnenviertel transformation). So, while the material and discursive governance, as well as the defined development goals of the three transformation processes point at either entrepreneurial approaches to planning or the continuation of a social democratic planning tradition, the link between all three is the exercise of power of an urban elite through planning with culture.

The analysis of actors has revealed another notable fact as well. Actors intervening in urban development processes have largely shifted their interest from erecting new cultural landmark institutions to local culture-led processes aiming at the re-interpretation of city space, while cultural politics has not. This difference stands out from the analysis of Imagineering actors and the discursive coalitions revolving around them. Here a dividing line can be drawn between actors discursively intervening in planning with cultural *processes*, and those actors intervening in planning with cultural *institutions*. The first implies a varying pool of representatives of the political-administrative system, state-affiliated agencies, market actors, and cultural and civil society actors, while the second is determined by a cultural-political elite of cultural managers, the Vienna Tourism Agency and the city councilor of culture. The permanence of the latter constellation largely corresponds with the above introduced coalition of strategically intervening actors in the construction of a Viennese cultural imaginary. Their appearance hence allows for the construction of a powerful imaginary of culture-led planning that influences all three case study transformations in material terms – a fact to be further detailed in the following chapter.

CULTURE-LED HEGEMONIC ECONOMIC AND IDEOLOGICAL PROJECTS

Building on case study findings, it can be pointed out how the combination of certain material cultural preconditions and powerful cultural imaginaries facilitates the realization or stabilization of specific economic and ideological projects in Vienna's development. Indeed, empirical analysis was able to identify certain transformed material practices that serve hegemonic interests, new modes of cultural planning, and patterns of exclusion that are all critical from the point of a culturized planning view, thereby already indicating the challenges concerning the city's future cultural development.

Art-led public space aestheticization as hegemonic representation

The empirical analysis of Cultural Vienna unhides that the City of Vienna actively pursues a very typical policy of cultural planning, which is, utilizing the historic city center for the material representation of a hegemonic cultural vision that aims at the promotion of a touristic image. Herewith, inner city areas are discursively re-formulated from central public spaces for the interaction and cultural expression of an urban society into representational spaces of an exclusive commodity culture that shall represent an accessible image for a global capitalist class.

This value construct becomes the hegemonic representation of Cultural Vienna mainly for three reasons. First, in Karlsplatz transformation, a local cultural-political elite successfully engages in discourse to promote the art-led, touristic cultural imaginary and the determined role of inner city public space in this regard. Second, recent strategic planning documents predominantly refer to heritage architecture, art institutions, and aestheticized public spaces as the city's cultural development potential, pointing to a culture of consumption for global tourism. And third, the envisioning of Cultural Vienna is still largely determined by its historic center, hence leaving no doubt that the culture-led transformation of Karlsplatz is symbolic for and determinant of the whole city. Even the Seestadt Aspern development and a general re-orientation of Vienna's development approaches towards a more polycentric structural and functional development couldn't change that circumstance recently.

This stabilization of hegemonic Cultural Vienna is not only materially reflected by the re-making of Karlsplatz into another representative space of an anyway dominant culture, but as well by innovations in the city's institutional setting. The foundation of departure, the city's creative economy agency, and KÖR, the public fund for art in public space, are two sings of an increased awareness of the importance of culture as a planning tool – both economically and in terms of ideological representation. The institutionalization of creative city and public space strategies in Vienna's planning must be considered as approaches of the local state to steering culture spatially and promote or regulate the transformation of certain places of the (inner) city with culture. This is indicated also by the increasing promotion of projects that deal with places of state-induced urban transformation, particularly Karlsplatz and Seestadt Aspern (KÖR, n.d.b). The 2012 issued regulation of street performances in Vienna (wien.at, 2012) is another piece of the puzzle in the city's growing interest for promoting the transformation of Vienna's (central) public spaces into representations of a top-down determined, marketable cultural identity.[16]

Remarkably, while classic physical planning in Vienna seems to be both materially and discursively shaped by the political re-orientations in governing urban change, i.e. a shift from government to governance, the emerging instruments of and discourses on culture-led public space transformation still widely comply with the characteristics of classic government and a top-down constructed urban cultural vision. In this regard, all three case study analyses confirm that public space development is increasingly understood not only as an important planning object per se, but – at least in the case of Vienna – as one of the last resorts of government and an instrument to stabilize cultural hegemony, ideological supremacy and power over space.

Culturalization for capitalization in (re)urbanization processes

As case study analysis has shown, the cultural imaginaries consolidating in the three place-specific discourses all predominantly refer to culture as an agent of change in planning. Evidently, expressions of cultural identity and difference are actively linked to distinct places in order to utilize them in diverse accumulation strategies. In Karlsplatz transformation, culture-led material regeneration is a means to promote a marketable image of a global city of the arts in order to attract attention and economic capital from a global tourism market. In Brunnenviertel, socio-economic and cultural diversity are re-interpreted into a political mandate *for* urban regeneration and utilized by the real estate sector to create economic surplus value. And in Seestadt Aspern, both cultural events and a hegemonic urban (architectural) identity are communicative tools and thematic pillars of a place branding strategy heading an entrepreneurial urbanization approach.

Notably, Brunnenviertel and Seestadt Aspern are contested processes as concerns the materialization of cultural imaginaries in local material practice. In both cases, an opposing imaginary exists that attempts to redefine the dominant links between cultural processes and urban development. In Brunnenviertel, it is the early broad framing of place-based artistic approaches as representation instruments of cultural difference and socio-political critique. The respective material transformations and adjacent culturized discourses form a counter-hegemonic approach to the increasing utilizations of local cultural processes.

---

16 Interview with Christian Dzwonkowski and Richard Natiesta from Buskes Festival Vienna.

Recently they are overlaid both by market mechanisms of capitalization on cultural difference and the incorporation of civic engagement in the political representation of a hegemonic planning-political approach. In Aspern, it is the conceptualization of culture as a locally distinct urbanity that contributes to a city's identity and urban culture, combined with the claim for a more open planning practice. Yet, this imaginary is less of a counter-discourse to economic and political utilizations of culture, but as well serves as a culturalization strategy stabilizing the uncontested continuation of a development strategy determined by economic principles. Hence, both Brunnenviertel and Seestadt Aspern are endangered of becoming bad practice examples of instrumentalizations – even of a broad approach to culture in planning – for the sake of capitalizing on (re)urbanization processes in Vienna.

Empirical research also pointed out that the constructions that became dominant in discourse evidently influenced the materializations in the analyzed place transformation processes. Be it the culturalization of urban life and the conversion of material cultural difference into a culture of consumption (Brunnenviertel), the marketing of a first discursively, then materially constructed "culture of place" for legitimizing and stabilizing a large-scale urbanization process (Seestadt Aspern), or the regeneration of a central public space upon a hegemonic art-led interpretation of the city's common cultural identity and image (Karlsplatz) – they all uncover the materialization of a culturalized imaginary for the capitalization in economic accumulation strategies, or schemes of hegemonic ideological representation.

Anyhow, the dominant approaches to planning the city with culture hence point to largely uncontested, mostly art-led cultural processes. Here culture is merely considered as a tool in top-down determining place identity for either representations of hegemonic power over space, or transformations of cultural into economic capital for individual economic projects. If, at all, material cultural processes emerge upon civic engagement in Vienna's processes of culture-led urban transformation (see particularly Seestadt Aspern and Brunnenviertel transformation), they are instantly incorporated by the anyway dominant coalition of Vienna's extended political-administrative system. This not only consolidates ideological supremacy, but also guarantees the invulnerable continuation of a chosen path in planning. Consequently, evolving niche cultures can only develop within the boundaries of a strict framework that is determined by a hegemonic cultural and planning-political agenda for Vienna's urban development. And this agenda is powerfully facilitated both materially and discursively by an extended local state in all projects analyzed. But the immediate incorporations revealed in the case studies diminish the potential for social innovation (cf. Moulaert et al.,

2004 among others) and the chance of establishing pluralist hegemony (Mouffe, 2007) upon self-determined cultural initiatives.

The displacement of "non-marketable" cultures in Cultural Vienna

A related phenomenon to be detected in the investigation of culture-led place transformation in Vienna is the active displacement of cultural signifying practices that do not add to pre-defined accumulation strategies. In this regard, case study analysis again reveals the power of the above introduced interpretation of cultural processes as tools in hegemonic capitalization strategies. In each of the place transformations, different forms of niche cultural expression and public space appropriation through "other" cultures than the ones promoted by the local state or developer appear. Yet, the hegemonic strategy and adjacent imaginary of culturalization for capitalization excluded these niche cultures from materializing in urban space, thereby reflecting badly on Vienna's cultural planning practice and the openness of the local state towards cultural difference in general.

In Brunnenviertel, "other" migrants, i.e. hard-to-reach groups that did not suit the lifestyle-based imaginary of ethnic diversity and ethnic economies as a neighborhood-specific culture of consumption were largely displaced very early in the transformation process.[17] In Aspern, the dominance of the capitalization objective did not allow for the continuation of the early cultural intervention concept that aimed at continuously accompanying the urban development process to establish networks, identities, and urbanity. Also, the "Wagenplatz Gänseblümchen", a community of nomadic artists representing an experimental lifestyle, is only reluctantly allowed to appropriate a small part of the construction ground temporarily, as they do not fit the brand image of cultural Seestadt Aspern (Gänseblümchen, 2013; wien 3420 Aspern Development AG, n.d.f). And, Karlsplatz stands out as the most critical case of Cultural Imagineering for constructing an exclusive cultural urbanity. The inner city aestheticization of the traffic node into an art space went along with the increasing displacement of drug addicts, who appeared at Karlsplatz in large numbers. The prior solution to this problematic situation combined a contact point for addicts with the engagement of social workers and was thus a declared political belief and symbolic statement of the City of Vienna that the problems of an urban society must be at the center of its attention – both mentally and spatially. The recent displacement of drug addicts to other, more peripheral and dispersed places and facilities,

---

17 Interview with Hans Staud, owner of Brunnenviertel-based company Staud's.

though, is a symbol of a politics of planning that increasingly aestheticizes the city, clearing the ground for a global capitalist class by moving social problems to the margin. Yet, herewith the socio-spatial fragmentation of the city is only increased instead of reduced and the problem still unsolved.

It is remarkable that no public discourse about the obvious conflict in Vienna's place transformations between a number of fringe groups, alternative lifestyles and the development visions of a political and economic elites exists. This is largely due to the already debated planning-political tradition in Vienna, which is still emphasized in all local planning discourses today, constructing a hegemonic planning imaginary of a strong and socially sensitive local state. These recurring construals mute any critical voices that would allow for the establishment of a counter-hegemonic cultural imaginary or even the materialization of niche cultural processes in state-led urban transformation. The habitual practice of a consensus-oriented planning model in Vienna (Novy et al., 2001) is also not helpful in this regard, as it leads to a sometimes incomprehensible behavior of decision-makers in conflictive situations, such as the displacement of "the others" as a strategy of conflict avoidance. Consequently, decisions are reasonably criticized for being non-transparent, effectuating in resentments towards the political-administrative system as concerns its approaches to governing culture-led urban development processes.

From state-led cultural planning to market-led neighborhood branding

Cultural planning in Vienna was long characterized by a top-down, state-led development approach. This was mainly due to the dominant framing of cultural planning policies as the provision of large-scale public infrastructures, which was of course shaped by the city's heritage institutions and the Federal cultural amenities located in the capital that served as built-in-stone determinants of this policy. Yet, it was further enforced by a combination with the general ideological claim in Vienna's planning of publicly providing these amenities for safeguarding equal access and equal opportunities among the city's residents. The current culture discourse and planning strategies still reflect this dominant interpretation by almost exclusively promoting cultural planning in the context of cultural infrastructures and state-led institutions. Even more, the recent discursive re-scaling from national capital to European metropolis adds a new strategic tone to planning the city with culture in Vienna.[18] The political-administrative

---

18 Cf. "Wien wächst – das Comeback einer Metropole" (Kurier, May 23, 2007).

system increasingly sees a chance to utilize the city's hegemonic art-led imaginary in transnational inter-place competition for tourists, hence discursively constructing *one* cultural identity that is to be promoted as the city's cultural image.

On the other hand, the widened perception of culture as everyday practices, identity representations and lifestyle expressions points to a completely different interpretation, which considers culture as constant processes evolving, blending, and vanishing in close relation to urban development. These, of course, can be discerned in Vienna's processes of place transformation as well – all three case studies revealed such self-determined, civic interventions. At Karlsplatz, it is the annual festival of street artists that attempts to counter the top-down determined culturalization of Vienna's inner city with a grassroots event of counter-hegemonic public space appropriation.[19] At Brunnenviertel, Soho In Ottakring is both the event and platform to communicate and critically reflect the demands and problems emerging in a socio-economically diverse neighborhood through bottom-up initiated artistic interventions.[20] And at Seestadt Aspern, both a performing artist collective and a nomadic group leading an experimental lifestyle insist on equally participating in the process of cultural identity construction for new Vienna.[21]

Although such processes are often marginalized or even excluded, they are recently incorporated in accumulation strategies in Vienna. Notably, the discourse of a metropolis in the making facilitates this incorporation. It sketches Vienna as a city of increasing cultural diversity and, consequently, an increasing variety of demands. Yet, this does not effectuate a more culturized approach to planning in the first run. Instead, it serves as a legitimation of market-oriented development strategies, which utilize cultural difference in the construction of distinct urban neighborhoods. These place brandings form clear-cut cultural identities for specific target audiences by re-interpreting the distinct cultures of place into marketable images. Ultimately, these images are the tools for creating surplus value in urban transformation. As case study analysis has revealed, processes of niche cultural expression are either instantly incorporated in such accumulation strategies in Vienna's processes of culture-led place transformation,

---

19 Interview with Christian Dzwonkowski and Richard Natiesta from Buskes Festival Vienna.
20 Interview with Ula Schneider and Beatrix Zobl from the association Soho In Ottakring.
21 Interview with Daniel Aschwanden, performing artist from the artist collective content.associates.

or they are marginalized because they do not fit the capitalist cultural development vision.

A second important influence in this regard is Vienna's development trajectory. In this concern, *"Vienna is different"* is the recurring legitimation for realizing particular planning considerations by pointing to the city's socially oriented planning tradition.[22] This framing mutes critical or oppositional voices that warn of the social consequences of emerging market-oriented planning efforts and allows paving a planning path that is increasingly biased by individual economic interests. Interestingly though, in the context of the city's *economic development*, the argument is reversed. Here, Vienna is not different from other cities and its past development not a path-shaping factor. Instead, the city would have to accommodate to an external competitive pressure for economic success.[23] Empirical analysis showed that this second contextualization is a particularly influential planning imaginary for place transformation in Vienna. There is a consensus between powerful actors that due to this taken-for-granted context the approach of maintaining the city's actual social mix needs to be dropped. In order to be successful in transnational economic competition in the long run, urban quarters in transition should instead be discursively constructed as distinct cultural places. This would lead to a city with a variety of faces for a variety of outward audiences, while only attracting wished-for target groups within each quarter, hence being economically efficient.

These approaches to active place transformation become a dominant consideration in Vienna's culture-led urban development discourse. They skillfully combine two contextualizations of Vienna's urban development to promote a planning-ideological shift from state-led cultural planning "for all" to market-led neighborhood branding for specific target audiences: first, the framing of Vienna as a metropolis in the making, which would cause increasing diversity and, hence, demand openness towards societal differentiation, and second, the axiomatic planning ideological framing that Vienna is different, i.e. a city determined by a strong and socially caring local state, hence legitimizing market-led approaches to planning.

Yet, these neighborhood branding approaches are problematic for at least three reasons. First, the often non-economic goals of processes of local cultural expression are utilized in for-profit planning strategies. The transformations of both Seestadt Aspern and Brunnenviertel point to such developments. Second,

---

22 Cf. "Grätzel & Ghetto: Warum Wien nicht Paris wird" (Die Presse, September 19, 2006).
23 Cf. "Wir müssen die Stärken weiter stärken" (WirtschaftsBlatt, October 06, 2011).

communicating distinct cultural neighborhood images for attracting only particular target audiences will increase segregation tendencies within the city, which can become problematic, if societal conflicts begin to reflect spatially as well. This will be particularly problematic, the more the cultures of place construct an exclusive picture of urbanity. The distinct cultural imaginaries of the three case studies already indicate an increasing discursive differentiation between parts of the city – from inner city high-brow culture to the creative middle class in new urban Vienna. And third, it weakens the local state by promoting the notion that citywide planning ideological visions would be anachronistic in a diverse metropolis. This largely aims at de-politicizing urban planning, while strengthening market actors and developers as decision-makers and ideological path-shapers in planning Cultural Vienna.

By now, the latter of these threats is skillfully countered by the City of Vienna through maintaining the prerogative of interpretation of the city's culture-led place transformations. The city's planning-political agenda concerning its urban cultural development is carried on by the politics-influenced semi-public cultural institutions and economic agencies. Hence, the political administrative system is still largely determinant of the culture-led construction of the city. Consequently, culture-led place transformation in Vienna can promote both competition-oriented entrepreneurial planning, and the notion of a strong and socially oriented local state without seeming self-contradictory, which in fact makes Vienna different. And as the analysis has shown, the dominance of this ambiguous combination is to a large degree legitimized and stabilized upon skillful Cultural Imagineering.

Towards a culturized planning practice
Conclusions on Cultural Imagineering

THE CULTURAL IMAGINEERING OF VIENNA

This research asked whether cultural imaginaries would actually influence the material city in terms of planning outcomes and material cultural processes. The above analysis clearly revealed modes of discursively legitimizing urban change or stabilizing hegemonic material practices. It was also revealed that Cultural Vienna is determined by different imaginaries of planning with culture, depending on what each place constituted for the city in material terms so far, and what a dominant coalition envisions for its future. The following section summarizes the revealed characteristics of Imagineering Cultural Vienna.

- **Definitions and utilizations of culture in place transformation**: The discursive narrowing down to a prevailing interpretation of culture in Vienna's planning discourses points to art-led projects in all case studies. This construct is randomly linked to place-related cultural materialities, depending on whether they support the claims made by a dominant discourse coalition or not. In all cases the cultural imaginaries are a means to legitimize new or stabilize existing hegemonic economic projects upon utilizations of culture. In Karlsplatz and Brunnenviertel these imaginaries also successfully promote the consolidation of ideological supremacy of a Social Democratic planning-political regime, while only in Brunnenviertel cultural processes can be employed for community building and social innovation as well. Hence, the role of culture in Vienna's development is reduced to a tool for facilitating powerful accumulation interests of a capitalist class or the ideological projects of a ruling political regime.

- **Prevalent contextualizations and scalings**: Place transformation is deeply linked with contextualizations of the city and scalings of urban development that are shaped by dominant actor coalitions. Undoubtedly, when it comes to culture as the arts, Vienna is referred to by a cultural-political elite as a global city in inter-urban competition with one hegemonic cultural identity and art-led image. References to culture as lifestyle diversity are largely shaped by market-oriented actors, who then conceptualize the city as a kaleidoscope of neighborhoods with ever distinct (commodified) cultural identities and arbitrary contexts – depending on the respective target audience. Speaking of lifestyle diversity through migration though, a broader, yet less powerful variety of state and civil society actors points to Vienna's social responsibility as European metropolis towards migrants and integrative measures. Thus, the contextualizations underline the cleavage in Vienna's strategic development between pro-active planning upon a powerful art-led imaginary and reactive accommodation to unswayable outward influences.

- **Influential material regulations**: The planning-ideological traditions of Vienna are the most influential material path-shaping factor in culture-led place transformation. The strong local state and long tradition of Social Democratic planning principles decisively influence planning approaches and outcomes in all three case studies, regardless of respective material cultural preconditions. Almost equally important is the city's past as capital of an Empire and European melting pot, which particularly legitimizes the transformation of Brunnenviertel and Aspern. Vienna's monocentric urban structure stabilizes Karlsplatz's hegemonic re-making into a representational place of the arts and simultaneously explains why Seestadt Aspern needed to be legitimized upon another material context, namely that of constant urban growth. On the other hand, the material practice of civic engagement in Brunnenviertel's development unintentionally stabilizes a hegemonic political representation strategy.

- **Audiences of and exclusions in place transformation**: All case study processes showed that planning with culture is meant to attract specific target audiences upon a reductive application of culture in discourse and material place transformation. While Karlsplatz regeneration clearly aims at global tourists, the other two examples point to a new middle-class of dwellers in search for places charged with cultural capital. A related and equally problematic point is the exclusion and displacement of certain interest groups or material cultural processes. In all three cases, non-institutionalized cultural actors are either actively or unintentionally excluded from the economic cycle that was initiated through place transformation. Even worse, in each case study a distinct mode of exclusion of certain cultures was revealed as part of the Imagineering process. Be it the displacement of unaesthetic drug addicts from Karlsplatz, the rejection of non-marketable lifestyles in Seestadt Aspern development, or the early exclusion of badly integrated hard-to-reach groups from Brunnenviertel – they all point to a problematic dichotomy between dominant planning visions and the actual material cultural diversity of Vienna.

- **Transformed material practice**: Cultural Imagineering shaped the materialities of place in each of the case studies. Transformed material practice at Karlsplatz points to the consolidation of a culture that serves the attraction of global tourism. It hence sustains an accumulation strategy upon cultural processes that represent the hegemonic city image to serve an established cultural economy. In Seestadt Aspern the materialization of cultural projects is the realization of an entrepreneurial planning approach, hence serving as the tool to safeguard the individual capitalization interests of profit-oriented developers and investors. In Brunnenviertel two different material practices collide: first, the self-determined signifying practices of a local community as a representation of identity and difference, and second, the instrumentalization of just these processes for dominant political interests and exclusive economic benefits of an urban elite. Overall, the influence of an economic elite and, even more, of a powerful planning-political regime on cultural place transformation through Imagineering gets obvious from the transformed materialities in all three case study projects.

- **Power over space and power over planning**: Hence, we can conclude on the question of who has power over space and power over planning in Vienna's culture-led development as follows. As concerns the transformation of inner city representative Karlsplatz, selective local state representatives and cultural and tourism managers with high reputation were able to jointly push through their development vision of Touristic Vienna upon the shoulders of a narrow interpretation of culture without any opposition. In Seestadt Aspern, symbol of a new, pro-active planning in Vienna, a corporatist governing coalition of actors from the political-administrative system of planning and the state-affiliated economic agencies teamed up to realize a large-scale development project. By employing cultural processes as marketing tools they not only secure aspired surplus value upon an urbanization process, but successfully create acceptance to maintain the power over planning. Only Brunnenviertel is contested as concerns power over space and power over planning. Being a symbol of diversity, integration, and Vienna's path towards becoming a lively and livable European metropolis, the local state, the real-estate sector, and local civil society actors compete for the prerogative of interpretation in this neighborhood. While counter-hegemonic ephemeral cultural actors are increasingly excluded due to growing development pressures, the institutionally empowered local civil society might remain a symbolic and thus irreplaceable quality of place, hence serving the cultural development of Brunnenviertel. Yet, this process must be carefully observed in the near future to prevent it from becoming another case of uncontested hegemonic culturalization for exclusive benefits. Within all that, the local state is a constant factor in culture-led place transformation. It intervenes in the physical regeneration of urban space in all three cases, thereby indirectly influencing the cultural materialities of place and their development opportunities. Yet, the active involvement with material cultural processes is left to others, which enables powerful non-state actors to utilize them for facilitating their individual interests. It is due to path-dependencies and long traditions in Vienna's planning that the political-administrative system understandably struggles with supporting cultural processes in a similar manner as it supports cultural institutions. At the same time, respective decision-makers do not always seem to desire such a policy shift, as the consolidation of a physical planning approach and an institution-oriented cultural planning better serves their representation interests and the maintenance of power over planning than temporary processes probably would. The consequence is an imbalance between a state-led cultural planning as planning with arts and institutions for promoting a global capital of culture, and market-led planning as neighborhood branding upon local cultural specificity for individual economic profits. Yet, it is clear that both cannot adequately serve a principle that considers planning as a tool for paving the way to a city's cultural development.

Tab. 4: Deconstructing Vienna's Cultural Imagineering

	KARLSPLATZ	SEESTADT ASPERN	BRUNNENVIERTEL
Definition of culture	- Art-led projects - Heritage - Cultural economy	- Art-led projects - Creative economy - Urban identity	- Art-led projects - Lifestyle diversity - Ethnicity
Utilization of culture for …	- Stabilizing economic and ideological project	- Legitimizing economic project	- Legitimizing economic and ideological project - Community building
Context and scaling	- Inter-urban competition (global)	- Inter-urban competition - Increasing diversity	- Increasing diversity
Material regulations	- (Cultural) planning traditions - Monocentric urban structure	- Planning traditions - Urban growth	- Planning traditions - Metropolitan history ("melting pot") - Civic engagement
Audiences	- Global tourists	- New middle-class dwellers - New businesses - Urbanists	- New middle-class dwellers - Local residents
Exclusions	- Ephemeral cultural actors - Fringe groups	- Ephemeral cultural actors - Non-marketable lifestyles	- Ephemeral cultural actors - Hard-to-reach groups
Material practice	- Hegemonic representation for accumulation	- Culturalization for capitalization	- Culturalization for capitalization - Representation of difference
Power over space and power over planning	- Cultural-political elite coalition: local state + cultural elite (uncontested)	- Corporatist governing coalition: local state + affiliated agencies (uncontested)	- Empowered civil society, local state, developers (contested)

Empirical analysis has shown that there is more than one model of planning the city with culture in Vienna. We can observe the targeted construction of distinct places on the shoulders of an *ever specific* construction of culture and its role in urban development. On the one hand, this is due to the respective (cultural) materialities of place, on the other hand though, it is determined by the actors who engage in discourse to push through their ever specific development visions.

However, the analysis has clearly confirmed the assumption that discourse is also in the context of Vienna's planning used as a political arena to place ideological beliefs and simplistic constructs in the public debate in order to influence urban development paths and practices. In this regard it became obvious that culture is both discursively and materially utilized as an agent of change. Even more, it was shown through case study analyses that imaginaries are an important link in the process of place transformation; that they have the power to inform material practice, and that, in fact, they need to be understood as important discursive regulations of culture-led place transformation.

It was also pointed out several times that culture-led place transformation indeed is a question of power also in Vienna, where an urban elite can – largely without any contestation – determine the city's planning processes and cultural future. Whether it does so by employing traditional Social Democratic approaches, or by borrowing from entrepreneurialism is not of importance in this regard. What remains, and this backs the initial hypothesis, are the projects that satisfy the capitalist and ideological interests of this elite in the first run, while the actual cultural pluralism of Vienna is not supported with enough emphasis in current planning practice.

PLANNING FOR CULTURAL DEVELOPMENT: TOWARDS A CULTURIZED PLANNING PRACTICE IN VIENNA

In Vienna, cultural planning was long considered as an instrument of social reform (Schorske, 1981; Mattl, 2000). The top-down imposed institutionalization of history, heritage, traditions, and the arts, the implementation of cultural programs and development plans, and the support of diverse cultural processes were meant to serve a local population as educational and representational resources and, hence, as a means to supply citizens with the tools to acquire greater freedom. As the present analysis of the politics of planning with culture pointed out though, actors of the city often turn to culture for different reasons today. On the one hand, cultural planning is increasingly considered as a tool to foster social and economic innovation in cities, where prior approaches failed due to the decline of Fordism and a transformed urban sphere. On the other hand, culture is utilized by powerful forces as a tool to re-generate, promote, or even sell urban space in order to secure individual benefits. Consequently, planners are today confronted with various potential paths of steering urban development and place transformation in combination with the cultures that are determinant of cities.

As the above elaborations have also clearly pointed out, planners and urban practitioners have a pivotal role to play on another front – not in planning the city *with* culture, but in empowering the diversity of cultures that constitute a city to express their difference in order to democratize urban development.

Hence, we planners should instead regard our task as planning *for* cultural development, thereby making a valuable contribution to the realization of pluralist hegemony in the appropriation of urban space for ideological representation and for urban social and economic development at large.

By employing such a planning view, this research has analyzed culture-led place transformations in Vienna to understand the current path of the city's cultural development. Building on these findings, the following section gives recommendations on how a culturized planning practice might be realized, and how the revealed utilizations of cultural processes for reductive ends might be countered in future planning in Vienna. To conclude, it also specifies general potential future roles and points of intervention of planners in processes of culture-led urban development to contribute to current planning practice.

- **Reconsider cultural planning I – from institutions to processes**: Due to Vienna's cultural planning traditions, the focus of urban and cultural politics and urban planning is on art-led projects and the institutions representing them. Yet, cultural processes need to be equally fostered in economic and organizational terms. Currently the processes constituting Vienna's distinct urban life are underrepresented politically, economically, and strategically, except when being utilized in top-down determined marketing strategies. Their potential for social innovation and community building though is not emphasized enough or supported properly. Even more, although our current understanding of culture as a signifying practice of individual and collective identities should build on civic cultural processes, cultural planning is by and large determined by political and economic elites. But the civic cultural practices emerging constantly need to be materially empowered and explicitly featured in the city's planning strategies. In this regard, Vienna's planning-political system needs to employ a more open approach to other forms of cultural expression that are not yet established or institutionalized, as these are vital ingredients to critique, learning and innovation, community, identity and image.

- **Reconsider cultural planning II – from mono-centricity to polycentricity and "culture for all"**: Vienna's old city center has always been and still is the one representative place of the city for the construction and consolidation of a dominant urban identity and cultural image. Hence, future (cultural) planning strategies in Vienna must be seriously committed to two things: first, measures that promote the appropriation of inner city public spaces by the diverse non-institutionalized cultures of the city, and second, the refocusing on other parts of the city for these spaces to become equally representative places of the city in the long run. This is also particularly important if Vienna wants to cope with predicted growth and diversification scenarios. The two case studies of Brunnenviertel and Seestadt Aspern are already on their way to supporting such a polycentric urban cultural vision. The latter, though, demands more than a thought through housing scheme or the recently promoted smart city strategy to become a culturally charged place and counterpoint to the culturally representative inner city. It demands explicit cultural measures as part of the development process. Yet, the currently dominating policy focus on structures, i.e. institutions, won't be sufficient in this regard, as cultural institutions can hardly ever enhance participation. Instead, low-threshold civic processes should be fostered with way more emphasis. Consequently, the underlying rationale of all cultural policies in Vienna, the Social Democratic claim of providing "culture for all", meaning the equal spatial distribution of cultural infrastructures, must be reformulated into "culture from all" as a policy objective. Only this reconsideration can do justice to the ideal of equally distributed *opportunities* of cultural representation throughout an urban society.

- **Develop a comprehensive joint cultural planning strategy for Vienna**: The detailed analysis of strategic documents on Vienna's planning-political approach to culture revealed that the only explicit cultural planning strategy is the Tourism Concept for Vienna, published by the Vienna Tourism Agency. And understandably, it has a narrow focus on culture's role in the city's development. Although Vienna is renowned for its status as a global city of the arts, there is no other future-oriented strategy on its cultural development. Hence, the city needs to initiate a process of developing a more comprehensive cultural planning strategy that employs a broad culture definition and consequently includes actors from a wide range of spheres – from cultural politics and a local cultural economy to grassroots movements, interest groups, planners and urban researchers. It would hence demand a joint effort of the political decision-makers from the fields of planning, housing, culture, and integration, the agencies advocating the interests of a local (cultural) economy and a tourism economy, and the NGOs and activist groups endorsing niche cultural representation demands. Such a strategy would form the basis to the development of distinct policies for cultural planning and the evaluation of cultural politics, while at the same time serving as a guideline for urban planning alike.

- **Re-define tourism as a factor for intercultural learning and social innovation**: The dominant interpretation of culture as the arts and the consideration of tourism as an economic resource are mutually dependent in Vienna's development. While tourism planning builds upon the city's art-led projects, it simultaneously constructs the art-led images of Vienna that stabilize a cultural planning dominated by the narrow culture definition. What is largely ignored in Vienna's recent strategic debate on tourism development though, are the other positive effects of promoting tourism in a city. Instead of solely pointing to the economic outcomes, we should emphasize tourism as a form of knowledge exchange as well. From this viewpoint, projects like Centrope are important, as they have the potential to foster intercultural learning upon intense knowledge exchange in order to facilitate the future integration of Vienna and Bratislava into a joint metropolitan region. This give-and-take has the ability to foster social innovation within a territory as well. Therefore, tourism planning in Vienna must attempt to broaden its scope from public relations, marketing, and lobbying for an established local economy to becoming an advocate of the interests of the many niche cultures of a local population as well. To this end, it is necessary to actively integrate these cultures in the development process of touristic concepts for Vienna, instead of merely utilizing them for marketing distinct locations of the city as it is done now. This not only allows a broad population to directly experience the monetary effects of a flourishing tourism economy, but enables intercultural learning beyond city limits that might be useful to coping with integration problems within the city.

- **Secure inclusion of Vienna's diverse cultures in economic cycles**: In close relation to the claim for a widened scope in tourism planning, urban planning must as well broaden its approach to participation to secure inclusion in urban development. If inter-urban competition is considered a determinant planning context also in terms of a city's cultural development, we planners must define strategies that allow for the participation of all cultures of the city in the so-created economic cycles. By now, the promoted and marketed culture of Vienna is a rather elitist imaginary, with positive economic effects flowing back largely to an elitist, narrowly defined cultural economy. Yet, cultural planning should create the stage for new cultural formats, artistic approaches, and civic processes that are not only bottom-up created, but function as processes that integrate a local population to secure its inclusion in the positive social and economic effects of cultural development. To this end, projects like Soho In Ottakring in Brunnenviertel, or content.associates' accompaniment of Seestadt Aspern's development should be fostered and invited in, as they are valuable resources to promoting the inclusion of diverse citizens.

- **Make clearer commitments to socio-economic and socio-cultural differentiation**: Population growth and increasing diversity have indeed shaped the material development of Vienna in the past two decades and will most likely be decisive of its future transformation as well. Yet, a culturized planning approach demands taking not only the resulting spatial challenges of a growing agglomeration into account. It demands considering the socio-political and socio-economic consequences as well. In Seestadt Aspern, symbol of a growing city and metropolis in the making, the envisioned diversity seems to be largely detached from the city's actual cultures. Migration, ageing, or alternative lifestyles are widely overlooked or disregarded, although they should be more intensely debated – not as development challenges, but as qualities of a 21st century metropolis. Increasing lifestyle diversity and its support in the strategic development of an urban future must hence be integrated in future policy debates and strategy developments. And it should become a path-shaping element of new urban development projects like Seestadt Aspern, if we understand the recently evolving "smart city" efforts to be grounded there not only as technologically, but as socially sensitive as well.

- **Treat references to the past sensitively – history between path-shaping and path-breaking**: History was conceived as one of the determinant contexts in place transformation processes, and indeed, it is important, particularly if considered as a memorial culture in the case of Vienna and its burdened past. On the other hand though, recurring references to history strengthen path-dependencies, thus often inhibiting creativity and openness in envisioning urban futures and path-breaking in the development trajectory of a city. Consequently, history is frequently utilized for the solidification of hegemony as all case studies have shown. Hence, it is one context, but just one among many. And pointing to heritage studies, we should be aware that history is also a hegemonic narrative and not an exact image of a city's past that represents all interests, experiences, and cultures equally. So if we want to achieve open processes in planning as a precondition to planning for cultural development, we need to be cautious to not exclude potentially imaginable futures by predetermining urban development paths upon powerful framings of history. Instead, we need to collect a broad variety of historic narratives of those, who are involved in our planning endeavors in order to carve out what they have in common and what might become a collective identity or culture of place in the future. So, history might facilitate path-breaking, i.e. the envisioning of a completely new development path that was unimaginable before. But it might as well facilitate path-shaping, meaning the construction of an imaginary that serves individual benefits only. Anyhow, being a practitioner, one must be aware of this duality inherent in references to the past in planning to safeguard democratic outcomes in place transformation.

- **Redefine urbanity and public space: from structure to process, from exclusion to inclusion**: Urbanity is a buzz-word in Vienna's planning discourse and a determinant of place transformation. Yet, the urbanity referred to most often builds on a somewhat anachronistic notion. It considers high densities and the diversity of uses, people, and goods as the only characteristics that would constitute urban environments. This view solely points to structures and is hence still embedded in the outdated envisioning of the city as a static object. Today we know that urban space must be regarded as a constant process of change and transformation that is at least as much constituted by everyday practices, the cultural processes that evolve as a result of social and economic innovation, and democracy and citizenship as guiding principles of the European city. In this regard, the increasing turn to actively developing the public spaces of Vienna should be reconsidered as well. By now, it is largely top-down determined by the local state, its lately founded institutions (for instance KÖR), and the recently established regulations (for instance the regulation of street performances in Vienna). But public space development should as well be a participatory act – also in the representative inner city areas such as Karlsplatz, and not only in Brunnenviertel, where public space regeneration successfully included a local population. And it must be embedded in a different understanding of space and planning, too. The largely pre-determined visions of a certain end-state in the top-down transformation of public spaces cause that those groups having difficulties to articulate themselves are excluded from planning processes or even displaced as they don't fit the envisioned outcomes of place transformation. Yet, if we promote the idea of planning and urban space as being *constant processes*, our approaches to (public) space transformation must be flexible enough to include niche cultures and fringe groups still at a later stage of development. Interestingly, in Karlsplatz transformation, the seemingly most pre-determined of the three case studies in cultural terms, this was possible for the Buskers Festival Vienna due to the openness of the curators of karlsplatz.org (while the displacement of the drug scene cannot be endorsed). Decision-makers have in all cases reacted unskillfully on unplanned appropriations or niche cultures that don't fit the envisioned development concepts. Hence, the active construction of urbanity and transformation of public spaces in Vienna's planning needs to be redefined as participatory, open processes that can never reach an end-state. Planning approaches must be tolerant of difference, the potentially non-marketable lifestyles, and struggling fringe groups in order to create the ground for an urban future where these are not marginalized, but part of an urban sphere that builds on the principles of democracy and inclusion.

- **Counter Vienna's increasing neighborhood branding and micro-scale differentiation**: The analysis of Brunnenviertel has revealed that real estate sector representatives increasingly engage in promoting a greater differentiation between the neighborhoods and quarters of the city upon their distinct cultural materialities. From a culturized planning view, this development must be sanctioned. It potentially leads to greater socio-economic segregation in Vienna and the displacement of certain lifestyles upon the exploitation of the image value of only some selected local cultural processes. Furthermore, it disempowers the local planning system in steering the city's spatial development and elaborating useful neighborhood development strategies upon more comprehensive criteria, as external market actors begin to gain the prerogative of interpretation of these neighborhoods, their identities, and demands. The city's division into districts as a traditional cognitive categorization into moderately better or worse neighborhoods seems sufficient to satisfy both the real-estate sector's economic interests and the local state's attempts to keep disparities between urban quarters low and diminish the stigmatization of single urban quarters.

- **Institutionalize support for non-institutionalized cultural processes**: The cultural processes shaping the identity of place are being instrumentalized for exclusive economic projects in all analyzed case studies of culture-led place transformation in Vienna. And as research has shown, these processes – small as they may be – are confronted with bureaucratic restrictions, financial and organizational uncertainties, and a simple lack of knowledge about who they might reasonably address in the city's institutional jungle. All this hinders new ideas, new cultural formats and innovative practices from being realized in the city. Hence, these non-institutionalized cultural processes demand a competent contact point. They demand institutional support, which is currently not existent in the needed form. This support is necessary to safeguard that these processes are not exploited for the benefits of individual actors while their positive social effects (e.g. community and network building, identity and image creation) cannot unfold. From the application of permit to applying for public and private subsidies, from organizational support for events to mitigating the liability for cultural projects the spectrum of activities should range. Vienna's cultural development demands a service institution for non-profit cultural actors, just like it has established the Vienna Business Agency as the one-stop-shop for businesses thirty years ago, and departure for supporting the city's creative industries two decades later. Now it is time to institutionalize the support for cultural processes that represent the non-commercial cultures of Vienna, as they are equally essential to Vienna's cultural development.

- **Create on-the-ground neighborhood assistance as platforms of civic empowerment**: Planning-ideological traditions have framed Vienna's culture-led place transformations as they did in many other cities. But this path-dependency was rather of use for the anyway powerful actors in Vienna's development and hence resulted in the prevalence of hegemonic projects on the shoulders of the city's cultural development. A local population has hardly ever been the target audience of the analyzed culture-led place transformations, although it should be. Consequently, what is needed are more on-the-ground planning institutions in the city such as the Urban Renewal Offices, yet, with less top-down pre-determined tasks from urban politics, but as "on-site neighborhood assistance" for the self-determined development of local places. While Urban Renewal Offices are almost fully engaged with being service institutions for the day-to-day problems of a local population, neighborhood assistance should engage in active, empowering work to foster processes like Soho In Ottakring and their up-scaling to become models of citizen participation for the whole city. Hence, building on both the positive and negative experiences from Urban Renewal Offices, Local Agenda 21 projects, and Local Area Management ("Grätzelmanagement") in Vienna, the expansion of on-the-ground offices is highly recommended to encourage civic engagement, enable grassroots movements, and support the materialization of innovative cultural processes that together constitute cultural pluralism and pluralist hegemony over space and urban development.

- **Place educated planners at the interface of cultural processes and contested planning**: For the most part, culture-led processes in place transformation cannot be conducive to the public good. Their potential benefits to society are weakened due to their recurring utilizations for individual profits. Yet their instrumentalization for individual ideological or representation interests in Vienna's planning and their influence on the transformed materialities of place uncover that they can actually be effective forming forces of the city. Hence, culture-led place transformation processes demand mediators as objective interfaces and communicative links between civic cultural projects on the one hand, and the contests over their utilization in planning on the other hand. Emerging niche cultures, everyday practices, and the cultural materialities of place in general need to be actively protected from culturalization, i.e. their economic or political exploitation. At the same time, they need to be integrated as potentials in strategies towards social and economic innovation in cities. This balancing act needs thoughtfulness as it needs constant participation of actors who are familiar with the theory and practice of contests over urban space, the operations of a public and market sector, and the complexities of a local civil society. The expertise of educated planners is an indispensable resource in this regard. They can provide the impetus for civic processes, safeguard the implementation of cultural projects after democratic planning principles, and subsequently ensure outcomes of culture-led planning that satisfy a public interest, while not ignoring individual demands.

- **Raise awareness for links between cultural processes and planning in planning education**: This research has pointed out both in theory and the empirical analysis that there are multiple lines of reasoning that can explain the deep links between cultural processes and urban development. While the cultural turn has captured planning practice for the most part, this is still by and large learning by doing. In planning education though, we do not emphasize the relationship between culture and planning sufficiently, nor do we consider urban planning itself a cultural practice at all. Yet, we need to raise the awareness for the proximities, commonalities, as well as the dividing lines between planning practice and cultural practice to pave the way for a culturized understanding of the city, its development, and planning.

List of Figures & Tables

Fig. 1: ALCOA's Imagineering: imaginary, materialization, hegemony | 13
Fig. 2: Conceptualizing the process of Cultural Imagineering | 28
Fig. 3: Locating case studies of culture-led transformation in Vienna | 37
Fig. 4: Population development and forecast for Vienna and the Vienna urban region (1953-2030) | 116
Fig. 5: Employment development in Vienna, 1964-2001 | 118
Fig. 6: Vienna's scales of metropolitan governance | 127
Fig. 7: Annual public subsidies for cultural activities (2001-2011) | 136
Fig. 8: Advertising "Cultural Vienna" as competitive business location | 137
Fig. 9: Top-10 terms per year in Karlsplatz mediatic discourse |149
Fig. 10: Theme-based mapping of actors in Karlsplatz discourse | 151
Fig. 11: Visualizing the chronology of Karlsplatz discourse | 153
Fig. 12: Top-10 terms per year in Seestadt Aspern mediatic discourse | 168
Fig. 13: Theme-based mapping of actors in Seestadt Aspern discourse | 170
Fig. 14: Visualizing the chronology of Seestadt Aspern discourse | 172
Fig. 15: Top-10 terms per year in Brunnenviertel mediatic discourse | 191
Fig. 16: Theme-based mapping of actors in Brunnenviertel discourse | 193
Fig. 17: Visualizing the chronology of Brunnenviertel discourse | 195
Fig. 18: Top-10 reference cities in Vienna's cultural planning discourse | 210

Tab. 1: A culturized planning view. Critically reviewing the capitalist culturalization of the city | 21
Tab. 2: Revisiting the regulation-accumulation-representation coupling of Cultural Imagineering in the duality of urban space | 101
Tab. 3: Analytical variables in Critical Discourse Analysis | 107
Tab. 4: Deconstructing Vienna's Cultural Imagineering | 229

Bibliography

Aglietta, M. (1979): *A theory of capitalist regulation. The U.S. experience.* London and New York: Verso.
Albers, G. (2008): *Stadtplanung. Eine illustrierte Einführung.* Darmstadt: Primus Verlag.
Albrechts, L. (2004): Strategic (spatial) planning reexamined. In: *Environment and Planning B: Planning and Design 2004, 31,* 743-758.
Allmendinger, P. (2002): Marxism and critical theory. In: Allmendinger, P. (ed.): *Planning theory.* Basingstoke: Palgrave Macmillan.
Amin, A. & Graham, S. (1997): The ordinary city. In: *Transactions of the Institute of British Geographers, New Series, 22(4),* 411-429.
Anderson, J. & O'Dowd, L. (1999): Borders, border regions and territoriality: contradictory meanings, changing significance. In: *Regional Studies, 33(7),* 593-604.
Appignanesi, R. (2003): *Introducing Postmodernism.* Cambridge: Icon Books.
Ashworth, G.J., Graham, B., Turnbridge, J.E. (2007): *Pluralising pasts. Heritage, identity and place in multicultural societies.* London & Ann Arbor: Pluto Press.
Bahn, C., Potz, P., Rudolph, H. (2003): Urbane Regime. Möglichkeiten und Grenzen des Ansatzes. *Discussion Paper SP III 2003 - 201.* Wissenschaftszentrum Berlin für Sozialforschung.
Barnett, C. (2008): Theorising democracy geographically. In: *Geoforum, 39,* 1637-1640.
Bassett, K., Smith, I., Banks, M., O'Connor, J. (2005): Urban dilemmas of competition and cohesion in cultural policy. In: Buck, N., Gordon, I., Harding, A., Turok, I. (eds.): *Changing cities. Rethinking urban competitiveness, cohesion and governance.* Hampshire and New York: Palgrave Macmillan
Bastian, M., Heymann, S., Jacomy, M. (2009): Gephi: an open source software for exploring and manipulating networks. *International AAAI Conference on Weblogs and Social Media.*

Bauman, Z. (2011): *Culture in a liquid modern world.* Cambridge and Malden: Polity Press.

Beazley, M., Loftman, P., Nevin, B. (1997): Downtown redevelopment and community resistance: an international perspective. In: Jewson, N. & MacGregor, S. (eds.): *Transforming cities: contested governance and new spatial divisions.* London and New York: Routledge.

Beck, U. (2006): The cosmopolitan age: redefining power in the global age. In: *International Journal of Politics, Culture, and Society, 2005(18),* 143-59.

Benneworth, P. & Hospers, G. (2009): Introduction: culture, economy and "old industrial regions". In: Benneworth, P. & Hospers, G. (eds.): *The role of culture in the economic development of old industrial regions.* Zurich & Berlin: LIT.

Berger, P.L. & Luckmann, T. (1980): *Die gesellschaftliche Konstruktion der Wirklichkeit. Eine Theorie der Wissenssoziologie.* Frankfurt am Main: Fischer Verlag.

Berking, H. (2006): Raumtheoretische Paradoxien im Globalisierungsdiskurs. In: Berking, H. (ed.): *Die Macht des Lokalen in einer Welt ohne Grenzen.* Frankfurt & New York: Campus Verlag.

Berndt. C. & Pütz, R. (2007): Kulturelle Geographien nach dem Cultural Turn. In: Berndt. C. & Pütz, R. (eds.): *Kulturelle Geographien. Zur Beschäftigung mit Raum und Ort nach dem Cultural Turn.* Bielefeld: transcript.

Best, J. & Paterson, M. (2010): *Cultural political economy.* Oxon and New York: Routledge.

Best Practices Hub Wien (ed.) (2004): Best Practices der Stadt Wien – UN-HABITAT Best Practices Programm. *Werkstattbericht der Stadtentwicklung Wien, vol.66.* Published by City of Vienna, Municipal Department 18.

Bianchini, F. (1993): Remaking European cities: the role of cultural policies. In Bianchini, F. & Parkinson, M. (eds.): *Cultural policies and urban regeneration. The West European experience.* Manchester: Manchester University Press.

Bieling, H.J. (2006a): Die politische Theorie des Neo-Marxismus: Antonio Gramsci. In: Brodocz, A. & Schaal, G.S. (eds.): *Politische Theorien der Gegenwart I.* Opladen & Farmington Hills: Verlag Barbara Budrich.

Bieling, H.J. (2006b): Die politische Theorie des Neo-Marxismus: Bob Jessop. In: Brodocz, A. & Schaal, G.S. (eds.): *Politische Theorien der Gegenwart I.* Opladen & Farmington Hills: Verlag Barbara Budrich.

Bihl, G. (2006): Wien 1945-2005. Eine politische Geschichte. In: Csendes, P. & Oppl, F. (eds.): *Wien. Geschichte einer Stadt. Von 1790 bis zur Gegenwart.* Vienna and others: Böhlau.

Binns, L. (2005): Capitalising on culture: an evaluation of culture-led urban regeneration policy. In: *Futures Academy Articles, Dublin Institute of Technology*. Article available at http://arrow.dit.ie/futuresacart/5.
Bloomfield J. & Bianchini, F. (2001): Cultural citizenship and urban governance in Western Europe. In: Stevenson, N. (ed.): *Culture & citizenship*. London and others: Sage.
Bourdieu, P. (1986): The forms of capital. In: Richardson, J. (ed.): *Handbook of theory and research for the sociology of education*. New York: Greenwood.
Boyer, R. & Saillard, Y. (2002): *Régulation theory. The state of the art*. London & New York: Routledge.
Breiger, R.L. (2004): The analysis of social networks. In: Hardy, M. & Bryman, A. (eds.): *Handbook of data analysis*. London: Sage.
Brenner, N. (2000): The urban question as a scale question: reflections on Henri Lefebvre, urban theory and the politics of scale. In: *International Journal of Urban and Regional Research, 24(2)*, 361-378.
Brühl, H., Echter, C., Frölich von Bodelschwingh, F., Jekel, G. (2005): Wohnen in der Innenstadt – eine Renaissance?. *Difu-Beiträge zur Stadtforschung, vol.41*. Berlin: self-published by Deutsches Insitut für Urbanistik.
Buck, N. (2005): Social cohesion in cities. In: Buck, I., Gordon, I., Harding, A., Turok, I. (eds.): *Changing Cities. Rethinking urban competitiveness, cohesion and governance*. London: Palgrave Macmillan.
Carp, S. (2009): Im themenpark der Hochkultur. In: Becker, K. & Wassermair, M. (eds.): *Phantom Kulturstadt. Texte zur Zukunft der Kulturpolitik II*. Wien: Erhard Löcker GesmbH.
Castells, M. (1998): *The information age: economy, society and culture: The rise of the network society*. Malden: Wiley-Blackwell.
Castells, M. (2000): Materials for an exploratory theory of the network society. In: *British Journal of Sociology, 51(1)*, 5-24.
Castells, M. (2005): Space of flows, space of places: materials for a theory of urbanism in the information age. In: Sanyal, B. (ed.): *Comparative planning cultures*. New York: Routledge.
Cataldo, S. (2009): Promoting culture as a dimension of strategic urban planning in Italy. In: Eckardt, F. & Nyström, L. (eds.): *Culture and the city*. Berlin: BWV Berliner Wissenschaftsverlag.
Comunian, R. (2009): Challenging the creative city: the role of local identity, networks and support in the creative economy. In: Benneworth, P. & Hospers, G. (eds.): *The role of culture in the economic development of old industrial regions*. Zurich & Berlin: LIT.
Cresswell, T. (2004): *Place. A short introduction*. Malden and others: Blackwell.

Crevoisier, O. (2001): Der Ansatz des kreativen Milieus. Bestandsaufnahme und Forschungsperspektiven am Beispiel urbaner Milieus. In: *Zeitschrift für Wirtschaftsgeographie, 45(3-4)*, 246-256.

Crouch, C. (2004): *Post-democracy*. Cambridge and Malden: Polity Press.

Dahl, R.A. (1994): A democratic dilemma: system effectiveness versus citizen participation. In: *Political Science Quarterly, 109(1)*, 23-34.

Davidoff, (1965): Advocacy and pluralism in planning. In: Faludi, A. (ed.). (1975): *A reader in planning theory*. Oxford and others: Pergamon Press.

Davoudi, S. & Strange, I. (2009): Space and place in twentieth century planning. An analytical framework and an historical review. In: Davoudi, S. & Strange, I. (eds.): *Conceptions of space and place in strategic spatial planning*. London and New York: Routledge.

De Frantz, M. (2005): From cultural regeneration to discursive governance: constructing the flagship of the "Museumsquartier Vienna" as a plural symbol of change. In: *International Journal of Urban and Regional Research 29(1)*, 50-66.

De Frantz, M. (2011): *Capital city cultures: reconstructing contemporary Europe in Vienna and Berlin*. Brussels: P.I.E. Peter Lang.

Dicken, P. (1998): *Global shift: mapping the changing contours of the world economy*. London: Sage.

Du Gay, P. & Pryke, M. (2002): Cultural economy: an introduction. In: Du Gay, P. & Pryke, M. (eds.): *Cultural economy. Cultural analysis and commercial life*. London and others: Sage Publications.

Du Gay, P., Hall, S., Janes, L., Koed Madsen, A., Mackay, H, Negus, K. (2013): *Doing cultural studies. The story of the Sony Walkman*. Los Angeles and others: Sage Publications.

Eade, J & Mele, C. (2002): Understanding the city. In: Eade, J & Mele, C. (eds.): *Understanding the city. Contemporary and future perspectives*. Malden: Blackwell.

Eckardt, F. & Nyström, L. (2009): Introduction: urban culture. In: Eckardt, F. & Nyström, L. (eds.): *Culture and the city*. Berlin: BWV Berliner Wissenschaftsverlag.

El Khafif, M. (2008): Inszenierter Urbanismus: Stadtraum für Kunst, Kultur und Konsum im Zeitalter der Erlebnisgesellschaft. *Dissertation at Vienna University of Technology*.

Elliott, A. (2001): The reinvention of citizenship. In: Stevenson, N. (ed.): *Culture & citizenship*. London and others: Sage.

Ermann, U. (2007): Magische Marken – Eine Fusion von Ökonomie und Kultur im globalen Kapitalismus. In: Berndt. C. & Pütz, R. (eds.): *Kulturelle Geo-*

graphien. Zur Beschäftigung mit Raum und Ort nach dem Cultural Turn. Bielefeld: transcript.

Evans, G. (2001): *Cultural planning. An urban renaissance?* London: Routledge.

Evans, G. (2003): Hard-branding the cultural city – from Prado to Prada. In: *International Journal of Urban and Regional research 27(2)*, 417-440.

Evans, G. (2006): Branding the city of culture – the death of city planning?. In: Monclùs, J. &Guàrdia, M. (eds.): *Culture, urbanism and planning.* Aldershot: Ashgate.

Faludi, A. (2005): The Netherlands: a culture with a soft spot for planning. In: Sanyal, B. (ed.): *Comparative planning cultures.* New York & Oxon: Routledge.

Fassbinder, H. (1993): Zum Begriff der strategischen Planung. In: Fassbinder, H. (ed.): *Strategien der Stadtentwicklung in europäischen Metropolen. Berichte aus Barcelona, Berlin, Hamburg, Rotterdam und Wien.* Hamburger Berichte zur Stadtplanung, vol.1. Hamburg: self-published by TUHH.

Fessler Vaz, L. & Berenstein Jacques, P. (2006): Contemporary urban spectacularisation. In: Monclùs, J. &Guàrdia, M. (eds.): *Culture, urbanism and planning.* Aldershot: Ashgate.

Fincher, R. & Jacobs, J. (1998): Introduction. In: Fincher, R. & Jacobs, J. (eds.): *Cities of difference.* New York: Guilford Press.

Florida, R. (2002): *The rise of the creative class. And how it's transforming work, leisure, community and everyday life.* Cambridge: Basic Books.

Flyvbjerg, B. (1998): Habermas and Foucault: thinkers for civil society? In: *British Journal of Sociology, 49(2)*, 210-33.

Flyvbjerg, B. (2000): Ideal theory, real rationality: Habermas versus Foucault and Nietzsche. *Paper for the Political Studies Association's 50th Annual Conference, The Challenges for Democracy in the 21st Century, London School of Economics and Political Science, 10-13 April 2000.*

Flyvbjerg, B. (2002): Bringing power to planning research. One Researcher's Praxis Story. In: *Journal of Planning Education and Research, 21*, 353-366.

Flyvbjerg, B. (2003): Rationality and power. In: Campbell, S. & Fainstein, S. (eds.): *Readings in planning theory.* Malden and others: Blackwell.

Flyvbjerg, B. (2004): Phronetic planning research: theoretical and methodological reflections. In: *Planning Theory & Practice, 5(3)*, 283-306.

Föhl, P.S. (2009): Regionale Kooperationen im Kulturbereich. Begriffe und Systematisierungen. In: Föhl, P.S. & Neisener, I. (eds.): *Regionale Kooperationen im Kulturbereich. Theoretische Grundlagen und Praxisbeispiele.* Bielefeld: transcript.

Fohrbeck, K. & Wiesand, A.J. (1989): *Von der Industriegesellschaft zur Kulturgesellschaft? Kulturpolitische Entwicklungen in der Bundesrepublik Deutschland.* München: C.H. Beck'sche Verlagsbuchhandlung.

Franck, G. (1998): *Ökonomie der Aufmerksamkeit.* Munich and Vienna: Carl Hanser Verlag.

Freestone, R. & Gibson, C. (2006): The cultural dimension of urban planning strategies: an historical perspective. In: Monclùs, J. &Guàrdia, M. (eds.): *Culture, urbanism and planning.* Aldershot: Ashgate.

Friedmann, J. (1986): The world city hypothesis. In: *Development and Change, 17(1),* 69-83.

Friedmann, J. (2011): *Insurgencies: essays in planning theory.* London: Routledge.

Friesen, N. & Hug, T. (2009): The mediatic turn: exploring concepts for media pedagogy. In: Lundby, K. (ed.): *Mediatization. Concept, changes, consequences.* New York: Peter Lang Publishing.

Füller, H. & Marquardt, N. (2009): Gouvernementalität in der humangeographischen Diskursforschung. In: Glasze, G. & Mattissek, A. (eds.): *Handbuch Diskurs und Raum. Theorien und Methoden für die Humangeographie sowie die sozial- und kulturwissenschaftliche Raumforschung.* Bielefeld: transcript.

García, B. (2004): Cultural policy and urban regeneration in Western European cities: lessons from experience, prospects for the future. In: *Local Economy, 19(4),* 312-26.

Geschäftsgruppe Stadtplanung (1981): Der Karlsplatz in Wien. In: *Beiträge zur Stadtforschung, Stadtentwicklung und Stadtgestaltung, vol.8.* Self-published by the Municipal Authority of the City of Vienna.

Gibson, L. & Stevenson, D. (2004): Urban space and the uses of culture. In: *International Journal of Cultural Policy 10(1),* 1-4.

Giffinger, R. & Hamedinger, A. (2009): Metropolitan competitiveness reconsidered: the role of territorial capital and metropolitan governance. In: *Terra Spectra – Planning Studies – Central European Journal of Spatial and Landscape Planning, 1(20),* 3-12.

Giffinger, R. & Wimmer, H. (2002): Segregation von ausländischer Wohnbevölkerung als Barriere der sozialen Integration?. In: Fassmann, H., Kohlbacher, J. & Reeger, U. (eds.): *Zuwanderung und Segregation. Europäische Metropolen im Vergleich.* Klagenfurt: Drava.

Giffinger, R. & Wimmer, H. (2005): Cities between competition and cooperation in Central Europe. In: Giffinger, R. (ed.): *Competition between cities in Central Europe: Opportunities and risks of cooperation.* Bratislava: Road.

Glasze, G., Husseini, S., Mose, J. (2009): Kodierende Verfahren in der Diskursforschung. In: Glasze, G. & Mattissek, A. (eds.): *Handbuch Diskurs und Raum. Theorien und Methoden für die Humangeographie sowie die sozial- und kulturwissenschaftliche Raumforschung.* Bielefeld: transcript.

Glasze, G. & Mattissek, A. (2009): Diskursforschung in der Humangeographie: Konzeptionelle Grundlagen und empirische Operationalisierungen. In: Glasze, G. & Mattissek, A. (eds.): *Handbuch Diskurs und Raum. Theorien und Methoden für die Humangeographie sowie die sozial- und kulturwissenschaftliche Raumforschung.* Bielefeld: transcript.

Glogner, P. & Föhl, P.S. (2010): Publikumsforschung im Kulturbereich: Relevanz, Herausforderungen, Perspektiven. In: Glogner, P. & Föhl, P.S. (eds.): *Das Kulturpublikum. Fragestellungen und Befunde der empirischen Forschung.* Wiesbaden: VS Verlag für Sozialwissenschaften.

Goodwin, M (1993): The city as commodity: the contested space of urban development. In: Kearns, G. & Philo, C. (eds.): *Selling places. The city as cultural capital, past and present.* Oxford and others: Pergamon Press.

Gordon, I., & Buck, N. (2005): Cities in the new conventional wisdom. In: Buck, I., Gordon, I., Harding, A., Turok, I. (eds.): *Changing Cities. Rethinking urban competitiveness, cohesion and governance.* London: Palgrave Macmillan.

Göschel, A. (2009): Die kulturelle Produktivität von Städten: Thesen zu unterschiedlichen Potentialen in Ost- und Westdeutschland. In: Quenzel, G. (ed.): *Entwicklungsfaktor Kultur. Studien zum kulturellen und ökonomischen Potential der europäischen Stadt.* Bielefeld: transcript.

Göschel, A. & Kirchberg, V. (1998): Einleitung: Kultur der Stadt – Kultur in der Stadt. In: Göschel, A. & Kirchberg, V. (eds.): *Kultur in der Stadt.* Opladen: Leske + Budrich.

Gotham, K.F. (2005): Theorizing urban spectacles. In: *City, 9(2)*, 225-46.

Gottdiener, M. (2000): Approaches to consumption: classical and contemporary perspectives. In: Gottdiener, M. (ed.): *New forms of consumption. Consumers, culture, and commodification.* Lanham: Rowman & Littlefield.

Gottdiener, M. & Budd, L. (2005): *Key concepts in urban studies.* Los Angeles: Sage.

Grodach, C. & Silver, D. (2013): Urbanizing cultural policy. In: Grodach, C. & Silver, D. (eds.): *The politics of urban cultural policy. Global perspectives.* London and New York: Routledge.

Grubbauer, M. (2011a): *Die vorgestellte Stadt. Globale Büroarchitektur, Stadtmarketing und politischer Wandel in Wien.* Bielefeld: transcript.

Grubbauer, M. (2011b): Räume der Wirtschaft: Das Bürohochhaus als Bedeutungsträger in der visuellen Konstruktion ökonomischer Vorstellungswelten. In: Hofmann, W. (ed.): *Stadt als Erfahrungsraum der Politik*. Berlin: LIT.

Gruber, H. (2008): Analyzing communication in the new media. In: Wodak, R. and Krzyzanowski, M. (eds.): *Qualitative discourse analysis in the social sciences*. Hampshire: Palgrave Macmillan.

Gualini, E. (2005): Reconnecting space, place, and institutions: inquiring into "local" governance capacity in urban and regional research. In: Albrechts, L. & Mandelbaum, S.J. (eds.): *The network society: a new context for planning?*. Oxon and New York: Routledge.

Gunter, B. & van der Hoeven, R. (2004): The social dimension of globalization: A review of the literature. *International Labour Review, 143(1-2)*, 7-43.

Gupta, A. & Ferguson, J. (1997a): Culture, power, place: ethnography at the end of an era. In: Gupta, A. & Ferguson, J. (eds.): *Culture, power, place. Explorations in critical anthropology*. Durham and London: Duke University Press.

Gupta, A. & Ferguson, J. (1997b): Beyond "culture": space, identity, and the politics of difference. In: Gupta, A. & Ferguson, J. (eds.): *Culture, power, place. Explorations in critical anthropology*. Durham and London: Duke University Press.

Hajer, M. (2003): A frame in the fiels: policymaking and the reinvention of politics. In: Hajer, M: & Wagenaar, H. (eds.): *Deliberative policy analysis*. Cambridge and others: Cambridge University Press.

Hajer, M. & Versteeg, W. (2005): A decade of discourse analysis of environmental politics: achievements, challenges, perspectives. In: *Journal of Environmental Policy & Planning, 7(3)*, 175-184.

Hajer, M. & Wagenaar, H. (2003): Introduction. In: Hajer, M. & Wagenaar, H. (eds.): *Deliberative policy analysis. Understanding governance in the network society*. Cambridge and others: Cambridge University Press.

Hall, S. (1997): The work of representation. In: Hall, S. (ed.): *Representation: cultural representations and signifying practices*. London and others: Sage Publications.

Hall, T. & Hubbard, P. (1996): The entrepreneurial city: new urban politics, new urban geographies? In: *Progress in Human Geography, 20(2)*, 153-174.

Hall, T. (1998): *Urban geography*. London: Routledge.

Hannemann, c. & Sewing, W. (1998): Gebaute Stadtkultur: Architektur als Identitätskonstrukt. In: Göschel, A. & Kirchberg, V. (eds.): *Kultur in der Stadt*. Opladen: Leske + Budrich.

Harding, A. (2005): Governance and socio-economic change in cities. In: Buck, I., Gordon, I., Harding, A., Turok, I. (eds.): *Changing Cities. Rethinking urban competitiveness, cohesion and governance*. London: Palgrave Macmillan.

Harrison, J. (2009): Breaking down the barriers to growth: economic development, culture, and "old industrial regions". In: Benneworth, P. & Hospers, G. (eds.): *The role of culture in the economic development of old industrial regions*. Zurich & Berlin: LIT.

Harvey, D. (1985): *The urbanization of capital. Studies in the history and theory of capitalist urbanization 2*. Oxford: Basil Blackwell.

Harvey, D. (1989): From managerialism to entrepreneurialism: The transformation in urban governance in late capitalism. In: *Geografiska Annaler. Series B, Human Geography, 71(1)*, 3-17.

Harvey, D. (1990): *The condition of postmodernity. An enquiry into the origins of cultural change*. Cambridge & Oxford: Blackwell.

Harvey, D. (1997): Contested cities: social process and spatial form. In: Jewson, N. & MacGregor, S. (eds.): *Transforming cities: contested governance and new spatial divisions*. London and New York: Routledge.

Harvey, D. (2002): The art of rent: globalization, monopoly rent and the commodification of culture. In: *Socialist Register, vol.38*, 93-110.

Hatz, G. (2009): Kultur als Instrument der Stadtplanung. In: Fassmann, H., Hatz, G., Matznetter, W. (eds.): *Wien – Städtebauliche Strukturen und gesellschaftliche Entwicklungen*. Vienna and others: Böhlau.

Häußermann, H. & Siebel, W. (1993): *Festivalisierung der Stadtpolitik. Stadtentwicklung durch große Projekte*. Wiesbaden: Springer.

Häußermann, H., Läpple, D., Siebel, W. (2008): *Stadtpolitik*. Berlin: Suhrkamp.

Healey, P. (1992): Planning through debate: the communicative turn in planning. In: *The Town Planning Review, 63(2)*, 143-162.

Healey, P. (1997): *Collaborative planning. Shaping places in fragmented societies*. Vancouver: UBC Press.

Healey, P., Khakee, A., Motte, A., Needham, B. (1999): European developments in strategic spatial planning. In: *European Planning Studies, 7(3)*, 339-355.

Healey, P., de Magalheas, C., Madanipour, A., Pendlebury, J. (2003): Place, identity and local politics: analysing initiatives in deliberative governance. In: Hajer, M: & Wagenaar, H. (eds.): *Deliberative policy analysis*. Cambridge and others: Cambridge University Press.

Heineberg, H. (2005): Die Erforschung der Stadt – von "lokal" bis "global". In: *Geographie heute, 236*, 2-5.

Helbrecht, I. (1993): Innovation Stadtmarketing: Ausverkauf des Politischen oder Demokratisierung der Planung?. In: *Wissenschaftliche Zeitschrift der Hochschule für Architektur und Bauwesen Weimar, 39(1/2)*, 151-155.

Helbrecht, I. (1994): *Stadtmarketing. Konturen einer kommunikativen Stadtentwicklungspolitik.* Basel: Birkhäuser Verlag.

Helbrecht, I. (2001): Sokrates, die Stadt und der Tod. Individualisierung durch Urbanisierung. In: *Berichte zur deutschen Landeskunde, 75(2-3)*, 103-112.

Heywood, A. (2013): *Politics.* Hampshire: Palgrave Macmillan.

Hofmann, W. (2011): Vorbemerkung. In: Hofmann, W. (ed.): *Stadt als Erfahrungsraum der Politik. Beiträge zur kulturellen Konstruktion urbaner Politik.* Berlin: LIT Verlag.

Hornig, P. (2011): *Kunst im Museum und Kunst im öffentlichen Raum. Elitär versus demokratisch?.* Wiesbaden: VS Verlag für Sozialwissenschaften.

Hunter, F. (1983): Die Machtstruktur von Regional City. In: Schmals, K.M. (ed.): *Stadt und Gesellschaft. Ein Arbeits- und Grundlagenwerk.* München: Edition Academic Verlags-GmbH.

Jacobs, J. (1969): *The economy of cities.* New York: Vintage Books.

Jacobs, J. (1998): Staging difference: aestheticization and the politics of difference in contemporary cities. In: Fincher, R. & Jacobs, J. (eds.): *Cities of difference.* New York: Guilford Press.

Jacobs, K. (2006): Discourse analysis and its utility for urban policy research. In: *Urban Policy and research, 24(1)*, 39-52.

Jameson, F. (1991): *Postmodernism, or, the cultural logic of late capitalism.* Durham: Duke University Press.

Jameson, F. (1998): *The cultural turn. Selected writings on the postmodern, 1983-1998.* London & New York: Verso.

Jewson, N. & MacGregor, S. (1997): Transforming cities: social exclusion and the reinvention of partnership. In: Jewson, N. & MacGregor, S. (eds.): *Transforming cities: contested governance and new spatial divisions.* London and New York: Routledge.

Jessop, B. (1990): Regulation theories in retrospect and prospect. In: *Economy and Society, 19(29)*, 153-216.

Jessop, B. (1993): Towards a Schumpeterian workfare state? Preliminary remarks on post-Fordist political economy. In: *Studies in Political Economy, 40*, 7-40.

Jessop, B. (1997): The entrepreneurial city: re-imaging localities, redesigning economic governance, or restructuring capital?. In: Jewson, N. & MacGregor, S. (eds.): *Transforming cities: contested governance and new spatial divisions.* London and New York: Routledge.

Jessop, B. (2004): Critical semiotic analysis and cultural political economy. In: *Critical discourse studies, 1(1)*, 1-16.
Jessop, B. (2008): *State power. A strategic-relational approach.* Cambridge and Malden: Polity Press.
Jessop, B. (2013): Recovered imaginaries, imagined recoveries: a cultural political economy of crisis construals and crisis-management in the North Atlantic Financial Crisis. In: Brenner, M. (ed.): *Beyond the global economic crisis: economics and politics for a post-crisis settlement.* Cheltenham: Edward Elgar.
Jessop, B. & Oosterlynck, S. (2008): Cultural political economy: on making the cultural turn without falling into soft economic sociology. In: *Geoforum, 39(3)*, 1155-1169.
Jessop, B. & Sum, N.L. (2006): *Beyond the regulation approach. Putting capitalist economies in their place.* Cheltenham & Northampton: Edward Elgar.
Jones, P. & Wilks-Heeg, S. (2004): Capitalising culture: Liverpool 2008. In: *Local Economy, 19(4)*, 341-360.
Jones, S. (2006): *Antonio Gramsci.* Oxon and New York: Routledge.
Jung, M.M. (2010): *Raumimage – Imageräume. Marketing von (urbanen) Räumen ans Instrument von Gemeinwesenentwicklung. Series „Studien im Rahmen der Schriftenreihe des Masterstudiengangs Gemeinwesenentwicklung, Quartiermanagement und lokale Ökonomie.* Munich: Fakultät für angewandte Sozialwissenschaften an der Hochschule München.
Kaufmann, T. (2009): Jenseits des visibility-Mantras. In: Becker, K. & Wassermair, M. (eds.): *Phantom Kulturstadt. Texte zur Zukunft der Kulturpolitik II.* Wien: Erhard Löcker GesmbH.
Kavaratzis, M. (2004): From city marketing to city branding: towards a theoretical framework for developing city brands. In: *Place Branding 1(1)*, 58-73.
Kearns, G. (1993): The city as spectacle: Paris and the bicentenary of the French Revolution. In: Kearns, G. & Philo, C. (eds.): *Selling places. The city as cultural capital, past and present.* Oxford and others: Pergamon Press.
Kearns, G. & Philo, C. (1993): Culture, history, capital: a critical introduction to the selling of places. In: Kearns, G. & Philo, C. (eds.): *Selling places. The city as cultural capital, past and present.* Oxford and others: Pergamon Press.
Keller, R. (2011): *Diskursforschung. Eine Einführung für SozialwissenschaftlerInnen.* Wiesbaden: VS Verlag für Sozialwissenschaften.
Kelly, P. (1999): The geographies and politics of globalization. *Progress in Human Geography, 23(3)*, 379-400.

Kirchberg, V. (1998): Stadtkultur in der Urban Political Economy. In: Göschel, A. & Kirchberg, V. (eds.): *Kultur in der Stadt*. Opladen: Leske + Budrich.

Kloostermann, R. & van der Werff, M. (2009): Culture: a local anchor in a world of flows? A critical assessment of cultural spatial planning in the Netherlands. In: Benneworth, P. & Hospers, G. (eds.): *The role of culture in the economic development of old industrial regions*. Zurich & Berlin: LIT.

Knierbein, S. (2010): *Die Produktion zentraler öffentlicher Räume in der Aufmerksamkeitsökonomie: Ästhetische, ökonomische und mediale Restrukturierungen durch gestaltwirksame Koalitionen in Berlin seit 1980*. Wiesbaden: VS Verlag für Sozialwissenschaften.

Kofman, E. (1998): Whose city? Gender, class and immigration in globalizing European cities. In: Fincher, R. & Jacobs, J. (eds.): *Cities of difference*. New York: Guilford Press.

Kohlbacher, J. & Reeger, U. (2002): Zuwanderung und Segregation in Wien. In: Fassmann, H., Kohlbacher, J. & Reeger, U. (eds.): *Zuwanderung und Segregation. Europäische Metropolen im Vergleich*. Klagenfurt: Drava.

Kohlbacher, J. & Reeger, U. (2011): Geringqualifizierte Migration und sozialräumliche Polarisation. Das Fallbeispiel Wien. In: Matznetter, W. & Musil, R. (eds.): *Europa: Metropolen im Wandel*. Wien: Mandelbaum Verlag.

Koolhaas, R. (1995): The generic city. In: Koolhaas, R. & Mau, B. (eds.): *S, M, L, XL*. New York: Monacelli Press.

Krätke, S. (2003): Global media cities in a world-wide urban network. In: *European Planning Studies, 11(6)*, 605-628.

Krzyzanowski, M. (2008): Analyzing focus group discussions. In: Wodak, R. and Krzyzanowski, M. (eds.): *Qualitative discourse analysis in the social sciences*. Hampshire: Palgrave Macmillan.

Kühn, M. & Fischer, S. (2010): *Strategische Stadtplanung. Strategiebildung in schrumpfenden Städten aus planungs- und politikwissenschaftlicher Perspektive*. Detmold: Rohn.

Kunzmann, K.R. (2009): Kreativwirtschaft und strategische Stadtentwicklung. In: Lange, B., Kalandides, A., Stöber, B., Wellmann, I. (eds.): *Governance der Kreativwirtschaft. Diagnosen und Handlungsoptionen*. Bielefeld: transcript.

Küpper, U.I. (1990): Zum Wandel der verfahren und Entscheidungsstrukturen in Stadtentwicklung und Stadtplanung. In: Sieverts, T. (ed.): *Zukunftsausgaben der Stadtplanung*. Düsseldorf: Werner-Verlag.

Lagendijk, A. (2004): Global "lifeworlds" versus local "systemworlds": how flying winemakers produce global wines in interconnected locales. In: *Tijdschrift voor Economische en Sociale Geografie, 95(5)*, 511-526.

Landry, C. (2000): *The creative city. A toolkit for urban innovators*. Bournes Green: Comedia.
Lange, B. (2007): Konzeptionalisierungen von „Markt" als Gegenstand der Neuen Kulturgeographie – Der Fall emergierender Märkte in Kreativökonomien. In: Berndt. C. & Pütz, R. (eds.): *Kulturelle Geographien. Zur Beschäftigung mit Raum und Ort nach dem Cultural Turn*. Bielefeld: transcript.
Lange, B., Kalandides, A., Stöber, B., Wellmann, I. (2009): Fragmentierte Ordnungen. In: Lange, B., Kalandides, A., Stöber, B., Wellmann, I. (eds.): *Governance der Kreativwirtschaft. Diagnosen und Handlungsoptionen*. Bielefeld: transcript.
Lee, N. (2009): The creative industries as "distinctiveness strategy". In: Eckardt, F. & Nyström, L. (eds.): *Culture and the city*. Berlin: BWV Berliner Wissenschaftsverlag.
Lees, L. (2004): Urban geography: discourse analysis and urban research. In: *Progress in human Geography, 28(1)*, 101-107.
Lewitzky, U. (2005): *Kunst für alle? Kunst im öffentlichen Raum zwischen Partizipation, Intervention und neuer Urbanität*. Bielefeld: transcript.
Lindblom, C.E. (1959): The science of "muddling through". In: Faludi, A. (ed.) (1973): *A reader in planning theory*. Oxford and others: Pergamon Press.
Logan, J.R. & Molotch, H.L. (1987): *Urban fortunes. The political economy of place*. Berkeley & Los Angeles: University of California Press.
Lundby, K. (2009): Introduction: "Mediatization" as key. In: Lundby, K. (ed.): *Mediatization. Concept, changes, consequences*. New York: Peter Lang Publishing.
Madanipour, A. (1998): Social exclusion and space. In: LeGates, R.T. & Stout, F. (eds.) (2007): *The city reader*. Oxon and New York: Routledge.
Madanipour, A. (1999): Why are the design and development of public spaces significant for cities?. In: *Environment and Planning B. Planning and Design, 1999(26)*, 879-891.
Madanipour, A. (2003): Marginale öffentliche Räume in europäischen Städten. In: *disP – The Planning Review, 39(155)*, 4-17.
Maderthaner, W. (2006): Von der Zeit um 1860 bis zum Jahr 1945. In: Csendes, P. & Oppl, F. (eds.): *Wien. Geschichte einer Stadt. Von 1790 bis zur Gegenwart*. Vienna and others: Böhlau.
Madgin, R. (2009): Using culture to transform de-industrial cities: a British-French comparison. In: Eckardt, F. & Nyström, L. (eds.): *Culture and the city*. Berlin: BWV Berliner Wissenschaftsverlag.

Marcuse, P. (2011): The three historic currents of planning. In: Bridge, G. & Watson, S. (eds.): *The new Blackwell companion to the city*. Malden and Oxford: Blackwell.

Marcuse, P. & van Kempen, R.(2000): Conclusion: a changed spatial order. In: Marcuse, P. & van Kempen, R. (eds.): *Globalizing cities: a new spatial order?*. Oxford: Blackwell.

Markusen, A. & Gadwa, A. (2009): Arts and culture in urban or regional planning: a review and research agenda. In: *Journal of Planning Education and Research, 29(3)*, 379-391.

Martin, D., McCann, E., Purcell, M. (2003): Space, scale, governance, and representation: contemporary geographical perspectives on urban politics and policy. In: *Journal of Urban Affairs, 25(2)*, 113-121.

Martinelli, F. & Novy, A. (2013): Urban and regional trajectories between pathdependency and path-shaping: structures, institutions, discourses and agency in contemporary capitalism. In: Martinelli, F., Moulaert, F., Novy, A. (eds.): *Urban and regional development trajectories in contemporary capitalism*. London & New York: Routledge.

Massey, D. (2006): Keine Entlastung für das Lokale. In: Berking, H. (ed.): *Die Macht des Lokalen in einer Welt ohne Grenzen*. Frankfurt/Main: Campus Verlag.

Mattissek, A. (2007): Diskursive Konstitution städtischer Identität – Das Beispiel Frankfurt am Main. In: Berndt. C. & Pütz, R. (eds.): *Kulturelle Geographien. Zur Beschäftigung mit Raum und Ort nach dem Cultural Turn*. Bielefeld: transcript.

Mattissek, A. (2009): Die Aussagenanalyse als Mikromethode der Diskursforschung. In: Glasze, G. & Mattissek, A. (eds.): *Handbuch Diskurs und Raum. Theorien und Methoden für die Humangeographie sowie die sozial- und kulturwissenschaftliche Raumforschung*. Bielefeld: transcript.

Mattl, S. (2000): *Wien im 20. Jahrhundert*. Wien: Pichler Verlag GmbH & Co KG.

Mattl, S. (2009): City Brandings. In: Becker, K., Wassermair, M. (eds.): *Phantom Kulturstadt. Texte zur Zukunft der Kulturpolitik II*. Wien: Löcker.

Mautner, G. (2008): Analyzing newspapers, magazines and other print media. In: Wodak, R. and Krzyzanowski, M. (eds.): *Qualitative discourse analysis in the social sciences*. Hampshire: Palgrave Macmillan.

Mayerhofer, E. (2009): Cultural and creative industries. In: Becker, K. & Wassermair, M. (eds.): *Phantom Kulturstadt. Texte zur Zukunft der Kulturpolitik II*. Wien: Erhard Löcker GesmbH.

McCann, E. (2003): Framing space and time in the city: urban policy and the politics of spatial and temporal scale. In: *Journal of Urban Affairs, 25(2)*, 159-178.

McCann, E. (2004): Urban political economy beyond the "global city". In: *Urban Studies, 41(12)*, 2315-2333.

McGuigan, J. (2001): Three discourses of cultural policy. In: Stevenson, N. (ed.): *Culture & citizenship*. London and others: Sage.

Meißl, G. (2006): Ökonomie und Urbanität. Zur wirtschafts- und sozialgeschichtlichen Entwicklung Wiens im 20. Jahrhundert und zu Beginn des 21. Jahrhunderts. In: Csendes, P. & Oppl, F. (eds.): *Wien. Geschichte einer Stadt. Von 1790 bis zur Gegenwart*. Vienna and others: Böhlau.

Miles, M. (2007): *Cities and cultures*. Oxon: Routledge.

Miles, M., Hall, T., Borden, I. (2000): Introduction. In: Miles, M., Hall, T., Borden, I. (eds.): *The city cultures reader*. London & New York: Routledge.

Miles, S. & Paddison, R. (2005): Introduction: the rise and rise of culture-led urban regeneration. In: *Urban Studies, 42(5/6)*, 833-839.

Mills, S. (2007): *Der Diskurs*. Tübingen: Narr Francke Attempto Verlag.

Molotch, H.L. (1976): The city as growth machine: toward a political economy of place. In: *American Journal of Sociology, 82(2)*, 309-332.

Molotch, H.L. (1998): Kunst als das herzstück einer regionalen Ökonomie. In: Göschel, A. & Kirchberg, V. (eds.): *Kultur in der Stadt*. Opladen: Leske + Budrich.

Monclús, J. (2006): International exhibitions and planning. Hosting large-scale events as place promotion and as catalysts of urban regeneration. In: Monclús, J. & Guàrdia, M. (eds.): *Culture, urbanism and planning*. Aldershot & Burlington: Ashgate.

Monclús, J. & Guàrdia, M. (2006): Introduction. In: Monclús, J. & Guàrdia, M. (eds.): *Culture, urbanism and planning*. Aldershot & Burlington: Ashgate.

Morgan, K. (2004): The exaggerated death of geography: learning, proximity and territorial innovation systems. In: *Journal of Economic Geography, 4(1)*, 3-21.

Mossberger, K. (2009): Urban regime analysis. In: Davis, J. & Imbroscio, D.L. (eds.): *Theories of urban politics*. London: Sage Publications.

Mouffe, C. (2007): *Über das Politische. Wider die kosmopolitische Illusion*. Frankfurt/Main: Suhrkamp.

Moulaert, F., Demuynck, H., Nussbaumer, J. (2004): Urban renaissance: from physical beautification to social empowerment. In: *City, 8(2)*, 229-35.

Mumford, L. (1970): *The culture of cities*. San Diego and others: Harcourt Brace & Company.

Municipal Department 7 (2005): *Kunst- und Kulturbericht der Stadt Wien*. Vienna: self-published by the Municipal Authority of the City of Vienna.

Municipal Department 7 (2008): *Kunst- und Kulturbericht der Stadt Wien*. Vienna: self-published by the Municipal Authority of the City of Vienna.

Municipal Department 7 (2012): *Kunst- und Kulturbericht & Frauenkulturbericht der Stadt Wien 2012*. Self-published by the Municipal Authority of the City of Vienna.

Municipal Department 17 (2012): *Integrations- und Diversitätsmonitor der Stadt Wien 2009 - 2011*. Vienna: self-published by the Municipal Department 17.

Municipal Department 18 (1985): *Stadtentwicklungsplan Wien*. Vienna: self-published by the Municipal Authority of the City of Vienna.

Municipal Department 18 (1994): *Stadtentwicklungsplan Wien 1994*. Vienna: self-published by the Municipal Department 18.

Municipal Department 18 (2001): *Strategieplan für Wien – Strategische Projekte*. Werkstattbericht der Stadtentwicklung Wien, vol.32A. Published by City of Vienna, Municipal Department 18.

Municipal Department 18 (2004a): *Strategieplan 2004*. Self-published by the Municipal Authority of the City of Vienna, Municipal Department 18.

Municipal Department 18 (2004b): *Wiener Wohnstudien – Wohnzufriedenheit, Mobilitäts- und Freizeitverhalten*. Werkstattbericht der Stadtentwicklung Wien, vol.71. Published by City of Vienna, Municipal Department 18.

Municipal Department 18 (2005): *STEP 05. Stadtentwicklung Wien 2005*. Self-published by City of Vienna, Municipal Department 18.

Municipal Department 18 (2007): *Draußen in der Stadt – Öffentliche Räume in Wien*. Werkstattbericht der Stadtentwicklung Wien, vol.89. Published by City of Vienna, Municipal Department 18.

Municipal Department 18 (2008): *Neuinterpretation öffentlicher Raum – Eine Studienreihe für die Wiener Bezirke*. Werkstattbericht der Stadtentwicklung Wien, vol.93. Published by City of Vienna, Municipal Department 18.

Municipal Department 18 (2009): *freiraum stadtraum wien – Der Weg zum Leitbild für den öffentlichen Raum*. Werkstattbericht der Stadtentwicklung Wien, vol.98. Published by City of Vienna, Municipal Department 18.

Municipal Department 18 (2010): *StEP 05 Fortschrittsbericht 2010*. Self-published by City of Vienna, Municipal Department 18.

Municipal Department 18 (2011): *Jahresbericht 2011 der Abteilung Stadtentwicklung und Stadtplanung (MA18)*: Published by Municipal Authority of Vienna, Municipal Department 18.

Municipal Department 18 (2012a): *stadt bauen – Beispiele für und aus Wien*. Werkstattbericht der Stadtentwicklung Wien, vol.124. Published by City of Vienna, Municipal Department 18.
Municipal Department 18 (2012b): *Städtepolitik in der Europäischen Union – Ein Handbuch*. Werkstattbericht der Stadtentwicklung Wien, vol.123. Published by City of Vienna, Municipal Department 18.
Municipal Department 18 (2012c): *Zielgebiet Gürtel. Wiens größtes Bürgerbeteiligungsverfahren 2002-2007. Die Verwirklichung der Projekte 2007-2010*. Werkstattbericht der Stadtentwicklung Wien, vol.122. Published by City of Vienna, Municipal Department 18.
Municipal Department 19 (2006): *Vienna, world heritage – the state of the art*. Published by City of Vienna, Municipal Department 19.
Musner, L. (2006): Ist Wien anders? Zur Kulturgeschichte der Stadt nach 1945. In: Csendes, P. & Oppl, F. (eds.): *Wien. Geschichte einer Stadt. Von 1790 bis zur Gegenwart*. Vienna and others: Böhlau.
Novy, A., Redak, V., Jäger, J., Hamedinger, A. (2001): The end of Red Vienna. Recent ruptures and continuities in urban governance. In: *European Urban and Regional Studies, 8(2)*, 131-144.
Novy, A. (2011): Unequal diversity – on the political economiy of social cohesion in Vienna. In: *European Urban and Regional Studies, 18(3)*, 239-53.
Novy, A., Coimbra Swiatek, D., Lengauer, L. (2013): Vienna between East and West: the construction of a new transborder Central European region. In: Martinelli, F., Moulaert, F., Novy, A. (2013): *Urban and regional development trajectories in contemporary capitalism*. London & New York: Routledge.
Oh, M. & Arditi, J. (2000): Shopping and postmodernism: consumption, production, identity, and the internet. In: Gottdiener, M. (ed.): *New forms of consumption. Consumers, culture, and commodification*. Lanham: Rowman & Littlefield.
Orum & Chen (2003): *The world of cities. Places in comparative and historical perspective*. Malden: Blackwell.
Peck, J. (2005): Struggling with the creative class. In: *International Journal of Urban and Regional Research, 29(4)*, 740-770.
Peters, J.D. (1997): Seeing bifocally: media, place, and culture. In: Gupta, A. & Ferguson, J. (eds.): *Culture, power, place. Explorations in critical anthropology*. Durham and London: Duke University Press.
Pierre, J. (1999): Models of urban governance. The institutional dimension of urban politics. In: *Urban Affairs Review, 34(3)*, 372-396.

Pirhofer, G. & Stimmer, K., (2007): *Pläne für Wien. Theorie und Praxis der Wiener Stadtplanung von 1945 bis 2005*. Self-published by City of Vienna, Municipal Department 18.

Pollak, A. (2008): Analyzing TC documentaries. In: Wodak, R. and Krzyzanowski, M. (eds.): Q*ualitative discourse analysis in the social sciences*. Hampshire: Palgrave Macmillan.

Porter, B.W. (2008): Heritage tourism: conflicting identities in the modern world. In: Graham, B. & Howard, P. (eds.): *The Ashgate research companion to heritage and identity*. Aldershot & Burlington: Ashgate.

Posova, D.& Sykora, L. (2011): Urbanisierung und Suburbanisierung. Die Stadtregionen Prag und Wien unter den Rahmenbedingungen unterschiedlicher politisch-ökonomischer Regime. In: Matznetter, W. & Musil, R. (eds.): *Europa: Metropolen im Wandel*. Wien: Mandelbaum Verlag.

Pott, A. (2007): Identität und Raum. Perspektiven nach dem Cultural Turn. In: Berndt. C. & Pütz, R. (eds.): *Kulturelle Geographien. Zur Beschäftigung mit Raum und Ort nach dem Cultural Turn*. Bielefeld: transcript.

Pratt, A.C. (1998): The challenge of governance in the creative and cultural industries. In: Lange, B., Kalandides, A., Stöber, B., Wellmann, I. (eds.): *Governance der Kreativwirtschaft. Diagnosen und Handlungsoptionen*. Bielefeld: transcript.

Puhan-Schulz, F. (2005): *Museen und Stadtimagebildung. Amsterdam – Frankfurt/Main – Prag. Ein Vergleich*. Bielefeld: transcript.

Puype, D. (2004): Arts and culture as experimental spaces in the city. In: *City, 8(2)*, 295-301.

Quenzel, G. & Lottermann, A. (2009): Kulturelle Produktivität von Städten – ein Zusammenspiel von Kultur, Politik und Ökonomie. In: Quenzel, G. (ed.): *Entwicklungsfaktor Kultur. Studien zum kulturellen und ökonomischen Potential der europäischen Stadt*. Bielefeld: transcript.

Reicher, C. (2009): Industriekultur: Gespeicherte Erinnerung und kulturelles Potential. In: Quenzel, G. (ed.): *Entwicklungsfaktor Kultur. Studien zum kulturellen und ökonomischen Potential der europäischen Stadt*. Bielefeld: transcript.

Ribera-Fumaz, R. (2009): From urban political economy to cultural political economy: rethinking culture and economy in and beyond the urban. In: *Progress in Human Geography, 33(4)*, 447-465.

Rhodes, R.A.W. (1996): The new governance: governing without government. In: *Political Studies, 44*, 652-667.

Rode, P., Wanschura, B., Kubesch, C. (2010): *Kunst macht Stadt. Vier Fallstudien zur Interaktion von Kunst und Stadtquartier*. Wiesbaden: VS Verlag für Sozialwissenschaften.

Rojek, C. (2000): Mass tourism or the re-enchantment of the world? Issues and contradictions in the study of travel. In: Gottdiener, M. (ed.): *New forms of consumption. Consumers, culture, and commodification*. Lanham: Rowman & Littlefield.

Sackmann, R., Jonda, B., Reinhold, M. (2008): Demographie als Herausforderung. In: Sackmann, R., Jonda, B., Reinhold, M. (eds.): *Demographie als Herausforderung für den öffentlichen Sektor*. Wiesbaden: VS Verlag für Sozialwissenschaften.

Sadler, D. (1993): Place-marketing, competitive places and the construction of hegemony in Britain in the 1980s. In: Kearns, G. & Philo, C. (eds.): *Selling places. The city as cultural capital, past and present*. Oxford and others: Pergamon Press.

Salet, W. & Faludi, A. (2000): Three approaches to strategic spatial planning. In Salet, W. & Faludi, A. (eds.): *The revival of strategic spatial planning*. Amsterdam: University of Amsterdam.

Sanyal, B. (2005): Hybrid planning cultures: the search for the global cultural commons. In: Sanyal, B. (ed.): *Comparative planning cultures*. New York & Oxon: Routledge.

Sassen, S. (1994): The new inequalities within cities. In: Miles, M., Hall, T., Borden, I. (eds.) (2000): *The city cultures reader*. London and New York: Routledge.

Sassen, S. (2001): *The global city: New York, London, Tokyo*. Princeton: Princeton University Press.

Sassen, S. (2011): Informelles politisches Wissen in Netzwerken. Die Rolle der neuen Technologien. In: Becker, K & Wassermair, M. (eds.): *Nach dem Ende der Politik. Texte zur Zukunft der Kulturpolitik III*. Wien: Löcker.

Schäfers, B. (2009): Entwicklung und Selbstverständnis der europäischen Stadt. In: Quenzel, G. (ed.): *Entwicklungsfaktor Kultur. Studien zum kulturellen und ökonomischen Potential der europäischen Stadt*. Bielefeld: transcript.

Schäflein, S. (1994): *Freizeit als Faktor der Stadtentwicklungspolitik und -planung. Stadtmarketing für mehr Lebensqualität?*. Frankfurt/Main: self-published by Institut für Kulturgeographie, Stadt- und Regionalforschung and Institut für Physische Geographie, Johann Wolfgang Goethe-Universität Frankfurt/Main.

Schipper, S. (2012): Zur Genealogie neoliberaler Hegemonie am Beispiel der „unternehmerischen Stadt" in Frankfurt am Main. In: Dzudzek, I., Kunze, C.,

Wullweber, J. (eds.): *Diskurs und Hegemonie. Gesellschaftskritische Perspektiven*. Bielefeld: transcript.

Schmid, H. (2007): Ökonomie und Faszination: Aufmerksamkeitsstrategien und unternehmensorientierte Stadtpolitik. In: Berndt. C. & Pütz, R. (eds.): *Kulturelle Geographien. Zur Beschäftigung mit Raum und Ort nach dem Cultural Turn*. Bielefeld: transcript.

Schmid, C. (2008): Henri Lefebvre's theory of the production of space. Towards a three-dimensional dialectic. In: Goonewardena, K., Kipfer, S., Milgrom, R., Schmid, C. (eds.): *Space, difference, everyday life. Reading Henri Lefebvre*. New York & London: Routledge.

Schneider, H. (1997): *Stadtentwicklung als politischer Prozess. Stadtentwicklungsstrategien in Heidelberg, Wuppertal, Dresden und Trier*. Opladen: Leske + Budrich.

Schorske, C.E. (1981): *Fin-de-siecle Vienna. Politics and culture*. New York & Toronto: Vintage Books.

Schroer, M. (2008): „Bringing space back in" – Zur Relevanz des Raums als soziologischer Kategorie. In: Döring, J. & Thielmann, T. (eds.): *Spatial turn. Das Raumparadigma in den Kultur- und Sozialwissenschaften*. Bielefeld: transcript.

Schulz, D. (2006): Die politische Theorie symbolischer Macht: Pierre Bourdieu. In: Brodocz, A. & Schaal, G.S. (eds.): *Politische Theorien der Gegenwart I*. Opladen & Farmington Hills: Verlag Barbara Budrich.

Schulze, G. (2005):. *Die Erlebnisgesellschaft: Kultursoziologie der Gegenwart*. Frankfurt/Main: Campus Verlag.

Scott, A.J. (1997): The cultural economy of cities. In: *International Journal of Urban and Regional Research 27(2)*, 323-339.

Scott, A.J. (2000): *The cultural economy of cities*. London and others: Sage.

Scott, J. (2001): *Power*. Cambridge and Malden: Blackwell.

Scott, J.W. (2012): European politics of borders, border symbolism and cross-border cooperation. In: Wilson, T.M., Donnan, H. (eds.): *A companion to border studies. Blackwell companions to anthropology*. West Sussex: Wiley-Blackwell, 83-99.

Sennett, R. (2008): *Handwerk*. Berlin: Berlin Verlag.

Sieverts, T. (1990): Neue Aufgaben für den Städtebau im alten Europa – Voraussetzungen, Prinzipien, Beispiele. In: Sieverts, T. (ed.): *Zukunftsausgaben der Stadtplanung*. Düsseldorf: Werner-Verlag.

Sklair, L. (2006): Iconic architecture and capitalist globalization. In: *City, 10(1)*, 21-47.

Smith, G.D. (1988): *From monopoly to competition. The transformation of AL-COA, 1888-1986.* Cambridge and others: Cambridge University Press.
Smith, A. (2005): Conceptualizing city image change: the "re-imaging" of Barcelona. In: *Tourism Geographies, 7(4),* 398-423.
Smith, M.P. (2002): Power in place: retheorizing the local and the global. In: Eade, J. & Mele, C. (eds.): *Understanding the city. Contemporary and future perspectives.* Malden: Blackwell.
Smith, D. A., & Timberlake, M. F. (2001): World city networks and hierarchies, 1977-1997. In: *American Behavioral Scientist, 44(10),* 1656–1678.
Soja, E. (2008): Vom „Zeitgeist" zum „Raumgeist". New twists on the spatial turn. In: Döring, J. & Thielmann, T. (eds.): *Spatial Turn. Das Raumparadigma in den Kultur- und Sozialwissenschaften.* Bielefeld: transcript.
Spiegel, E. (1990): Schwerpunkte des sozialen Wandels. Perspektiven und Konflikte. In: Sieverts, T. (ed.): *Zukunftsausgaben der Stadtplanung.* Düsseldorf: Werner-Verlag.
Springer, B. (2007): *Artful transformation. Kunst als Medium urbaner Aufwertung.* Berlin: Kulturverlag Kadmos.
Stalder, F. (2009): Nischen im Flickenteppich. In: Becker, K. & Wassermair, M. (eds.): *Phantom Kulturstadt. Texte zur Zukunft der Kulturpolitik II.* Wien: Erhard Löcker GesmbH.
Stäheli, U. (2006): Die politische Theorieder Hegemonie: Ernesto Laclau und Chantal Mouffe. In: Brodocz, A. & Schaal, G.S. (eds.): *Politische Theorien der Gegenwart I.* Opladen & Farmington Hills: Verlag Barbara Budrich.
Steinert, H. (2009): Culture industry cities: from discipline to exclusion, from citizen to tourist. In: *City, 13(2),* 278-291.
Stevenson, N. (2001): Culture and citizenship: an introduction. In: Stevenson, N. (ed.): *Culture & citizenship.* London and others: Sage.
Stöber, B. & Kalandides, A. (2009): Orte, Städte und Kreativökonomien als Brand. In: Lange, B., Kalandides, A., Stöber, B., Wellmann, I. (eds.): *Governance der Kreativwirtschaft. Diagnosen und Handlungsoptionen.* Bielefeld: transcript.
Stoker, G. (1995): Regime Theory and Urban Politics. In: Judge, D., Stoker, G., Wolman, H. (eds.): *Theories of urban politics.* London: Sage Publications.
Stoker, G. (1998): Governance as theory: five propositions. In: *International Social Science Journal, 50(155),* 17-28.
Strauss, C. (2006): The imaginary. In: *Anthropological Theory, 2006(6),* 322-344.

Suitner, J. (2010): *Local.art – global.image. Zur Rolle der Planung zwischen lokalen, kunstbasierten Aufwertungsprozessen und globaler Stadtimageproduktion*. Saarbrücken: VDM.

Suitner, J. (2014): Cultures of image construction. Approaching planning cultures as a factor in urban image production. In: *European Spatial Research and Policy, 21(1)*, 39-52.

Swyngedouw, E. (1997): Neither global nor local: "glocalization" and the politics of scale. In: Cox, K.R. (ed.): *Spaces of globalization. Reasserting the power of the local*. New York: The Guilford Press.

Swyngedouw, E., & Kaïka, M. (2003): The making of "glocal" urban modernities. *City, 7(1)*, 5-21.

Taylor, C. (2004): *Modern social imaginaries*. Durham & London: Duke University Press.

Time (1942): The place they do Imagineering. Advertisement of the Aluminum Company of America, ALCOA. *Time Magazine, February 16, 1942*, p.59.

Tockner, L. (2012): Wohnpolitische Strategien: Liberalisierung oder politische Intervention?. In: *Wirtschaft und Gesellschaft, 38(1)*, 57-75.

Torfing, J (1999): *New theories of discourse. Laclau, Mouffe and Zizek*. Oxford and Malden: Blackwell.

Tovatt Architects & Planners & Projektteam Fluigfeld Aspern (2007): *Masterplan Flugfeld Aspern*. Self-published by Projetkteam Flugfeld Aspern.

Turnbridge, J.E. (2008): Plural and multicultural heritages. In: Graham, B. & Howard, P. (eds.): *The Ashgate research companion to heritage and identity*. Aldershot & Burlington: Ashgate.

Turok, I. (2005): Cities, Competition and Competitiveness: Identifying New Connections. In: Buck, I., Gordon, I., Harding, A., Turok, I. (eds.): *Changing Cities. Rethinking urban competitiveness, cohesion and governance*. London: Palgrave Macmillan.

Urry, J. (2006): Globale Komplexitäten. In: Berking, H. (ed.): *Die Macht des Lokalen in einer Welt ohne Grenzen*. Frankfurt/Main: Campus Verlag.

Van Heur, B. (2010a): Beyond regulation: towards a cultural political economy of complexity and emergence. In: *New Political Economy, 15(3)*, 421-44.

Van Heur, B. (2010b): *Creative networks and the city. Towards a cultural political economy of aesthetic production*. Bielefeld: transcript.

Van Houtum, H. (2011): The mask of the border. In: Wastl-Walter, D. (ed.): *The Ashgate research companion to border studies*. Surrey & Burlington: Ashgate.

Van Leeuwen, T. (2008): *Discourse and practice. New tools for critical discourse analysis*. Oxford and New York: Oxford University Press.

Vienna Tourism Agency (2005): *50 Jahre Wien-Tourismus & die Zukunft 1995-2005*. Vienna: self-published by Vienna Tourism Agency.
Vienna Tourism Agency (2009): *Tourismuskonzept 2015 – Langfassung*. Vienna: self-published by Vienna Tourism Agency.
Ward, K. (2003): The limits to contemporary urban redevelopment. "Doing" entrepreneurial urbanism in Birmingham, Leeds and Manchester. In: *City, 7(2)*, 199-211.
Ward, S.V. (1998): *Selling places. The marketing and promotion of towns and cities 1850-2000*. London and New York: Routledge.
Ward, S.V. (2006): "Cities are fun!": inventing and spreading the Baltimore model of cultural urbanism. In: Monclùs, J. & Guàrdia, M. (eds.) *Culture, urbanism and planning*. Aldershot: Ashgate.
Weber, G. (2006): *Metropole Wien. Technik – Urbanität – Wandel. Geschichte der Stadtbaudirektion Wien 1986-2006*. Wien: Carl Gerold's Sohn.
Werlen, B. (2008): Körper, Raum und mediale Repräsentation. In: Döring, J. & Thielmann, T. (eds.): *Spatial Turn. Das Raumparadigma in den Kultur- und Sozialwissenschaften*. Bielefeld: transcript.
Wien 3420 Aspern Development AG (2010): *The city + the brand. aspern brandbook*. Self-published by Wien 3420 Aspern Development AG.
Wien 3420 Aspern Development AG (2011): *Vision + Wirklichkeit. Die Instrumente des Städtebaus*. Werkstattbericht der Stadtentwicklung Wien, vol.118. Published by Wien 3420 Aspern Development AG & City of Vienna, Municipal Department 18.
Wodak, R. (2008): Introduction: discourse studies – important concepts and terms. In: Wodak, R. and Krzyzanowski, M. (eds.): *Qualitative discourse analysis in the social sciences*. Hampshire: Palgrave Macmillan.
Yeung, H. (1998): Capital, state and space: contesting the borderless world. In: *Transactions of the Institute of British Geographers, 23(3)*, 291-309.
Yin, R.K. (2009): *Case study research. Design and methods*. Los Angeles and others: Sage.
Young, G. (2006): Speak, culture! – Culture in planning's past, present and future. In: Monclùs, J. & Guàrdia, M. (eds.) *Culture, urbanism and planning*. Aldershot: Ashgate.
Young, G. (2008): *Reshaping planning with culture*. Aldershot and Burlington: Ashgate.
Zukin, S. (1982): *Loft living: culture and capital in urban change*. Baltimore: John Hopkins University Press.
Zukin, S. (1995): *The cultures of cities*. Cambridge: Blackwell.

Zukin, S. (1996): Space and symbols in an age of decline. In: King, A.D. (ed.): *Re-presenting the city. Ethnicity, capital and culture in the 21st century metropolis*. New York: New York University Press.

Zukin, S. (1998): Urban lifestyles: diversity and standardization in spaces of consumption. In: *Urban Studies, 35(5-6)*, 825-39.

ONLINE REFERENCES

ALCOA Inc. (2002): It all starts with dirt. The making of aluminum at ALCOA. Retrieved April 16, 2013 from: www.alcoa.com/global/en/about_alcoa/pdf/startswithdirt.pdf.

ARGE CENTROPE Agency (2013): Multilaterale Partnerschaft. Retrieved August 29, 2013 from: www.centrope.com/de/projekt-centrope/multilaterale-partnerschaft.

brainds (n.d.): *Stadt trifft Marke – City Branding Flugfeld Aspern*. Retrieved September 10, 2013 from: www.brainds.com/projekte/159,aspern-marken positionierung.html.

City-regional Management (n.d.): *Stadt-Umland Management – Organisation*. Retrieved August 29, 2013 from: www.stadt-umland.at/index.php?id=76.

Departure – Die Kreativwirtschaftsagentur der Stadt Wien (n.d.): *Departure business promotion in Vienna*. Retrieved August 31, 2013 from: www.departure.at/en/departure/departure.

ESPON (2012): *POLYCE. Metropolisation and polycentric development in Central Europe. Targeted Analysis 2013/2/12. Final report*. Retrieved July 14, 2013 from: www.espon.eu/export/sites/default/Documents/Projects/Targeted Analyses/POLYCE/FR/POLYCE_FINAL_MAINREPORT.pdf.

gerner°gerner plus (n.d.): *Kulturpassage Karlsplatz – Neugestaltung Passage Karlsplatz, Wien*. Retrieved September 03, 2013 from: www.gernergerner plus.com/karlsplatz.html.

Gänseblümchen (2013): *Gänseblümchen. Künstler*innen-Wagenburg*. Retrieved September 23, 2013 from: gaensebluemchen.wagenplatz.at.

Grüne Ottakring (2007): *Baustelle Brunnenmarkt*. Retrieved September 14, 2013 from: http://www.gruene-ottakring.at/themen/brunnenmarkt/559.html.

JP Immobilien (2012): *Der Grätzel Bericht. Vom Arsenal bis zum Yppenplatz*. Retrieved September 14, 2013 from: www.jpi.at/sites/default/files/presse/graetzl/Der_Graetzlbericht_Ausgabe_1.pdf.

karlsplatz.org (n.d.): *karlsplatz.org*. retrieved September 03, 2013 from: karls platz.org.

KÖR (n.d.a): *KÖR guiding principles*. Retrieved August 31, 2013 from: www.koer.or.at/cgi-bin/page.pl?id=3&lang=en.

KÖR (n.d.b): *Projects*. Retrieved September 03, 2013 from: www.koer.or.at/en/index.

Kunsthalle Wien (n.d.): *About us*. Retrieved September 03, 2013 from: www.kunsthallewien.at/about/en.

KunstSozialRaum Brunnenpassage (n.d.): *Über uns*. Retrieved September 13, 2013 from: www.brunnenpassage.at/ueber-uns.

Magistratsdirektion (n.d.): *Organisation der Wiener Stadtverwaltung*. Retrieved August 28, 2013 from: www.wien.gv.at/verwaltung/organisation/pdf/verwaltung.pdf.

Municipal Department 21A (n.d.): *Gürtelnews. Gründerzeitviertel – Westgürtel*. Retrieved September 14, 2013 from: www.wien.gv.at/stadtentwicklung/projekte/zielgebiete/westguertel/pdf/guertelnewssommer09.pdf.

Municipal Department 25 (n.d.a): *Brunnenmarkt, Yppenplatz*. Retrieved September 14, 2013 from: www.gbstern.at/wirtschaft-im-wandel/plakat standorte/brunnenmarkt-yppenplatz.

Municipal Department 25 (n.d.b): *Brunnenmarkt. Großflächige Sanierung in 5 Bauabschnitten*. Retrieved September 14, 2013 from: www.gbstern.at/projekte/bauliche-erneuerung/brunnenviertel/brunnenmarkt.

Planning Association East (n.d.a): *Aufgaben der Planungsgemeinschaft OST*. Retrieved August 29, 2013 from: http://www.pgo.wien.at/pgo1/aufgaben.htm.

Planning Association East (n.d.b): *Organe der PGO*. Retrieved August 29, 2013 from: http://www.pgo.wien.at/pgo_d.html.

Schulz, P.A. (2012): *Sprungbrett Aspern*. Retrieved September 13, 2012 from: http://www.ibo.at/de/artikel/documents/sprungbrett_aspern.pdf.

SPÖ Wien (2012): *Michael Häupl*. Retrieved October 14, 2012 from: http://www.wien.spoe.at/dr-michael-haeupl.

Statistik Austria (2010): *Statistisches Jahrbuch für Migration & Integration 2010: Integration je nach Zuwanderergruppe unterschiedlich vorangeschritten*. Retrieved September 13, 2013 from: http://www.statistik.at/web_de/dynamic/statistiken/bevoelkerung/bevoelkerungsstruktur/bevoelkerung_nach_migrationshintergrund/051839.

Sucht- und Drogenkoordination Wien gemeinnützige GmbH (2010): *Dressel: Niederschwellige Angebote für Suchtkranke wurden verdoppelt*. Retrieved October 06, 2013 from: drogenhilfe.at/3655/dressel-niederschwellige-angebote-fuer-suchtkranke-wurden-verdoppelt/.

The World Bank. (2010): *Systems of cities: harnessing urbanization for growth and poverty alleviation. The World Bank urban and local government strategy.* Retrieved August 13, 2012, from siteresources.worldbank.org/INT URBANDEVELOPMENT/Resources/336387-1269651121606/FullStrategy. pdf.

United Nations (2012): *The universal declaration of human rights.* Retrieved April 11, 2012, from www.un.org/en/documents/udhr-.

Urban Renewal Offices (n.d.): *Sanfte Stadterneuerung.* Retrieved August 29, 2013 from: www.gbstern.at/stadterneuerung/stadterneuerung-.

Vienna Business Agency (n.d.): *Economic development in Vienna.* Retrieved August 29, 2013 from: http://www.wirtschaftsagentur.at/en/vienna_business _agency_group/about_us-.

Wien 2025 (n.d.): *Die Themen.* Retrieved May 24, 2013 from: wien2025.at/ site/die-themen-.

wien 3420 Aspern Development AG (n.d.a): *Bauinfo.* Retrieved August 24, 2013 from: www.aspern-seestadt.at/mitgestalten-investieren/bauinfo-.

wien 3420 Aspern Development AG (n.d.b): *Die Eigentümer.* Retrieved September 10, 2013 from: www.wien3420.at/wien-3420.html#owners.

wien 3420 Aspern Development AG (n.d.c): *Historie.* Retrieved August 24, 2013 from: www.aspern-seestadt.at/mitgestalten-investieren/historie.

wien 3420 Aspern Development AG (n.d.d): *Publik – Kultur auf der Baustelle.* Retrieved September 10, 2013 from: www.aspern-seestadt.at/wohnen-andarbeiten/publik-kultur-auf-der-baustelle.

wien 3420 Aspern Development AG (n.d.e): *PUBLIK | aspern.blog.* Retrieved September 10, 2013 from: blog.aspern-seestadt.at/category/aspern-publik.

wien 3420 Aspern Development AG (n.d.f): *Zweites Entgegenkommen für Wagenplatzgruppe Gänseblümchen in der Seestadt.* Retrieved September 23, 2013 from: www.aspern-seestadt.at/presse-1/presseinfo/118,zweitesentgegenkommen-fuer-wagenplatzgruppe-gaensebluemchen-in.html.

wien.at (2012): *Verordnung des Magistrates der Stadt Wien betreffend die Bedingungen zur Darbietung von Straßenkunst in Wien (Straßenkunstverordnung 2012):* Retrieved September 23, 2013 from: www.wien.gv.at/ recht/landesrecht-wien/rechtsvorschriften/html/i5800700.htm.

wien.at. (n.d.a): *Aufgaben der Bezirksvorsteherinnen und Bezirksvorsteher.* Retrieved August 28, 2013 from: www.wien.gv.at/bezirke/dezentralisierung/ organe/bezirksvorstehung.html.

wien.at (n.d.b): *Gesetz betreffend die Tourismusförderung in Wien (Wiener Tourismusförderungsgesetz, WTFG.):* Retrieved August 29, 2013 from:

www.wien.gv.at/recht/landesrecht-wien/rechtsvorschriften/html/w1200000. htm.
Wiener Linien (2013): *Kulturpassage Karlsplatz*. Retrieved September 03, 2013 from: www.wienerlinien.at/eportal/ep/contentView.do/pageTypeId/9320/programId/9419/contentTypeId/1001/channelId/-26075/contentId/29629.

LIST OF INTERVIEWS[1]

Aschwanden, Daniel: performing artist from the artist collective content.associates (August 13, 2013).
Dzwonkowski, Christian & Natiesta, Richard: founding members of Buskers Festival Vienna (July 24, 2013).
Kettner, Norbert: CEO of the Vienna Tourism Agency (July 29, 2013).
Lueger, Josef: former planner at wien 3420 Aspern Development AG"(August 13, 2013).
Rießland, Bernd: former CEO of the Vienna Business Agency (July 30, 2013).
Schneider, Ula & Zobl, Beatrix: founding members of Soho In Ottakring (July 31, 2013).
Smetana, Kurt: head of the Urban Renewal Office in the 16th district of Vienna, Ottakring (July 19, 2013).
Staud, Hans: owner of the Brunnenviertel-based company Staud's (July 19, 2013).

---

1 Interview transcripts are not published due to research-ethical considerations.